KU-146-851

Wild Colonial Girl

Essays on Edna O'Brien

Edited by
LISA COLLETTA
and
MAUREEN O'CONNOR

THE UNIVERSITY OF WISCONSIN PRESS

The University of Wisconsin Press
1930 Monroe Street
Madison, Wisconsin 53711

www.wisc.edu/wisconsinpress/

3 Henrietta Street
London WC2E 8LU, England

Copyright © 2006
The Board of Regents of the University of Wisconsin System
All rights reserved

5   4   3   2   1

Printed in the United States of America

Library of Congress Cataloging-in-Publication Data
   Wild colonial girl : essays on Edna O'Brien / [edited by] Maureen
O'Connor and Lisa Colletta.
      p.   cm.—(Irish studies in literature and culture)
      ISBN-13: 978-0-299-21630-6 (alk. paper)
      ISBN-10: 0-299-21630-6 (alk. paper)
      ISBN-13: 978-0-299-21634-4 (pbk. : alk. paper)
      ISBN-10: 0-299-21634-9 (pbk. : alk. paper)
   1. O'Brien, Edna—Criticism and interpretation.   2. Women and
literature—Ireland.   3. Ireland—In literature.   4. Irish in literature.
I. O'Connor, Maureen, 1960-   II. Colletta, Lisa.   III. Series.
      PR6065.B7Z96   2006
      823'.914—dc22   2005022818

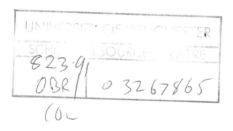

UNIVERSITY OF MANCHESTER
SCHOOL RESOURCE CENTRE
823.91
OBR   0 3267865
(0

This book was published with the support of
the Anonymous Fund for the Humanities of
the University of Wisconsin–Madison.

Contents

On the Side of Life: Edna O'Brien's Trilogy of

Acknowledgments

The editors wish to thank and acknowledge the authors of this volume of essays. While the exceptional quality of their work speaks for itself, what is less evident in the pages that follow is the unfailing patience and gracious professionalism that distinguished our every interaction with each one of them. We wish also to acknowledge those contributors to the book's production whose names do not appear in the table of contents. To return to the earliest days, we must thank Wendy Martin, the editor of *Women's Studies: An Interdisciplinary Journal,* where both of us had the good fortune to work as associate editors. This collection was inspired by a special issue on Irish women's writing, guest-edited by Maureen O'Connor in 2000, which resulted in an unexpected number and an impressive quality of submissions on Edna O'Brien. Danielle Hinrichs, associate editor of *Women's Studies* at that time, was of invaluable assistance in the early stages of the project; and Sharon Becker, the journal's subsequent associate editor, has been a lifesaver.

We are grateful to *Women's Studies* for granting permission to reprint Kristine Byron's essay, "Rereading and Revision in Edna O'Brien's *Country Girls Trilogy and Epilogue,*" and to *New Hibernia Review* for allowing us to reprint "On the Side of Life: Edna O'Brien's Trilogy of Contemporary Ireland," by Sophia Hillan.

There have been many others whose example and encouragement—professional and personal—have been indispensable, including Jim Rogers, Barbara Suess, Catherine Kasper, Neil Sammells, David T. Lloyd, Tom Shea, and Marc Redfield. We also would like to express our deep gratitude to Raphael Kadushin; Sheila Moermond; Adam Mehring; Michael Patrick Gillespie, editor of the Irish Studies in Literature and Culture series; and all the people at University of Wisconsin Press who have been so helpful in guiding this collection through the publication process. The editors would like to thank the Board of Research at Babson College and to acknowledge the Irish Research Council for the Humanities and Social Sciences Postdoctoral Fellowship for its generous support in the final stages of this project. Also, many thanks to Percy Clarke at the Jack Robinson Archive for his much appreciated generosity and good humor. And finally, we are happily indebted to Tadhg Foley and Stephen Croes, whose love and support make complete our enjoyment of the finished work.

Wild Colonial Girl

Introduction

LISA COLLETTA and MAUREEN O'CONNOR

Since the publication of her first novel, *The Country Girls* (1960), Irish writer Edna O'Brien has been both celebrated and maligned. Hailed for her lyrical prose and vivid female characters and attacked for her frank treatment of sexuality and alleged sensationalism, O'Brien and her work seem always to have spawned controversy. A prolific writer, O'Brien was awarded the 1995 European Prize for Literature in recognition of her life's work, as well as the 2002 American Medal of Honor for literature from the National Arts Club; however, she has long been under-regarded by scholars and is poised for serious and considerably overdue critical reevaluation. This essay collection marks a significant contribution to what promises to be the exciting retrieval of O'Brien's oeuvre. In the last five to ten years, a solid body of scholarly work on O'Brien has developed, though it has appeared so far almost exclusively as single entries in essay collections and journals. Some notable exceptions include the 1996 special issue of the *Canadian Journal of Irish Studies*, dedicated to O'Brien, and Amanda Greenwood's *Edna O'Brien*, published by Northcote in 2003, which was the first book-length text on the author since Grace Eckley's 1974 book of the same name.

According to James M. Cahalan, O'Brien is "rivaled in the scope of her international fame perhaps only by Brian Moore, among Irish novelists of either gender,"[1] and critical appreciation is, however slowly and belatedly, catching up to her popular acclaim. Her latest novel, *In the Forest*, published in 2002, received largely positive notices, but the *New York Times* review from April of that year demonstrates just how enduring are sexist, patronizing, and shockingly underdeveloped readings of O'Brien's work. The review furnishes this dismissive précis of the writer's earliest successes: "In her first three books . . . adultery nearly amounted to a developmental strategy. The reader sensed that young Kate would not mature without errant husbands, any more than flowers might be fertilized without errant bumblebees."[2] O'Brien's ensuing literary production is evaluated just as summarily: "The author was stuck in a rut." The review, punctuated with mock-exasperated, smugly belittling asides like "You see the pattern" and "Oh dear," dismisses O'Brien's latest novel as being too obvious. Finally, the novelist, whose ambition would appear to outstrip her limited—implicitly gendered—abilities, is advised to stick to the sexy stuff more appropriate to her affinities, to return to the "rut" previously deplored and go "back to a sin she like[s] better."

O'Brien's fiction has been associated with "sin" from the beginning of her career, when *The Country Girls* was met with scandalized outrage in her native country. Ireland, in fact, banned her books in 1969 on the grounds of their frank portrayal of female sexuality, a subject considered by Irish censors to be pornographic and obscene. Even outside of Ireland, O'Brien's attention to "women's" concerns, like sex, romance, marriage, and childbirth—and her expression of the inevitable frustrations and failures attending these unsatisfying, claustrophobic "female" preoccupations—has relegated her to, at best, critical neglect or, at worst, outright opprobrium. Some voices attempted to counter the official reaction of indignation and suppression to the sexual and emotional openness of O'Brien's early, groundbreaking fiction (which portrays men in uniformly unflattering terms). For instance, in 1969 Benedict Kiely twitted the hidebound Irish censors, characterizing their violent disapproval as being activated by "the feeling that while it's bad and very bad for a man to speak out and tell the truth, it is utterly unthinkable that a woman . . . should claim any such liberty."[3] But it wasn't only conservatives who objected to O'Brien's portrayal of women's experience. In 1974 fellow novelist Julia O'Faolain criticized feminists for their rejection of O'Brien and her hapless heroines, approvingly referring to O'Brien's stories as "bulletins from a front on which they [feminists] will not care to engage, field reports on the feminine condition at its most acute." Even O'Faolain's praise is radically qualified, however, as she goes on to decry the fact that "Miss O'Brien's range is narrow and obsessional. . . . What she does not seem to be able to do is to get experience into perspective. She cannot judge or structure it and so she seems forced. . . . The story is forever the same."[4] Ironically, in light of O'Faolain's somewhat tortuously construed feminist apologia, only a few years earlier, in 1967, O'Brien's work had been slighted by Sean McMahon for being "a kind of neo-feminist propaganda."[5] Frequently contradictory imputations of sameness, prodigality, narrowness, extravagance, silliness, emotionalism, dullness, and sensationalism dominated discussions of O'Brien and her work until the end of the twentieth century, and, as the *New York Times* review of *In the Forest* illustrates, do so even into the twenty-first.[6]

Critics often make recourse to O'Brien's biography with a casual sense of entitled appropriation and projection,[7] and the ad hominem nature of the most scathing condemnations of her work, from the 1960s to the present, demonstrates the transgressive power of the writer's canny performance of identity and her manipulation of personae. O'Brien's deliberate, stylized, highly theatrical stagings of the self have traditionally drawn the most critical fire, as they not only make porous the boundaries between author and text but also reveal the constructed nature of national and sexual identities, as well as the unacknowledged interdependence of those constructs. The wild runaway, the dreamy Irish colleen with porcelain skin and masses of auburn hair, the passive domestic slave with her harlequin-romance fantasies, the sexually voracious but emotionally unfulfilled fallen woman—these are all roles O'Brien has inhabited to parodic excess, an excess that calls attention to the implicit sexuality, as well as the oppressive brutality, of cultural/national gender stereotypes. Overdetermined identities that carry considerable historical, cultural, and political charge in postcolonial Ireland, these stereotypes are rendered undeniably volatile in O'Brien's operatic performance. Her flamboyant public self, relentlessly foregrounded, knowingly and gleefully marketed, places her in a tradition of insurgent, discomposing Irish writers in revolt against the masculinist dominant culture, which stretches back to Lady Morgan at the turn of the nineteenth century through Oscar Wilde at the cusp of the twentieth.[8]

Like those writers before her, the object of O'Brien's attack is diffuse and difficult to pin down, and it is this indeterminacy that has led to such widely divergent assessments of her work. Many critics and readers alike frequently miss the inherent irony and disturbing comedic aspects of her fiction as she explodes the romantic fantasies of many of her heroines, sometimes in the most violent ways, fundamentally critiquing cultural realities. Both irony and fantasy depend on the recognition of received patterns and structure for their force; O'Brien reproduces these sensationally but also maneuvers around the dominant discourse and challenges powerful cultural mythologies, including the ones women construct about their own lives. However, the exposure of romantic expectations as illusory doesn't do much to assuage the outrage of their inefficacy, and this leads to the frequent and often disturbing events that take place in O'Brien's fiction. Her heroines cling tenaciously to those illusions in the same way skeptics assert their beliefs, in order to create a fiction to live by. Questions of cause and effect are often at the heart of some of O'Brien's darkest occurrences, and no real answers are offered.

Though she left Ireland in 1959 for London, where she still resides, O'Brien's fiction is always in dynamic communication with the land of her birth. Her relationship to that country is an intimate and complicated one, poorly served by the clichéd and reductive narrative of rejection, flight, resentment, and victimization often imposed on the writer's biography. O'Brien constructs both a self and a nation through conscious acts of imagination and artistry grounded in a profound appreciation for history; a passionate investment in politics; and an unflinching dedication to a searching critique of her native country's custodial institutions of church, family, and state. When writing explicitly about Ireland, as she did in her first novels and has resumed doing in her latest work, O'Brien depicts the constricted, hardscrabble life of the villages and farms of the west. Anthropologist Nancy Scheper-Hughes has observed as recently as 1979 that "although all societies are characterized by sexual asymmetry to some extent, one would be hard put to find a society in which the sexes are as divided into opposing alien camps as they are in any small Irish village of the west." And, indeed, such gender distinctions in Ireland are pervasive and persistent, "profoundly rooted in mythology, history, and the interactions of fiction, fact, folklore."[9] A remote and atavistic west where the whole of Irish culture and history is preserved functions metonymically for the nation in O'Brien's fiction, which insists on the link between domestic and political colonization and between obsessions about the control of land and the control of women. These links inform the work of many contemporary women artists who have come to recognize that in Ireland "issues of gender and national identity intersect in multiple ways: in the gendering of the concept of the nation; in the idea of the national landscape as feminine; . . . and in the delimiting of gender roles in the idealization and representation of rural life."[10] The brutal need to contain female sexuality suggests the "double" colonization of a typical O'Brien protagonist, "the slave of a slave," as James Connolly, one of the martyrs of the 1916 Easter Uprising, articulated Irish women's cultural and material abjection nearly a hundred years ago.[11] Connolly, who was militant not only in his Irish nationalism, but in his socialism and feminism, envisioned a nation that would reject the social and sexual inequities that had defined and supported the despotism of British colonial rule. The Irish Free State, however, reproduced all of its previous master's oppressive structures, its technologies of control and prohibition. The exercise of power in independent Ireland has continued to be patriarchal and exclusionary. Ailbhe Smyth has provided a succinct mapping out of the gender paradigm of this fateful postcolonial power shift: "The liberation of the state implies male role-shift from that of Slave to Master, Margin to Centre, Other to Self. Women, powerless under patriarchy, are maintained as Other of the ex-Other, colonized of the post-colonized."[12]

The politics inherent in representations of female sexuality under such conditions command the attention of several of the essays that follow. In the first essay, "'In the Name of the Mother . . .': Reading and Revision in Edna O'Brien's *Country Girls Trilogy and Epilogue*," Kristine Byron asserts that by "dealing with issues such as motherhood, sexuality, religion, and marriage, the *Trilogy* exposes the ways feminine gender roles are constructed, offering a radical critique of capitalist patriarchy that is particularly Irish and Catholic." At the same time, O'Brien's text offers a commentary on the prescribed roles for women across literatures, and Byron contends that the 1986 reissue, with a new epilogue, of the *Country Girls Trilogy*—which comprises O'Brien's first three novels, *The Country Girls, The Lonely Girl* (1962; reprinted as *Girl with Green Eyes*, 1964), and *Girls in Their Married Bliss* (1964)—amounts to a questioning of the "adequacy of the female romance plot for representing women's experience in fiction." In the *Epilogue* and elsewhere, according to Byron, O'Brien's "treatment of her own work as a narrative in progress demanding revision challenges both the plots she works with and the critical impulse to find closure." More than merely showing women's struggle for self-determination in the face of constricting social and legal norms, O'Brien's *Trilogy* and *Epilogue* deconstructs the prescribed roles for women in patriarchal Irish society, interrogates, in Byron's words, "both literary and social scripts" available to women.

In her essay "Hysterical Hooliganism: O'Brien, Freud, Joyce," Helen Thompson discovers similar textual/sexual strategies at work in O'Brien's 1972 novel, *Night*, in which the narrator, Mary Hooligan, effectively rewrites James Joyce's fictional creation Molly Bloom, whose voice is the last we hear in Joyce's *Ulysses*. O'Brien frequently cites Joyce as one of her major literary influences, and in this essay Thompson argues that *Night* uses the trope of hysteria to parody and deauthorize Joyce's representation of female sexuality in the Penelope episode of *Ulysses*. According to Juliet Mitchell, "The woman novelist must be an hysteric. Hysteria is the woman's simultaneous acceptance and refusal of the organization of sexuality under patriarchal capitalism."[13] And in O'Brien's work we see that "the Irish patriarchy is anxious to control women's sexual and reproductive roles because by limiting women, they maintain the semblance of masculine dominance." Thompson argues, "It is in the overarticulations of women's social and sexual functions, which effectively silence any attempts Irish society has made to debate sexual issues, that patriarchal anxiety manifests itself." From out of this rigid framework, *Night*'s determinedly hysterical narrator pulls at the "seams where women cannot and will not be contained." O'Brien's self-conscious "plagiarism" of Joyce serves as an indictment of Joyce's plagiarism of the lives of his wife and daughter, whom he reduced to text, rendered readable and, therefore, susceptible to misreading and rewriting. Thompson maintains that O'Brien's "strategy works to demonstrate the shortcomings of Joyce's vision of female sexual and social roles as well as highlight the emancipatory possibilities of Mary's more fluid identity." In doing so, Thompson concludes, O'Brien "challenges the hegemony of both the [Irish] constitution and the canon."

Like Joyce, O'Brien figures Ireland as mother. However, unlike Joyce, who writes from the privileged position of patriarchal power despite his deliberate outsider stance, O'Brien creates a different metaphor for Ireland. Ireland is not an old sow that eats her farrow but, as described in her powerful memoir, *Mother Ireland*, a woman who has been raped by various enemies, a woman with whom other women can identify, indeed, must identify, and always to their sorrow. It is the mother who emerges in O'Brien's fiction as the most compelling love object, a figure at least as romantically and erotically cathected, and even more desirable, elusive, and destructive, finally, than any heterosexual object of desire. O'Brien's articulation of the problems of the female postcolonial subject begins in the context of the family. Taught by mothers to submit to men and warned by the church to remain chaste, O'Brien's women soon find themselves rejected by lovers and humiliated by husbands. The heightened eroticism of her work results in more than just "lyrics of the loins," as Stanley Kauffman once described her novels, but in a challenge to Catholic, patriarchal Irish culture that blights the lives of women by insisting on a hierarchy that denies them their desiring subjectivity. Her work is characterized by the child's search for a loving father—or father substitute—the young woman's ambiguous feelings toward a mother whose love she wants but whose legacy she rejects, a mother who clings to her children, seeking in them an antidote to her unhappiness. Tamsin Hargreaves has noted this "psychological umbilical cord between mother and child" that disempowers so many of O'Brien's protagonists who "desperately attempt to replace the safety and wholeness, the sense of identity and meaning found with the mother."[14]

In Ireland, as Rebecca Pelan observes in her essay "Edna O'Brien's 'Love Objects,'" an ironic elevation of motherhood is powerfully effected by the cult of the Virgin Mary, a nexus of religious, cultural, and social control. Taking the novelist's self-proclaimed major theme as being "loss . . . as much as love," Pelan's readings of O'Brien's primal narratives of loss consider the ways O'Brien's conflation of the mother, the self, and God, through a process of idealization, manifests itself in the figures of idealized "love objects," occasionally nuns, but more often mothers or god-like men, in her early (pre-1985) fiction. Pelan locates O'Brien's "iconoclastic mission of exposing the brutality of various insidious forms of oppression" in the context of modern Ireland and a tradition of Irish women writing within and against the religious and social orthodoxies of a rigidly Catholic, patriarchal culture. In this tradition, the dilemma presented by a binarized notion of female sexuality—with its contradictory dictates of chastity and fecundity, yoked in the unattainable fantasy figure of the Madonna—complicates the romance plot and its ethic of chivalry: the "love object" as vehicle for fulfillment, for locating or transcending the self, invariably proves a source of disillusion and failure. Sex may offer a kind of transcendence, but it is also revealed as the "ultimate disillusionment in search of selfhood," a theme always implicated in another recurring, if submerged, preoccupation in O'Brien's fiction, that is, "an acute awareness of writing within an existing, and predominantly male, literary tradition."

Christine St. Peter has diagnosed the specific "predominantly male, literary tradition" with which O'Brien and other Irish women writers contend: "Ireland is a tiny country with magnificent literary traditions.

Accordingly, the cult of the writer is a major cultural practice and export business, and the attention to the artist's merit and life a national pastime. Entrance to the sacred precincts is jealously guarded."[15] In his essay "Edna O'Brien and the Lives of James Joyce," Michael Patrick Gillespie persuasively argues that O'Brien has prevailed in this professional struggle, a triumph, Gillespie asserts, that the writer wears lightly and with exceptional intellectual aplomb and generosity. Gillespie delineates his portrait of O'Brien as self-contained, regally composed literary lion in the course of a reassessment of her much-maligned recent biography of James Joyce (*James Joyce*, 1999), a brave reassessment that does not spare even Gillespie's own earlier undervaluation of the text. After surveying the many Joyce biographies that came before, Gillespie judges O'Brien's authorial impulse to be distinct from those motivating earlier studies of Joyce's life and work. O'Brien's biography, a tribute to a writer whom she considers an important influence, is not so much a scholarly study as a work of imagination and artistry and, most significant, an interpretive guide to the aesthetic values and goals of O'Brien's own work. The biography takes, Gillespie maintains, "a very atypical Irish view of the man," one that is neither "reverential nor resentful" and one that reveals O'Brien's own considerable, refreshing artistic self-confidence.

O'Brien's practice of writing against patriarchal conventions also provides the focus of Wanda Balzano's essay, "Godot Land and Its Ghosts: The Uncanny Genre and Gender of Edna O'Brien's 'Sister Imelda.'" For a short story such as Edna O'Brien's "Sister Imelda" the meanings of the text are "as plural as are the traces followed by any patient reader of detective stories." Balzano, who reviews the various genres the story exploits—the bildungsroman, sentimental or religious literature, the feminist parable, narratives of exile, and the psychological thriller—concludes that the gothic and the fantastic are the major genres the story engages. In O'Brien's uneasiness with her native land, Balzano discovers an inchoate "Irishness" that grants access to an essentially fantastic world. O'Brien's statement that her own Irishness is a sometimes "awkwardly prescribed inheritance and guarantee of ghostliness" is Balzano's point of departure, and she shows how this ghostliness helps to create a genre that is characterized by the uncanny and difficult to define. What escapes definition in the story are the affiliations between and among women. Balzano sees "Sister Imelda" as rewriting, through its deployment of the trope of the uncanny double, the sexist and divisive Eve/Lilith myth of Judeo-Christian tradition, "break[ing] patriarchal conventions," and clearing a space for "the fantastic and the feminist [to] meet at the crossroads."

Danine Farquharson and Bernice Schrank, the authors of "Blurring Boundaries, Intersecting Lives: History, Gender, and Violence in Edna O'Brien's *House of Splendid Isolation*," discuss a more recent example of O'Brien's transgressive revisioning of genre, one they regard as an "indictment of the impotence of texts and storytelling" itself. The authors argue that *House of Splendid Isolation* (1994) is one of the writer's most politicized novels and that it is a departure in both style and content from the majority of her fictional work. Focusing on the novel's formal and thematic innovations, Farquharson and Schrank trace the text's ironization of the violent, masculinist metanarrative of Irish history from colonial times to modernity. Farquharson and Schrank locate four narrative lines in the novel that deconstruct narrative itself, troubling and disrupting Irish history's confident teleology. Through the plot lines of the Big House, the romance, the melodrama of the outlaw hero on the run, and stories about myth, folklore, rumor—storytelling itself—the novel reveals the reality of an endless cycle of imprisonment and death that undermines official history's blind and destructive faith in progress. The novel, Farquharson and Schrank contend, "interrogates the very notion of linear historical movement" in its proffering of a "revisionist history that refuses to endorse the discriminatory practices of the new Republic" and that suggests "no story is complete, including the story of Ireland."

The novels that make up the trilogy of which *House of Splendid Isolation* is a part have been criticized for being out of touch with modern Ireland, in ironic contradistinction to the outcry against her earliest fiction for being "too far in advance of the ordinary reader," as Sophia Hillan remarks in her essay "On the Side of Life: Edna O'Brien's Trilogy of Contemporary Ireland." Hillan also discusses *House of Splendid Isolation,* situating it in relation to the other novels in O'Brien's latest trilogy, *Down by the River* (1996) and *Wild Decembers* (1999). While acknowledging O'Brien's place in a tradition of politically engaged and controversial Irish writing dating back to Maria Edgeworth and William Carleton, Hillan's interest is in revealing the novelist's adherence in her latest work to those qualities O'Brien admires most in Joyce, his "total honesty and perseverance" when treating of the subject of Ireland. In addition to the familiar similarities often posited between O'Brien and Joyce—their self-exile from Ireland, their condemnation by Irish censors, their jouissant handling of language—Hillan poses a resemblance between the writers' fidelity to the moral themes and concrete details of Irish life. By bringing her characters back to Ireland after years of fictional exile, O'Brien's latest trilogy forges powerful and affecting links not only to the work of Joyce and to her own earlier fictions but also to the material, political, and psychological realities of contemporary Irish life. The trilogy that continues O'Brien's project of rocking "the safe certainties" and demolishing "the old myths," nevertheless culminates, unlike her first trilogy, in hope. The figure of Breege, who, pregnant at the end of *Wild Decembers*, is "holding it together," still able to believe in "the hope that there is communication between the living and dead, between those who even in their most stranded selves are on the side of life and harbingers of love." Hillan's reading restores the land and its promise of renewal to O'Brien's country girls.

Notes

1. James M. Cahalan, *The Irish Novel: A Critical History* (Boston: Twayne, 1988), 286.

2. Caleb Crain, "Edna O'Brien Investigates the Varieties of Murderous Experience," *New York Times*, 7 April 2002.

3. Benedict Kiely, "The Whores on the Half-doors," *Conor Cruise O'Brien Introduces Ireland*, ed. Owen Dudley Edwards (New York: McGraw-Hill, 1969), 148–61, esp. 158.

4. Julia O'Faolain, "A Scandalous Woman," review of *A Fanatic Heart: Selected Stories* by Edna O'Brien, *New York Times*, 22 September 1974.

5. Sean McMahon, "A Sex by Themselves: An Interim Report on the Novels of Edna O'Brien," *Éire-Ireland* 2.1 (1967): 79–87, esp. 79.

6. Some of the most frequently quoted excoriations of O'Brien and her work include Darcy O'Brien, "Edna O'Brien: A Kind of Irish Childhood," in *Twentieth-Century Women Novelists*, ed. Thomas F. Staley (Totawa, N.J.: Barnes and Noble, 1982), 179–90; Peggy O'Brien, "The Silly and the Serious: An Assessment of Edna O'Brien," *Massachusetts Review* 28.3 (1987): 474–88; John Foster Wilson, "Irish Fiction 1965–1990," in *The Field Day Anthology of Irish Writing*, ed. Seamus Deane (Derry: Field Day Publications, 1991), 3: 937–65; Robert Hogan, "Old Boys, Young Bucks, and New Women: The Contemporary Irish Short Story," in *The Irish Short Story: A Critical History*, ed James F. Kilroy (Boston: Twayne, 1984), 169–215.

7. See Eileen Morgan, "Mapping Out a Landscape of Female Suffering: Edna O'Brien's Demythologizing Novels," *Women's Studies: An Interdisciplinary Journal* 29.4 (August 2000): 449–76, for a helpful and illuminating discussion of this aspect of O'Brien's reception.

8. See Maureen O'Connor, "Edna O'Brien, Irish Dandy," *Irish Studies Review* 13.4 (November 2005): 469–78.

9. Quoted in James M. Cahalan, *Double Visions: Women and Men in Modern Contemporary Irish Fiction* (Syracuse, N.Y.: Syracuse University Press, 1999), 12, 14.

10. Catherine Nash, "Remapping the Body/Land: New Cartographies of Identity, Gender, and Landscape in Ireland," in *Writing Women and Space: Colonial and Postcolonial Geographies,* ed. Alison Blount and Gillian Rose (New York: Giulford Press, 1994), 227–50, esp. 229.

11. Quoted in Carol Coulter, *The Hidden Tradition: Feminism, Women, and Nationalism in Ireland* (Cork: Cork University Press, 1993), 11; see Coulter for a full account of the way the early Free State wrote women out of the history of the revolution and Ireland's accession to independence, their subsequent silencing and exclusion from governance. Pádraig Pearse, who was executed for his involvement in the 1916 Easter Uprising, expresses a similar sentiment in his poem "The Rebel": "My mother bore me in bondage, in bondage my mother was born."

12. Ailbhe Smyth, "The Floozie in the Jacuzzi: The Problematics of Culture and Identity for an Irish Woman," *Feminist Studies* 17.1 (1991): 16–24, esp. 11–12.

13. Juliet Mitchell, *Women: The Longest Revolution* (New York: Pantheon Books, 1984), 101.

14. Tamsin Hargreaves, "Women's Consciousness and Identity in Four Irish Women Novelists," in *Cultural Contexts and Literary Idioms in Contemporary Irish Literature,* ed. Michael Kenneally (Totawa, N.J.: Barnes and Noble, 1988), 290–305, esp. 291–92.

15. Christine St. Peter, *Changing Ireland: Strategies in Contemporary Women's Fiction* (New York: St. Martin's Press, 2000), 11.

"In the Name of the Mother . . ."

Reading and Revision in Edna O'Brien's Country Girls Trilogy and Epilogue

KRISTINE BYRON

Prologar cuentos no leídos aún es tarea casi imposible, ya que
exige el análisis de tramas que no conviene anticipar. Prefiero
por consiguiente un epílogo. . . . Espero que las notas apresura-
das que acabo de dictar no agoten este libro y que sus sueños
sigan ramificándose en la hospitalaria imaginación de quienes
ahora lo cierran.

[To preface still unread stories is an almost impossible task,
since it demands the analysis of plots not yet convenient to
disclose. I prefer, therefore, an epilogue. . . . I hope that these
hasty notes which I have just dictated do not exhaust the
meanings of this book; may its visions continue to unfold in
the receptive imaginations of those who now close it.]

       Jorge Luis Borges, *El libro de arena* [The Book of Sand]

Lynette Carpenter has noted that Edna O'Brien "has been criticized for
writing the same story over and over, and for not writing the story she
writes best. . . . In short, O'Brien's literary reputation is anything but
settled."[1] Carpenter's observation certainly corresponds to the mixed
critical reviews of what are perhaps O'Brien's best-known works—the

novels *The Country Girls* (1960), *The Lonely Girl* (1962), and *Girls in Their Married Bliss* (1964)—which were republished in 1986 as *The Country Girls Trilogy and Epilogue*. Along the way, O'Brien kept making revisions, rewriting, and thereby unsettling the story. In 1971, for instance, she dramatically altered the conclusion of *Girls in Their Married Bliss*, undercutting the optimism of the first ending. The epilogue to the *Trilogy* further annihilates any possibility of a stock happy ending by allowing us to see, twenty years later, exactly what has become of her two heroines. If O'Brien's reputation is unsettled, her treatment of her own works as a narrative in progress demanding revision challenges both the plots she works with and the critical impulse to find closure.

O'Brien made a conscious decision to have two heroines in the novels of the *Trilogy*. She explains: "Realizing that the earlier heroines [of the tradition of Irish writing] were bawdy and the later ones lyrical I decided to have two, one who would conform to both my own and my country's view of what an Irish woman should be and one who would understand every piece of protocol and religion and hypocrisy that there was."[2] The 1986 epilogue seems to offer a definitive ending to this double plot, one which suggests that women's position had not changed drastically since 1960, the year in which the first novel of the *Trilogy (The Country Girls)* was first published. In the epilogue, we learn that Kate has drowned, like her mother before her. Baba suspects Kate committed suicide, but can't bring herself to think too much about this possibility. As for Baba herself, she has become nurse and mother to her once abusive husband, Durack, who has suffered a stroke that has rendered him completely dependent on her. In spite of Baba's less-than-happy marriage, she survives, in part because she is the heroine who understands "every piece of protocol and religion and hypocrisy that there ever was."

More than merely showing women's struggle for self-affirmation in the face of constricting social and legal norms, O'Brien's *Trilogy and Epilogue* deconstructs the prescribed roles for women in patriarchal Irish society. Dealing with issues such as motherhood, sexuality, religion, and marriage, the *Trilogy* exposes the ways feminine gender roles are constructed, offering a radical critique of a capitalist patriarchy that is particularly Irish and Catholic. At the same time, O'Brien's text offers a commentary on the prescribed roles for women in literature, challenging the adequacy of the female romance plot for representing women's experience in fiction.

In her study of feminist writing, Nancy K. Miller outlines some of the problems women's writing has faced historically: "The attack on female plots and plausibilities assumes that women writers cannot or will not obey the rules of fiction. . . . It does not see that the maxims that pass for the truth of human experience and the encoding of that experience, in literature, are organizations, when they are not fantasies, of the dominant culture. To read women's literature is to see and hear repeatedly a chafing against the 'unsatisfactory reality' contained in the maxim."[3] In other words, women writers are often criticized for not following the "rules" of fiction, especially when their work goes against the grain of the dominant (male) literary culture. Moreover, Miller contends, "the plots of women's literature are not about 'life' and solutions in any therapeutic sense, nor should they be. *They are about the plots of literature itself,* about the constraints the maxim places on rendering a female life in fiction" (43, emphasis added).

Much scholarly work on O'Brien contains such attacks on the "plots and plausibilities" of her fiction, while refusing to hear the "chafing against the 'unsatisfactory reality'" evident in much of O'Brien's writing. Darcy O'Brien, for instance, has described the "paradox of the strong, independent woman writing of women as victims." Two possible explanations are offered for this, both of which are equally simplistic. Either "the author is being insincere in her presentation of women as fragile and dependent on men" or "these heroines do reflect Edna O'Brien's sense of herself in relation not only to men but to the professional world which she inhabits and they control."[4] Here, a literary analysis of characters is transformed into psychoanalysis of the author. Other critics have even gone so far as to "blame" O'Brien for her characters' miserable lives. Anatole Broyard has observed: "Like Kate's, Baba's extra-marital choices are conspicuously odd, and if Miss O'Brien means these men to stand for women's fate, she has certainly stacked the deck. . . . The women in the later books are attractive, intelligent, witty — surely they could do better if the author let them."[5] Though O'Brien's characters are fictional, they certainly are realistic. And of course they could "do better" if the author let them, but that is not the story O'Brien chooses to write. Other times O'Brien's fiction is reduced to a sort of psychoanalytic case study: "It seems that the need to recover Ireland imaginatively and from a distance is more deeply a need for union with her mother" (476). Peggy O'Brien describes O'Brien's characters as mere "projections of a turbulent authorial psyche" and banishes the writer herself to near nonexistence: "Given her irrepressible, perverse humanity, the voice that we hear in [Edna O'Brien's] interviews is even more fictional than that of her fiction" (479, 477). In this light, the attack on "plots and plausibilities" of O'Brien's fiction extends to the "plots and plausibilities" of O'Brien's life.

A frequent critical emphasis on authorial persona has led to a tendency to ignore not only the "cultural and political contexts" of Edna O'Brien's writing but also, I contend, her narrative techniques. O'Brien's writing has only recently been seriously examined by feminist critics, and critical work on O'Brien has all but ignored the significance of the epilogue. Two notable exceptions are the essays by James Haule and Rebecca Pelan.[6] Haule's analysis is primarily concerned with psychoanalytic functions of the mother/child relationship in O'Brien's work, taking the epilogue as an example. However, he does not examine other functions of the epilogue. Though Haule makes some interesting observations about the institution of motherhood in Irish society, his conclusion seems limiting and even more tragic than that of the *Trilogy* itself: "Perhaps the truth, then, is that there is no safe place for women born to a country that offers no chance for health or happiness. If so, to be born in Ireland at all is the worst of luck" (223).

In what is perhaps the first attempt to reconcile the differences between criticism of O'Brien's work and of O'Brien herself, Rebecca Pelan notes: "O'Brien's 'Irishness' offered for her critics an obvious strategy for keeping the cultural and political contexts peripheral. . . . The persona, then, allows the literary establishment to acknowledge the talent and success of a writer like O'Brien without ever having to investigate or interrogate the nature of either" (75). In their focus on the persona rather than the writing, Pelan argues, critics have overlooked the blatant sociocultural context and political critique imbedded in O'Brien's work. Pelan reads O'Brien's "stage-Irish" persona as an act of resistance, concluding that "an analysis of the personality cult surrounding O'Brien today indicates that the authorial persona became the critical focus in direct correlation with the perception of O'Brien as a writer who challenged the dominant discourses of Anglo-American literary criticism by failing to confine her work within the parameters set for it. . . . Too 'stage-Irish' for the Irish, too Irish for the English and too flighty and romantic for feminists, O'Brien continues to be neglected as a writer whose work merits serious critical attention" (68, 77–78).

Though the *Trilogy and Epilogue* should certainly be read as a critique of Irish society, we should also look carefully at the extent to which it represents an attack on the "encoding" of women's experience in literature. Form and content are tightly woven together in O'Brien's work. If we carefully examine the relationship between the two, we might understand the unhappy ending of the *Trilogy and Epilogue* to be much more than "a maudlin, melodramatic tale of woman's woe" as Peggy O'Brien once described it.[7] Indeed, the epilogue of the *Trilogy* is the most logical place to begin such an analysis, for an epilogue marks a literal "writing beyond the ending," what Rachel Blau DuPlessis has defined as the "attempt by women writers to call narrative forms into question . . . to scrutinize the ideological character of the romance plot (and related conventions in narrative), and to change fiction so that it makes alternative statements about gender and its institutions."[8] O'Brien's text explores and challenges the narrative conventions of the female romance plot, and Baba's irreverent voice in the epilogue serves as an ideological amplifier of the issues explored in the three novels.

The epilogue offers the reader an opportunity to reflect on the *Trilogy* as a whole. O'Brien explained that she felt compelled to write an epilogue, rather than simply republish the three novels together: "The characters remained with me as ghosts, but without the catharsis of death. I had never finished their story, I had left them suspended, thinking perhaps that they could stay young indefinitely or that their mistakes might be canceled out or they would achieve that much touted fallacy—a rebirth" ("Why Irish Heroines," 13). If the epilogue is meant to provide a sort of catharsis for the author, it also functions as the key for the reader to reading the novels, or more specifically, to *rereading* them.

Literary critics, narratologists in particular, frequently define epilogues in a traditional way. One of the most standard definitions employed is that laid out by the French narratologist Gérard Genette: "The epilogue has as its canonic function the brief exposition of a (stable) situation subsequent to the denouement, from which it results: for example, the two heroes are reunited after several years, and they tenderly and peacefully gaze at their numerous offspring."[9] This definition seems ironic if applied to O'Brien's text, in particular the "denouement" and subsequent "situation" of Kate and Baba. Though one of them is dead, the two heroines *are* reunited. The narrative situation, in this case, is anything but stable. In O'Brien's epilogue, the denouement of the end of *Girls in Their Married Bliss* is unraveled. O'Brien's epilogue embraces the doubleness of the term denouement, which can mean "unknotting" as well as "resolving" or "knitting together."

The present and its relation to the past are central to O'Brien's epilogue, and memory serves as the organizing force of its narrative structure. Baba narrates in the present tense actual events are taking place in the epilogue.[10] Between these events (or more precisely, during them), she shifts into the past tense, recounting events of the past twenty years. Genette describes these types of narrating as simultaneous, "narrative in the present contemporaneous with the action," and interpolated, or "between the moments of the action." O'Brien's epilogue combines these two forms, making the narrative form highly intricate. According to Genette, the interpolation of past events with present ones is the "most complex [type of narrating], since it involves narrating with several instances, and since *the story and the narrating can become entangled in such a way that the latter has an effect on the former.*"[11] This is clearly the case in the epilogue, where Baba's act of narrating shapes the story itself. The readers' reception of the events is mediated by Baba's narrative voice, which controls how much of the story is revealed. Rather than provide a neat chronological summary of what has become of "our heroines," as a traditional epilogue might do, Baba jumps from "now" to "then" and back again. The duration (speed) and frequency of narrated events varies tremendously because the narrated events are triggered by and filtered through Baba's memory.

To an extent, the denouement, or resolution, of the women's story has already occurred in the twenty years between the end of *Girls in Their Married Bliss* and the (present) epilogue. Unlike traditional epilogues, which provide narrative closure, O'Brien's epilogue further delays closure, playing instead with the idea of *disclosure.* Allison Booth has observed the importance of disclosure in novels written by and about women: "How women 'end up' is so often the story, just as 'How does it end?' is the readiest question (most pleasurably deferred in the answering) about narrative."[12] O'Brien's text plays on the tensions between suspense and revelation, past and present. We ask less *how* the story ends than how the protagonists "ended up" there. In this sense, I would argue, O'Brien's text resembles Jorge Luis Borges's definition of an epilogue quoted in my epigraph—it expands, rather than condenses, meaning.[13] Instead of providing neat closure, it offers new ways of reading. It surprises, inviting the reader to return to the beginning, to reread. It has a revelatory function, yet it suppresses as much as it reveals, leaving the reader to fill in the gaps.

This revelatory function, this play with disclosure, asserts itself throughout Baba's narrative. We see it clearly in the opening lines of the epilogue: "It goes on, by Jesus, it goes on. I am at Waterloo again, the railway station where Kate gashed her wrists, thinking daftly that someone might come to her rescue, a male Florence Nightingale might kneel and bandage and swoop her off to a life of certainty and bliss.

Nearly twenty years ago. Much weeping and gnashing in between. They've cleaned this place up; it's morbidly bright and neat" (511). "It goes on" could be read at two levels—literally, the "weeping and gnashing" that continue, and metafictionally, the epilogue that continues the narrative structure of the *Trilogy*. The *Trilogy* resists closure because the epilogue postpones it. O'Brien had already tampered with the narrative outcome of the traditional female romance plot, boldly suggested in the cutting irony of the title of *Girls in Their Married Bliss*.

Moreover, the opening lines of the epilogue contain narrative delays and gaps that further postpone closure in the text itself. Some of these are simply rhetorical, while others are real information gaps. In Baba's opening remarks, for instance, "I am at Waterloo again" prompts the reader to think back, as it were, to Baba's previous visit to Waterloo. Yet Baba has never said, "I am/was at Waterloo"; the previous event—"Kate gashing her wrists"—was narrated by a third-person omniscient narrator in the second part of *Girls in Their Married Bliss* (chapter 9). Baba had simply recounted Kate's phone call "from some hospital. She'd had a little argument with a weighing machine at Waterloo Station and took this to be the end of the world" (*Bliss*, chapter 10). Neither version of the event recounts Baba's presence at Waterloo. Here, in the epilogue, Baba briefly alludes to Kate's suicide attempt—an event already narrated twice in the previous text—but delays divulging the purpose of her present visit to Waterloo. She instead shifts back to the present tense, describing changes in the station itself: "They've cleaned this place up; it's morbidly bright and neat." Already the reader faces a past-oriented delay. Why is Baba again at Waterloo Station? What sort of "weeping and gnashing" has been going on for nearly twenty years? The following paragraphs not only withhold the answers to these questions but also pose additional ones. For the time being, the reader is left in suspense to wonder not only what will follow but also what has already happened in the previous two decades.

Baba's narrative is interspersed with these sorts of gaps that cause the reader to search the text for clues. For instance, after describing the sunny June weather, Baba remarks, "There's a letter for me, it seems." She then abruptly switches to a description of the people around her. On the following page, Baba explains that she has hired "two flunkies" to carry a coffin: "They're from foreign parts. Pakistan or maybe even somewhere farther. . . . They look at me from time to time as if to size me up. I think they think it's all a bit forlorn. In their country there would be wailing now, flocks of relatives beating their chests; in my country too, and Kate's" (512). Although by this point, careful readers have probably connected the letter, the coffin, and Kate, Baba does not explicitly reveal their relationship. She holds back telling us that Kate is dead. Most of these gaps in the story are temporary; they are eventually filled in through the narrative juxtapositioning of present and past events. Yet, even when we know this is Kate's coffin, we are left guessing how she died. We only are told Kate's cause of death—drowning—twelve pages later.

Baba's memories continue to structure the narrative pattern of the epilogue. She explains that a waitress in the coffee shop of the train station reminds her of a man she met earlier in the year "on a holiday to one of those tropical islands" (513). She then shifts from present to past tense, describing her thoughts and feelings while on this trip. Her temporary escape to a tropical scene enabled her to forget her unhappy present: "I forgot Durack, I forgot the fishmongers, I forgot our pickled-pine kitchen and whether the sofa needed fucking reupholstering, I even forgot my own telephone number" (514). Her memories of this trip are suddenly interrupted by her present thought: "Poor Durack, I didn't miss him at all. . . . Durack and I were man and wife again." Again, readers are temporarily left in the dark, until Baba relates in detail how she was called home from her tropical paradise because her husband had had a stroke. At this point, Baba relates numerous events from further in the past, filling in many of the "missing pieces" of the story. These are frequently interrupted by her present thoughts, her interpretation of the past. Many of these changes in narrative time revolve around larger themes of the *Trilogy* as a whole.

Another significant characteristic of O'Brien's epilogue is the narrator's use of direct address to an unnamed narratee, "you." This kind of conversational rhetorical mode, suggests Kathy Mezei, stresses the "importance of our role as readers both in untangling and in responding to . . . narrative strategies."[14] In her analysis of dialogic theory and women's writing, Lynn Pearce discusses the gendered positions constructed in literary texts, contrasting those that posit the reader as an adversary versus those that address the reader as a potential ally. She asserts that "in contemporary women's fiction [this has] frequently been brought to metafictional consciousness." The recognition, Pearce contends, also depends on "the conflation of the textual with the extratextual—in this case the woman reader's knowledge of the workings of patriarchy, both inside and outside [the] particular fictional narrative—that enable her to grasp the full connotations of the speaker's 'you.' . . . The specialized cultural knowledge that makes the female reader privy to the text's intonation and extratextual context . . . is also, therefore, the key to her entry and participation. The textual and the extratextual become, indeed, 'a territory shared.'" O'Brien's epilogue clearly posits the reader in such a position. Baba tells the story to a designated narratee, "you," whom we tend to identify with as readers. We see the orality of the text in Baba's frequent use of linguistic tags which mark the reader's presence as listener—"Mind you," "I can tell you," "You wouldn't be surprised," "you won't believe it," and "to tell you the truth," to name some examples. Such subtle forms of narrative address, Pearce contends, force "the reader to enter the text against her better judgment."[15] Obviously, not all readers of O'Brien's novels are female, but female readers are more likely to recognize the "you" in Baba's narration as a textual 'interpellation' in the Althusserian sense of the term.[16] Baba's conscious address to "you" creates gendered positions for both narrator and narratee. The tone of Baba's narrative discourse resembles that of what Robyn Warhol describes as an "engaging narrator," one who "usually assume[s] that their narratees (not to mention their actual readers) are in perfect sympathy with them."[17] Baba's narrative, through its oral, colloquial, intimate tone and its frank direct address thus engages the reader. As Baba herself reexamines past events, the reader, too, is invited to do so.

In addition to its use of complex structural and rhetorical devices, the epilogue serves as an interpretative frame for the *Trilogy,* offering a commentary on the female romance plot with all its connotations. Jeanette Roberts Shumaker has identified two kinds of romance in O'Brien's short stories—religious and sexual—and she argues that in her short fiction, O'Brien deconstructs religious and sexual romance by merging the two.[18] I find that O'Brien employs a similar strategy in the *Trilogy.* O'Brien's epilogue frames the stories of Kate and Baba in metaphors of religion and romantic love. The function of these metaphors, I contend, is not to reinforce prescribed roles for women but rather to draw attention to them. The *Trilogy* is a text interested in interrogating literary scripts as well as social ones.

Throughout the *Trilogy,* Kate appears in the role of mystic as defined by Simone de Beauvoir—she who confuses God with man and man with God in hopes of becoming the supreme object of a supreme subject. She notes, for example, that Mr. Gentleman's face "still had that strange holy-picture quality that made me think of moonlight and the chaste way he used to kiss me" (261), and she once described him as "my new God, with a face carved out of pale marble." Years later, Kate had a one-night fling with a man named Roger, who "licked his finger and placed it prayerwise on her pulse. A little baptism" (497). Of course, Eugene figures most prominently in Kate's role as mystic. The first time she meets him, she compares his face with "a saint's face carved out of gray stone which [she] saw in the church every Sunday" (185), and at one point she describes him as "a dark-faced God turning his back" on her. On another occasion, she recalls that Eugene "lay there, like a Christ, sipping tea, his head resting on the mahogany head-board" (304), and later she sees him as "a stranger, a mad martyr nailed to his chair, thinking and sighing and smoking" (351).

In the epilogue, Baba sarcastically describes Kate's final "love object" (a married man who abandons Kate to go home "to wife and kiddies"): "He was the Holy Ghost because of his fugitive ways" (528).[19] Baba recalls first learning from Kate about this man: "I knew . . . that he was probably married and that she saw him once a fortnight or less, but of course saw him in street lamps, rain puddles, fire flames, and all that kind of Lord Byron lunacy" (527). She goes on in this vein for two paragraphs, trying to understand why Kate believed there "was such a thing as twin-star perpetuity" (528). The epilogue articulates the welcome death of romanticism, subverting the traditional outcome of the romance plot; for Kate was waiting for a male Florence Nightingale, a Prince Charming, a Good Shepherd, who never arrived and, as Baba suggests, may have never existed.

The epilogue helps the reader trace the meanings of motherhood in the *Trilogy*, culminating in its deconstruction and rewriting as narrative. This plotting of motherhood again recalls one of the most common outcomes of the female romance plot: the heroine can only realize her potential as woman through marriage and childbearing. This idealized vision of motherhood is dismantled in the *Trilogy*, particularly in Baba's assessment of Kate's life. In the epilogue, Baba reveals evidence of Kate's deteriorating mental state in her reproduction of their final conversation, during which Kate "raved about some dream, some apocalyptic dream," quoted Rilke, mumbled about roses, and "put her hand to her heart and said she'd like to tear it out, stamp on it, squash it to death, her heart being her undoing" (530). Here, religious and romantic metaphors combine in the figure of the Mother, especially as doubled in the cultural myth of the Virgin Mary. In a possible allusion to the Sacred Heart, Kate's desire to destroy her heart symbolizes not only romantic but maternal love. In Jacopone's dramatic hymn on the Passion, *Donna del Paradiso,* Mary, upon hearing that Jesus is being stripped and nailed to the cross "cries out in pain, wishing that her heart had rather been torn from her body than she should witness such a Crucifixion."[20] Kate is the Mater Dolorosa, whom Baba describes as "drooling and holding out the old metaphorical breast, like a warm scone or griddle bread . . . that was Kate's mistake, the old umbilical love. She wanted to twine fingers with her son, Cash, throughout eternity" (515).[21] When Baba calls Cash to break the news of his mother's death, she notes that he doesn't sound really surprised, "because he knew she was prone to the old Via Dolorosa" (529).

In contrast, Baba recalls her own husband's nickname for her—"Little Mother." She sees the irony inherent in this, for Baba and her daughter have never formed an ideal maternal bond. She reflects, "Little mother for the one illegitimate kid that I had, a girl that had a will of her own and a mind of her own from the second she was born. Vomited the milk I gave her, rejected me, from day one" (515). Baba, unlike Kate, clearly rejects the role of Mater Dolorosa; she refuses to play into the religious and sociopolitical protocols. This irreverence toward motherhood is seen most starkly in her angry rant about the pope: "Now, when Pope John Paul II travels he says what Popes have been saying since *secula seculorum*—'Thou shalt not sin.' He's still for keeping women in bondage, sexual bondage above all. . . . The Pope is all for bevies of children within wedlock, more children to fill the slums and the buses and smash telephone kiosks, because it's usually the ones in the slums that breed so profusely, part of their routine. . . . The smarter ones know all the ropes, know how to keep in with the Pope and still swing from the old chandeliers" (522).[22] Baba understands the hypocrisy behind societal attitudes toward motherhood. She is scornful of the church's hypocritical position on contraception and its emphasis on motherhood as the essence of womanhood, particularly in the case of Irish motherhood, with all the cultural baggage that goes along with it. She recognizes that the Catholic ideal of womanhood, the Virgin Mary, is unrealistic and unfair. Likewise, she implicitly understands that failure to be submissive, chaste, and selfless often leads to women being labeled as impure, tainted, or simply evil. In Christian patriarchal societies, along with the exalted Mater, we find the fallen woman, be she Eve or Mary Magdalene. As Marina Warner has observed: "Together, the Virgin and the Magdalene form a diptych of Christian patriarchy's idea of woman. There is no place in the conceptual architecture of Christian society for a single woman who is neither a virgin nor a whore. . . . The Church venerates two ideals of the feminine—consecrated chastity in the Virgin Mary and regenerate sexuality in the Magdalene. Populous as the Catholic pantheon is, it is nevertheless so impoverished that it cannot conceive of a single female saint independently of her relations (or lack of relations) with men."[23] Not surprisingly, these two "ideals of the feminine" are as limiting as the conventional endings for female characters in novels: marriage or death. At first, O'Brien's text would seem to reinscribe these possibilities. Both Kate and Baba suffer because of their "regenerate sexuality." Baba reveals in the epilogue that she is still trapped in a less-than-satisfying marriage, and Kate's transgressions ultimately lead to her death—the stock closure of the transgressive female plot.

Yet O'Brien's *Trilogy and Epilogue* lays the groundwork for scrutiny of the literary, as well as social, scripts available to women. The numerous literary allusions, especially to novels that follow a traditional female plot, lay bare the inadequacy of those literary scripts. Some of these allusions seem to undercut the seriousness of the original text.[24] For example, near the beginning of *Girls in Their Married Bliss,* we find a clear reference to Charlotte Brontë's *Jane Eyre* when Baba declares, "Well, to cut a long story short, [Reader] I married him" (385). In the epilogue, too, Baba resembles Jane Eyre: she faithfully returns to her now invalid lover/husband. Baba appears to see the inherent irony in Kate's story, as well as in her own. In *Girls in Their Married Bliss,* Baba describes Kate's remorse over her problems with her husband Eugene: "She pitied Eugene, She said. He was a misfit. He loved his child. She couldn't be responsible if he went mad. *For whom the bell tolls.* I mean, I don't have to go over the rigmarole. *You've heard it millions of times before*" (421, emphasis added). In this passage, in addition to the Hemingway reference, we have evidence of Baba's consciousness that both she and Kate are trapped in the scripts laid out for them, both in literature and in society. Baba "knows" that her narratee has heard (or read) this story "millions of times before." It is as if Baba (and O'Brien) were winking at us as readers familiar with the tradition of the female plot in Western literature.

The epilogue explodes the meaning of such foretold and retold stories. Baba's irreverent, regenerate voice serves not only an ideological function (to critique social and literary institutions), but also a testimonial function (through which Baba desacralizes the myth of Kate as Mother through religious and romantic discourse). Whether or not Kate's death was indeed a suicide, Baba is forced to come to terms with it as the culmination of a self-destructive life. As Margaret R. Higonnet has noted, such a death must be addressed by other characters: "To take one's life is to force others to read one's death. . . . The act is a self-barred signature."[25] Baba's narrating process leads her not only to understand Kate's dilemma, but also to reevaluate her feelings for her husband: "I realized that I didn't hate him anymore and that maybe I never hated him" (520). In this way, the epilogue functions as a catharsis for Baba that enables her to begin the process of rewriting the story of her own life.

At the same time, the epilogue might be read as a sort of elegy for Kate, though certainly not in the traditional sense.[26] Baba mentions ghosts and spirits throughout the *Trilogy,* but her attitude toward spiritual return seems to undergo a change in the epilogue. Early on, an angry Baba addresses Kate in an apostrophe: "Oh, Kate, why did you let the bastards win . . . why buckle under their barbaric whims?" Her anger and frustration is mixed with fear and confusion, and she confesses: "I'm terrified that she'll appear to me some night, maybe when I'm out in the garden smelling the phlox, or she'll be plonked on my bidet in ashes and loincloth, telling me some dire thing such as repent. Repent what. People are fucking gangsters" (513). Baba dreads the thought of Kate coming back to haunt her. Interestingly, she imagines Kate would ask her to "repent." This might be read in both the literal sense (to repent one's sins) but also in a figurative, literary sense (that female characters must repent their transgressions or pay for them through death). Baba explicitly rejects this notion; she refuses to be blackmailed into following a script by people she sees as "fucking gangsters."

Baba's initial fear of Kate's return is transformed into a hope for vengeance. She proclaims, "I hope she rises up nightly like the banshee and does battle with her progenitors" (523). She hopes that Kate will come back to haunt those who have caused her to suffer, those representatives of Irish Catholic patriarchy who have driven her into the role of the heroine whose transgressions must be punished. This differs from the peaceful, pastoral tone of a traditional elegy. Instead, Baba uses an Irish version of the monstrous feminine, the banshee, to convey her rage with the cultural codes imposed upon her generation. Baba then refocuses her anger and confusion on Ireland itself. She complains that she and Cash (Kate's son) will have to take Kate's ashes to "the old sod . . . and scatter them between the bogs and the bog lakes and the murmuring waters and every other fucking bit of depressingness that oozes from every hectometer and every furlong of the place." Baba transfers her despair and contempt to the land itself. Though she and Kate had left Ireland, they were not able to escape it. The futility of trying to elude their cultural roots is symbolized by the landscape.

By the final page of the epilogue, Baba temporarily embraces the religious discourse she has spent the greater part of the *Trilogy* mocking: "Jesus, is there no end to what people expect? Even now I expect a courier to whiz in on a scooter to say it's been a mistake; I'm crazy, I'm even thinking of the Resurrection and the stone pushed away, I want to lift her up and see the life and the blood coming back into her cheeks, I want time to be put back, I want it to be yesterday, to undo the unwanted crime that has been done. Useless. Nothing for it but fucking hymns" (531). Although she believes it useless, she continues, narrating future events: "We'll go through all the motions and all the protocol, the wreaths and the roses and Mozart and Van Morrison, and then the coffin off on its rocky little ride" (531–32). Her ambivalence toward Ireland and Catholicism will not prevent her from performing all the rituals it requires. She will follow the rituals, although she clearly acknowledges that she knows they will not bring Kate back. Yet Baba's blasphemous depiction of the Irish and Catholic traditions in the epilogue is true to her rebellious spirit. Baba's narrative suggests the possibility of textual resurrection, if not a physical one. Its ambiguously elegiac qualities call for a different term, perhaps a female anti-elegy.

The final paragraphs of the epilogue become more and more poetic, more and more prayerlike, until Baba finally concludes: "and I'm praying that her son won't interrogate me, because there are some things in this world you cannot ask, and oh, Agnus Dei, there are some things in this world you cannot answer" (531). In this final passage, Baba's narrative authority is briefly undermined by her struggle to find answers to questions she cannot even bring herself to ask. Yet rather than close off the text, this ending leaves it open. This (dis)resolution of the story leaves the *Trilogy* open to interpretation. The epilogue ends with Baba's observation that there are questions that can be neither asked nor answered. The reader is left to try to formulate the missing questions and answers. As Alison Booth has noted, in women's texts concerned with narrative closure, "Even when the end does not pretend to have the last word, the emphasis will fall there for the reader."[27] Baba certainly does not pretend to have the last word, but the reader is invited to ponder Baba's final words and is tempted to go back, to reread the *Trilogy,* perhaps in an attempt to find those unaskable questions. The story may end here, but not the discourse.

O'Brien's epilogue strives to achieve the goals of Borges's ideal epilogue; it does "not exhaust the meanings" of the *Trilogy*, but rather continues "to unfold [meaning] in the receptive imaginations of those who now close it." O'Brien's text—both in its story and its design—attempts to move beyond the tragic fate of its heroines. At one point, Baba identifies the "Father [as] the crux of [Kate's dilemma]," but the narrative structure of the epilogue suggests that the crucial theme is that of the Mother. Baba and Kate are synthesized via Baba's act of narrating, and the epilogue might be read as a prayer "In the Name of the Mother" through which Baba hopes the figure of the Mother will be liberated, reassessed, rewritten, and even reinvented. Not only for Kate and Baba's sake, but for that of their mothers as well as all Irish women.

Notes

1. Lynette Carpenter, "Tragedies of Remembrance, Comedies of Endurance: The Novels of Edna O'Brien," in *Essays on the Contemporary British Novel,* ed. Hedwig Bock and Albert Wertheim (Munich: Maz Heuber, 1986), 263.

2. Edna O'Brien, "Why Irish Heroines Don't Have to Be Good Anymore," *New York Times Book Review,* 11 May 1986.

3. Nancy K. Miller, *Subject to Change: Reading Feminist Writing* (New York: Columbia University Press, 1988), 44. Miller's definition of female plot is "quite simply that organization of narrative event which delimits a heroine's psychological, moral, and social development within a sexual fate. . . . Female plot thus is both what the culture has always already inscribed for woman and its reinscription in the linear time of fiction. It is generally mapped by the heroine's engagement with the codes of the dominant ideology, her obligatory insertion within the institutions which in society and novels name her—marriage, for example." Though men as well as women produce novels with female plots, Miller argues, "female-authored literature generally questions the costs and overdetermination of this particular narrative economy with an insistence such that the fictions engendered provide an internal, dissenting commentary on the female plot itself" (208).

4. Darcy O'Brien, "Edna O'Brien: A Kind of Irish Childhood," in *Twentieth-Century Women Novelists,* ed. Thomas F. Staley (Totowa, N.J.: Barnes and Noble, 1982), 184, 185.

5. Anatole Broyard, as cited in Peggy O'Brien, "The Silly and the Serious: An Assessment of Edna O'Brien," *Massachusetts Review* 28.3 (1987): 477.

6. See James M. Haule, "Tough Luck: The Unfortunate Birth of Edna O'Brien," *Colby Library Quarterly* 23.4 (1987): 216–24; and Rebecca Pelan, "Edna O'Brien's 'Stage-Irish' Persona: An 'Act' of Resistance," *Canadian Journal of Irish Studies* 19.1 (July 1993): 67–78.

7. In her analysis of Edna O'Brien's article "Why Irish Heroines Don't Have to Be Good Anymore," Peggy O'Brien speaks of her "misappropriation of a native tradition. . . . Hers are sins of presumption and reduction. . . . Her egoism

robs other characters and events of their individuality and usually their stature. She transforms the seering [*sic*] story of Deirdre into a maudlin, melodramatic tale of woman's woe" (475). The implication that the heroic women of Ireland's past have become the Kates and Babas of Ireland's present troubles some critics, who seem to imply that Edna O'Brien isn't "Irish" enough to be worthy of the "native tradition."

8. Rachel Blau DuPlessis, *Writing Beyond the Ending: Narrative Strategies of Twentieth-Century Women Writers* (Bloomington: Indiana University Press, 1985), x–xi.

9. Gérard Genette, *Palimpsests,* trans. Channa Newman and Claude Doubinsky (Lincoln: University of Nebraska Press, 1997), 207–8.

10. All direct quotations from the *Trilogy* are taken from Edna O'Brien, *The Country Girls Trilogy and Epilogue* (New York: Farrar, Straus & Giroux, 1986). To help contextualize the narrative structure of the epilogue, it might be helpful to recall a few narrative characteristics of the novels of the *Trilogy. The Country Girls* and *The Lonely Girl* are narrated in the first person by Cait (later "Kate"). In *Girls in Their Married Bliss* there is a move from the innocence of Kate's narrative perspective as a child and adolescent to that of the more cynical, adult voice of Baba. Yet Baba is not the only point of focalization; her four chapters narrated in the first person are interspersed among eight others, which are narrated from the perspective of a third-person omniscient narrator. So *Bliss* begins with Baba explaining, "Not long ago Kate Brady and I were having a few gloomy gin fizzes up London, bemoaning the fact that nothing would ever improve, that we'd die the way we were—enough to eat, married, dissatisfied" (381), and it ends with the external narrator observing Kate and Baba in the hospital after Kate's sterilization: "It was odd for Baba to see Kate like that, all the expected responses were missing" (508). These curious shifts in point-of-view provide a kind of transition to the epilogue, which is narrated solely by Baba.

11. Gérard Genette, *Narrative Discourse: An Essay in Method,* trans. Jane E. Lewin (Ithaca: Cornell University Press, 1980), 217, emphasis added.

12. Alison Booth, introduction to *Famous Last Words: Changes in Gender and Narrative Closure,* ed. Alison Booth (Charlottesville: University Press of Virginia, 1993), 3.

13. Jorge Luis Borges. *El libro de arena. Obras completas III* (The Book of Sand. Complete works, Volume 3) (Barcelona: Emecé Editores, 1996), 72–73.

14. Kathy Mezei, introduction to *Ambiguous Discourse: Feminist Narratology and British Women Writers,* ed. Kathy Mezei (Chapel Hill: University of North Carolina Press, 1996), 14.

15. Lynne Pearce, *Feminism and the Politics of Reading* (London: Arnold, 1997), 69, 73, 69.

16. See Pearce, 73.

17. Robyn Warhol, *Gendered Interventions: Narrative Discourse in the Victorian Novel* (New Brunswick, N.J.: Rutgers University Press, 1989), 36.

18. Jeanette Roberts Shumaker, "Sacrificial Women in Short Stories by Mary Lavin and Edna O'Brien," *Studies in Short Fiction* 32 (1995): 196.

19. Baba is quite adept in her ironic and sometimes humorous use of religious metaphors. To cite just two examples, Baba bemusedly recalls how her

husband and mother would "drink to me: the bloody sacrificial lamb" (386), and she describes Kate's life "like a chapter of the inquisition" (387).

20. Marina Warner, *Alone of All Her Sex: The Myth and the Cult of the Virgin Mary* (New York: Vintage, 1983), 212.

21. Kate's entire concept of her identity seems to revolve around her role as mother. Her "umbilical love," as Baba describes it, contrasts starkly with her youthful ambivalence toward motherhood. Years before she had confessed, "There were some things which I was very touchy about: babies for instance. Babies terrified me" (233), and later, "Babies terrified me—I remembered the day Baba first told me about breast feeding, and I felt sick again, just as I had done that day" (317).

22. Compare with this previous passage from *Girls in Their Married Bliss*: "Relax! I was thinking of women and all they have to put up with, not just washing nappies or not being able to be high-court judges, but all this. All this poking and probing and hurt. And not only when they go to doctors but when they go to bed as brides with the men that love them. Oh, God, who does not exist, you hate women, otherwise you'd have made them different. And Jesus, who snubbed your mother, you hate them more. Roaming around all that time with a bunch of men, fishing; and Sermons on the Mount. Abandoning Women" (473).

23. Warner, *Alone of All Her Sex*, 235.

24. Other examples allude to the conventional death of the romantic heroine. Years before her death, and before her breakdown in Waterloo Station, Eugene told Kate that she looked like Anna Karenina in the coat he had bought her (203). In *Bliss,* we find an almost tragic irony in Baba's recounting of a phone call she had placed to Kate: "She wasn't there. Out drowning herself, I imagined" (431).

25. Margaret R. Higonnet, "Speaking Silences: Women's Suicide," in *The Female Body in Western Culture: Contemporary Perspectives,* ed. Susan Rubin Suleiman (Cambridge: Harvard University Press, 1986), 68–69.

26. A traditional elegy, in particular the pastoral elegy, laments the death of a loved one and includes literary conventions such as the invocation of the muses, questioning God's justice, and a procession of mourners. Usually the initial sadness and sense of loss is transformed into joy, for the departed is now in Heaven. See M. H. Abrams, *A Glossary of Literary Terms,* 5th ed. (New York: Holt, Rinehart, 1988), 47.

27. Booth, *Famous Last Words,* 12. Booth has argued that "the predominance of the romance plot, leading either to marriage or death, does not close the play of the *discourse* along with the *story.* How the novel ends often exposes the difference between the narrative 'expression' and its 'content,' and either or both of these intertwined elements may serve to undermine social and literary convention. The woman's story and the design of the text itself may find ways to contradict the last words that ostensibly control the meaning of the ensuing silence" (2–3).

Hysterical Hooliganism
O'Brien, Freud, Joyce

HELEN THOMPSON

Edna O'Brien's writing foregrounds women's psychological struggles with social institutions that wish to contain women in limited spheres and overarticulate their sexual roles. It is woman's burden to represent herself as the patriarchy wishes to see her; yet, in order to mirror the patriarchy's demands of her and to remove the potential for social ostracism and possibly punishment, she has to stifle herself. In O'Brien's work we see that the Irish patriarchy is anxious to control women's sexual and reproductive roles because by limiting women they maintain the semblance of masculine dominance. Anxiety is a significant term in this context. It is in the overarticulations of women's social and sexual functions, which effectively silence any attempts Irish society has made to debate sexual issues, that patriarchal anxiety manifests itself. Anxiety seems to reside in the suspicion that women constitute a hostile audience who would prefer not to conform. Indeed, from out of this rigid framework, O'Brien, in all of her work, points to the seams where women cannot and will not be contained.

O'Brien writes in reaction to the Irish Constitution, the master narrative that overdetermines women's bodies and frames women as mothers. Narratives like these, which desire mastery over women, reduce them and their bodies to surface texts to be read, understood, interpreted, and appended to masculine concerns. O'Brien also responds to the Irish canon, the list of master narratives that frame women as objects of literature, not subjects of it, and certainly not producers of it. Joyce's *Ulysses* and Freud's *Dora* are narratives that work to control female experience. In each of these cases, the writer finds it difficult to maintain his female character within the frame he has created. The bodily surfaces seem to speak a life of their own, despite the masculine attempts at mastery over body and text. The reader helps the female characters erupt from the texts; and, in this case, O'Brien's reading of Joyce reinterprets Molly's textual position through her use of the trope of hysteria.

According to Freud, hysteria is "the somatic representation of a repressed bisexual conflict, an unconscious refusal to accept a single and defined subject position in the Oedipal structuration of desire and identity."[1] Since hysteria is primarily a women's malady, it would seem that oscillation is the psychological work of women. Certainly, Freud thinks that they have more adjustments to make as they move their attentions from the primary love object, the mother, to the secondary love object, the father, in a healthy resolution of Oedipal conflict. Freud suggested that Dora's neuroses stemmed from her contrary love objects, Herr K. and Frau K. These oscillations have to be perceived as neuroses in order to protect the dominance of heterosexuality and the masculine love object. Yet, the contradictory movements of desire also make women's heterosexuality possible. Therefore, the oscillations are at once neurotic and healthy. Such a contradiction points to Freud's anxiety concerning female sexuality, his inability to understand it and, therefore, control it. Instead of exhibiting mastery, then, Freud reproduces in his case study his discomfort with feminine sexuality. Joyce exhibits similar ambivalence and desire for mastery in his presentation of female sexuality in *Ulysses*. O'Brien, on the other hand, sees women as more than case studies. In this respect, her treatments of Mary Hooligan and Virginia Woolf are similar, in that they are not framed by rigid narrative structures.

Claire Kahane argues that modernist writers such as Ford Madox Ford, Joseph Conrad, and T. S. Eliot use hysteria as a narrative technique in order to explore the fragmentation of identity in the modern world. By textualizing the hysteria, they are also attempting to control what they perceive as the chaotic nature of identity in the new century. She argues that these writers use first person narrators, not their own voices, to distance themselves from the fragmentation, even while they are creating it. Even though the writers do not directly speak in their texts and create voices to speak for them, these voices are not distant enough from their own consciousnesses and they are tainted by the hysteria. In a footnote she says that James Joyce gives "the illusion of unmediated first-person consciousness through interior monologues."[2] While the Penelope episode appears to be unmediated, actually it is not. Joyce hystericizes the text of Molly's monologue to seemingly represent a female voice, a female character, and a female sensibility. However, the experience of Molly's monologue is not distinctly feminine, because Joyce has created it; it is a version of femininity constructed by a male author for a male audience to demonstrate both modernity and femininity. Molly is not unrestrained; rather she is controlled by Joyce's metonymical focus on her mouth as a culmination of his presentation as well as other seemingly unmediated male perspectives of her via parts of her body glimpsed in other episodes and that break up Molly's body and contain it. The body parts also serve to tease and disappoint the reader who awaits her whole body. Kahane suggests that we can read between the lines of modernist texts to uncover the authorial subject's hysterical ambivalence, the passions of the voice, as she calls it.[3] If we read between the lines of Penelope and see that Joyce is putting hysterical words into Molly's metonymical mouth, then it is quite possible that Molly's monologue represents Joyce's chaotic and contradictory attitudes toward female sexuality, the female body, and the female speaking subject. In other words, Molly's hysteria could possibly be borrowed from Joyce.

We can read Molly and Dora as hysterics who, precisely because of their neuroses and their physical symptoms, cannot be contained within the narratives and subsequently erupt in the readings of the texts. As Toril Moi says, "just as the hysteric perturbs the orderly unfolding of family life, might she not likewise disturb the position of authorial mastery . . . ?"[4] Both Joyce and Freud attempt to frame female sexuality as a mystery to be solved, as unambivalent, easily defined, and therefore controlled by authoritative (and, therefore, male) narrative. Yet, the anxiety concerning their inabilities to do so—and even their own hysterical reactions created by this anxiety—seep through the narratives. Freud's anxiety manifests itself in his framing of the narrative as a fragment and his frequent reiterations of Dora's interruption of the narrative by ending her therapy. Joyce's anxiety exhibits itself in his thoroughly phallic rendering of female sexual desire through a female voice.

Edna O'Brien is frequently compared to James Joyce. Joyce's influence on O'Brien is evident even in her earliest novels, according to Fritz

Senn.[5] Yet, while critics often see the influence of Joyce in her characters, O'Brien herself is also described as Joycean. For example, in a review of *Lantern Slides*, Jack Fuller says, "if Molly Bloom had James Joyce's gift for story and didn't ramble on so, she might have written fiction like Edna O'Brien."[6] It is particularly telling that Fuller disengages Molly Bloom from her fictional role and thereby her creator in order to treat her as a writer and compare her to Edna O'Brien. In this way, Fuller gives Molly the autonomy that Joyce denies her by freeing her from the frame narrative. But also, we can read his statement another way. He simultaneously suggests that both Molly Bloom and Edna O'Brien have been shaped by James Joyce's vision and so O'Brien is perhaps just another character in one of Joyce's texts. Whichever way we read Fuller's commentary, it is clear that he believes Molly and Edna function on the same plane: both women are characters and exist as texts to be unpacked. Certainly, O'Brien does not deny Joyce's importance and stature in Irish letters; however, her own relationship to Joyce is more ambiguous that it appears on the surface.

In fact, O'Brien reverses Fuller's observation when she makes Joyce the subject of her text in a biography. Instead of taking an objective, academic position regarding her subject, O'Brien uses Joyce as her protagonist in a subjective narrative of his life. Indeed, the narrative structure of *James Joyce* mirrors that of *Night* in its opening words, which also constitute the title of the chapter, "Once upon a time," and this phrase foregrounds the fictional nature of O'Brien's text. Her language further transforms him into a malleable character via the mimicry of Joyce's style: "James Joyce, poor joist . . . a Joyce of all trades, a bullock befriending bard, a peerless mummer, a priestified kinchite, a quill-frocked friar, a timoneer, a pool-beg flasher and a man with the gift of the Irish majacule script."[7] In this first page, O'Brien makes Joyce the subject of his own language and further dilutes his mastery by deemphasizing his importance of subject by flaunting her own linguistic prowess.

In other texts, O'Brien makes no secret of the influence of Joyce on her work, yet she denies Molly Bloom as an influence on *Night*.[8] In various other contexts she has referred to Joyce as "dear Mr. Joyce," "my master," "beyond assessment—gigantic," "the first and indeed the foremost to enunciate female desire, desire as rampant as any man's, and moreover he rendered it in a woman's voice."[9] While it appears on the surface that her admiration for Joyce is abundant, the ebullience with which she praises him undercuts the admiration. In these quotations, she does not directly focus her attentions on his writing; instead, she speaks of his capabilities in vague terms. When she does mention his work, she is clear to explain that she is praising his ability to ventrilo-quize a female desire that is reminiscent of male desire. In other words, she is making it clear that Joyce does not authentically present feminine desire in the Penelope episode.

Furthermore, O'Brien's ambivalence is couched in homage-paying and irony, which further undermines her flattery of Joyce: "There is of course Molly Bloom, but she is the creation of a man. Only she boasts and raves about her indisputable power to arouse man's desire, to come-hither him and to make jest of him in the process. Instead of pil-grimages to Mary and Joseph, and Jude, Bridget and Ita, the women of Ireland ought to be down on their knees to Mister James Joyce, who not only made their sexuality more patent to the world at large but who stripped from them the shackles of their own bound souls."[10] At once, O'Brien dismisses and exalts Joyce's portrayal of female desire. Indeed, her reaction to Joyce oscillates between critique and praise and through these extremes she clearly indicates her reservations about Joyce's por-trayals of female sexuality. On the one hand, Molly Bloom's character is flawed because it is drawn from male perceptions of femininity, and thus she is more interested in sexual prowess, power, and bravado. Yet on the other hand, O'Brien suggests that Joyce should be canonized and worshiped for freeing women's sexuality from Irish repression.

These oscillations can also be seen in her biography. Indeed, we might argue that her text reverses the pattern of Penelope by allowing Molly to write Joyce because she focuses on his libido and his relation-ships with women as well as his writing. We see a Joyce who is ob-sessed with prostitutes and who exploits the other women in his life, in-cluding Nora, his mother, Harriet Shaw Weaver, and Sylvia Beach. Yet O'Brien also takes a critical stance regarding these relationships. She points out that even though Joyce preferred relationships with women to those with men, these women suffered with the attention (or lack of) they received, particularly Nora who was isolated and impoverished. O'Brien even suggests that Joyce's views of women were such that they were subjects to be molded by him, as "idealized creatures on pedes-tals, put there for his litanies" or in a comparison to William Blake, "out of a sublime egotism wanted to fashion the woman into a creation of his own."[11] Hence, Molly Bloom may have been based on a combination of his mother's letters and Nora's sexual appetites, but she is a Joycean creation shaped by his own desires. O'Brien's biography recognizes this impulse and informs *Night*.

In light of O'Brien's commentary on Joyce, I believe that the relationship between O'Brien and Joyce is not the simple, noncompetitive deference of a fledgling writer toward her mentor, as Michael Patrick Gillespie suggests.[12] In fact, O'Brien agrees with the critics about Joyce's influence on her work in order to critique his vision in her fiction. Yet, she also exaggerates the paternalism and mastery inherent in his influence and, by reenvisioning Irish women's subjectivity, undermines Joyce's Molly Bloom.

Critics frequently point out that O'Brien's *Night* bears great resemblance to the Penelope episode of *Ulysses*. Lotus Snow, as representative of these critics, says, "*Night* (1972) derives from Joyce: from the long soliloquy of Molly Bloom in the final pages of *Ulysses*. It is the repetitious and bawdy reminiscence of an aging Irish floozy."[13] Indeed, both Mary Hooligan and Molly Bloom are aging Irish floozies. Each woman spends a sleepless night in bed ruminating on the satisfactions and dissatisfactions of her life. While Molly is unhappy with her husband, Mary cannot find a lasting relationship with either a man or a woman. Molly and Mary both display multifaceted and demanding sexualities. Molly imagines sex with most men she meets, even wishing she were a man in order to penetrate a woman. Mary chooses lovers of all ages, of all social classes, and of both genders. In this respect, both characters defy Irish perceptions of femininity yet do so in the privacy of their bedrooms. These women speak through self-reflexive narratives that are experimental in form. Instead of chronology, their narratives are perpetuated by seemingly random thoughts; indeed, Joyce does away with punctuation to suggest the loose associative nature of Molly's thoughts.

It is clear that Molly and Mary are similar characters. They are even connected via their names; Molly is the familiar form of Mary.[14] In fact, *Night* is a response to and a critique of this last chapter of *Ulysses*. By mimicking the style and character of the Penelope episode, O'Brien effectively rewrites Joyce's stream-of-consciousness narrative and its hystericization of Molly Bloom by hystericizing Mary Hooligan and her narrative, but with a difference. While Molly's is the disembodied voice of a woman on the verge of her menses, Mary's body is integral to the content and form of her narrative. Such a difference is, in a sense, illustrative of O'Brien's plagiarism of her literary "father."[15] Her strategy works to demonstrate the shortcomings of Joyce's vision of female sexual and social roles as well as highlight the emancipatory possibilities of Mary's more fluid identity.

Plagiarism is an elitist crime. In fact, textual theft is only a crime if the subject intends to steal from another writer or thinker.[16] For O'Brien to leave such clear evidence of the theft in her work must mean that she wants to be caught. Indeed, Joyce's own anxieties evident in the monologue may stem from his own acts of plagiarism. While O'Brien plagiarizes Joyce, Joyce steals from the textuality he forces on the bodies of his wife and daughter.[17] By using hysteria as a narrative form and placing a female voice in the text as a representative of that hysteria, Joyce is reducing Molly to a surface text in which her bodily symptoms are textual and therefore readable and plagiarizable. We can, therefore, understand O'Brien's rendering of Molly Bloom as an act of stealing Molly's textuality/sexuality. Furthermore, through her revision of Molly as Mary Hooligan, O'Brien is effectively removing Molly and her text from the economic exchange of marriage and heterosexuality, just as Mary disavows her traditional gender roles and her place in the heterosexual market place. In this sense, her plagiarism has become a transgressive tactic. O'Brien is also undermining what Randall calls the "institutional authority"[18] of the Irish canon by emphasizing that Joyce's monologue lacks textual integrity and, worst of all, is unoriginal. He has, after all, stolen from hysterical women who are the authors of their own symptoms.

Readings of Molly Bloom and her narrative are copious and contentious. As Bonnie Kime Scott says, "for the critics, there has been, first, the dilemma of whether to assign Molly to a realistic or symbolic category, and then the decision of whether to exalt or denigrate her."[19] I would suggest that these critical oscillations mirror Joyce's own uncertainty about the femininity he was textualizing. Critics read Molly symbolically as Celtic goddess (Scott), feminine performance (Herr), masquerade (Devlin), and even housewife impersonating a prostitute (Froula).[20] She is perceived as emancipated because she discusses her sexuality quite openly, because as Scott suggests "she topples the masonry of sentimental, proper, polite interpretations of women's lives" by openly discussing her sexuality.[21] Yet, others, like Henke, consider her restricted and repressed because she is "framed" by a masculine gaze (Pearce), and her performance is for only a masculine audience (Henderson).[22] She is at once conventional (Henderson) and unconventional.[23] Similarly, her monologue has been read as an example of Irigaray's *écriture féminine* (McCormick, Levitt, Nolan), Kristeva's women's time (Harper), as a political weapon (Schloss), and a pornographic male fantasy (Ziarek).[24] Molly represents female desire, male desire, absolute freedom, absolute constriction. O'Brien responds to Molly Bloom by reading her as a figment of Joyce's sexual imagination. She is a female character who represents male fantasies of female desire in that both her body and her narrative are framed by this vision and by the frame of *The Odyssey*. Hence, her sexuality becomes a ventriloquized performance from the limited sphere of the bedroom she shares with her husband.

Unlike Molly Bloom, Mary Hooligan is not in her own home, her own bed, and her sleeping husband is not lying next to her. Instead, she is in the home of an English couple for whom she is house-sitting, and, furthermore, she is alone. Mary remembers her childhood in Coose, her relationship with her parents, her escape from Ireland to Liverpool and finally London, her marriage to Dr. Flaggler and the birth and upbringing of her son. Since her marriage ended, she has struggled to make a living and has pursued a string of lovers. At present, she is without a home, permanent job, or a relationship.

It is interesting that O'Brien uses the names of literary figures for the owners of the house and Mary's employers. Jonathan and Tig are names borrowed from John Middleton Murray and Katherine Mansfield, Tig being Mansfield's nickname. Hence, we could read this novel on an historical level, seeing the underside of Victorian literary culture—of which Joyce was a part, even though he was removed on the Continent. We could also read it as a commentary on ownership and mastery of geographic space. As Irish Mary dominates a house owned by an Englishman and a New Zealander and gets to know it better than Jonathan and Tig can possibly know it themselves, O'Brien may be suggesting that knowledge and power are illusions when based on the constructions of gender or nationality; what really matters is one's relationship to that space and whether one thoroughly inhabits it or not. The same can be said of the female body, and Mary inhabits hers in the same scrupulous way that she does this borrowed accommodation. Since her insomnia is the reason for her narrative, we can read her body and her story as interconnected symptoms of hysteria.

Hysterical Body

Hysteria is a disorder of the body that affects the sufferer's ability to communicate logically and coherently. Historically, it has been categorized as a disorder that primarily affects women. While the Greeks believed that hysteria was caused by a woman's wandering womb, creating physical ailments wherever it found itself lodged, Freud believed that hysterical women were suffering either from a repressed sexual trauma or an equally repressed sexual desire. In either case, when treating hysteria, the body was considered a text to be read and rewritten. As Bernheimer and Kahane explain, the surface of the body offered the symptoms as puzzles to be solved.[25] The disease was also considered a physiological manifestation of woman's moral sickness. According to Strong, doctors believed that a woman's menstrual cycle created the potential for hysteria; also, the symptoms of hysteria were associated with what Bernheimer and Kahane call "deviant sexual conduct."[26] The plethora of hysterical manifestations ranged from coughs, limps, pains in various parts of the body to the inexplicable appearance of bruises or inflammation that adopted the form of words, thus creating a more literal text of the body. The cure for hysteria involved the intervention of a doctor to remove, either directly or indirectly, the physical ailment. The Greeks and Romans placed various potions, made up of ingredients ranging from frankincense to male excrement, at the opening of the woman's vagina so that the fragrance would lure the womb back to its rightful place. Freud believed that the hysteric could be cured by encouraging her to verbalize the psychological problem. Once she had spoken, the physical pain associated with her trauma would disappear. It would seem, then, that the hysteric had the ability to cure herself. However, this was not the case; she needed a (male) listener to translate her thoughts and her symptoms.

Freud's most famous case study of the "talking cure" is Dora, the hysteric who refused to be cured. The story of Dora demonstrates masculine control of determinations of hysteria as Freud attempts to dominate Dora through his narrative even though she refused him in her treatment. When comparing Freud's *Dora* to the Penelope episode of *Ulysses*, we see that both Dora and Molly are silenced by forceful masculine narratives that determine their sexualities. Molly Bloom is silent until the last chapter of this epic novel; instead of speaking for herself, she is spoken about and seen metonymically through glimpses of parts of her body, such as her arm, as body is woven into the text. Similarly, Dora's voice is absent from Freud's case study. Furthermore, both Molly and Dora are framed in the context of Greek myth—Homer's *Odyssey* and Sophocles' *Oedipus*—and do not constitute the subject of the narratives. The subject of *Dora* is Freud's anger over his inability to close the case; in *Ulysses*, Molly's narrative is undermined by the uniting of a lost father and son, of Leopold Bloom and Stephen Dedalus.

In both cases, maternal influences are ignored. Hence, both Dora and Molly Bloom become spectacles in their respective narrative frameworks, controlled by the masculine gazes of Freud and Joyce.

Molly Bloom, Dora, and Mary Hooligan are hysterical women by virtue of their physical ailments. Dora's symptoms range from a nervous cough to vaginal discharge; Mary and Molly suffer from insomnia, and Molly's case is further exacerbated by the onset of her menses. However, Mary's narrative differs from Dora's and Molly's because she refuses to control or be controlled by her story. As Karen Morley Brennan suggests, "hysteria, which on one level transforms women into spectacles, at the same time allows them to specularize the interpretations which have 'framed' them."[27] O'Brien allows Mary to speak for herself without imposing a framework that marginalizes her voice or refuses her as subject of the narrative. Instead, Mary is the subject of the novel and, in this central position, reenvisions not only Molly Bloom but also the definitions of hysteria that threaten to confine women's sexualities. In other words, she is in a position to interrogate the equation of women's biological and sexual functions with hysteria and madness and the reduction of women's bodies to surface text.

The narrative of *Night* does not reduce Mary's body to textuality; instead, it derives from her body by utilizing its functions for the narrative form. In the first few pages of the text, she defines herself as a woman: "I am a woman, at least I am led to believe so: I bleed, et cetera." "Woman" and "bleed" demonstrate a limited construction of femininity, a conflation that also creates women as hysterics. The remainder of feminine definition is left to the silence of the "et cetera." However, as well as interrogating such a facile definition of woman, Mary elaborates the silent et cetera in her narrative. These tasks overlap as she further describes her body: "And those noises, and those sighs . . . those coo-coos issue from me faithfully, like buntings. Not to mention the more bucolic sounds . . . the choice slushings of the womb which have ogled many another by means of gurgle, nuance, melody, ditty, and crass babbling supplication" (4–5).[28] Her body is noisy, and her narrative derives from the sounds made by her womb. Mary plays with the Greek notion of the wandering womb to suggest that her uterus has displaced itself to her mouth. Furthermore, she parodies the notion outlined by Beizer that a woman is "slave to her secretions, unable to control her dripping, spurting, oozing [of] bodily fluids" by claiming this fluidity for the structure of her narrative.[29] In this respect, her womb's articulations are disruptive because they are compliant and pacifying; yet, as the narrative demonstrates, they attack masculine constructions of female sexuality and speak of a woman who has no clearly defined gender role to fulfill. She is not a mother anymore, not a wife; instead, she is being paid for her domestic function as caretaker, thus professionalizing the feminine function.

Molly Bloom gets her period during the course of her narrative. While we can view this as Joyce's liberation of the unspeakable functions of women, Molly's flow merely indicates, according to Attridge, that she is not pregnant.[30] In this respect, the appearance of Molly's menses in the text is less revolutionary than it would first appear. The narrative style of this episode can be read in terms of the more modern form of hysteria, premenstrual syndrome, which is defined by a woman's anger, irrationality, unreasonableness, and general mutability and has been described by Karen Horney as woman's disavowal of her desire for a pregnant body.[31] Hence, we can view Molly's narrative excitability as stemming directly from her menses and, perhaps, from her wish and subsequent denial of that wish to be pregnant.

The primary difference between O'Brien's and Joyce's narratives lies in Molly's and Mary's attitudes toward their bleeding. While Mary Hooligan reverses the notion of female bleeding as problematic by correlating the fluidity of her narrative with her menstrual cycle and its generative power, Molly is angry with her body: "God knows theres always something wrong with us 5 days every 3 or 4 weeks usual monthly auction isn't it simply sickening . . . have we too much blood up in us or what O patience above its pouring out of me like the sea."[32] Not only does she view her period as a great inconvenience because it has thwarted her desire to have sex with Blazes Boylan, but also she believes it to be a sickness that women suffer from every month. Hence, a normal bodily function is assigned the role of a physical disorder caused by too much blood in the woman's body. Such an interpretation of Molly's menses at once breaks the taboo on discussing menstruation and relegates it to the domain of masculine (and quite possibly Joyce's) anxiety. As Karen Horney suggests, "the prime object of male dread is menstrual blood";[33] bleeding is associated with sickness and uncleanliness, therefore, sex is prohibited during menstruation. The acts of menstruation and childbearing also break down the division between inside and outside the body; a woman menstruating or giving birth is fearful precisely because her body fluids are not contained within the body.

Both Mary Hooligan and Molly Bloom have the self-dramatizing potential that characterizes hysteria. Yet while Mary struggles with memories of her former selves in order to divest herself of these roles, Molly insists on orgasmic pleasure. Her narrative, like a hysterical fit, is as Freud articulates, "an equivalent of coitus."[34] In other words, Molly is interested in pleasure, and she critiques femininity only to the extent that it denies her complete satisfaction. For example, she complains that women are rarely satisfied during sex, that multiple pregnancies are draining, and she is frustrated with her body. Yet the only act of emancipation is to give primacy to her sexual urges and manipulate her husband in order to satisfy her material needs. Furthermore, her view of women is negative: "I hate that in women no wonder they treat us the way they do we are a dreadful lot of bitches I suppose its all the troubles we have makes us so snappy."[35] Not only does Molly dislike women's roles, she also is not fond of what she perceives as women's temperamental emotions as they are associated with the reproductive functions. While Joyce is farsighted in that he distinguishes women's cultural conditioning from their biology, he creates a female character who dislikes many aspects of her own sex and, by using the pronoun "we" to discuss women's physical and emotional hindrances, Molly implies that she dislikes herself.

Mary Hooligan's relationship to her female organs constitutes the style of her narrative and the starting point for her self-analysis, while Molly Bloom's period signifies for her a digression in a narrative that ultimately celebrates her clearly defined role in marriage and in society. In fact, Molly's identity is unified by the social and sexual roles of wife, mother, and heterosexual lover. Mary's self, on the other hand, is fragmented because she is no longer a wife, mother, or dutiful daughter. This fragmentation is a classic symptom of hysteria. Such uncertainty is useful to Mary for it is a source of what Maureen Gaffney claims as "power to be able to experiment with many possible selves . . . [by] expanding the environments in which each of the sexes has traditionally operated."[36] Her experimentation takes the form of a polymorphous sexuality as well as with the adoption of a variety of costumes and roles.

Both Mary Hooligan and Molly Bloom have large sexual appetites and often find sex with men unsatisfying. However, while Molly's desire revolves around orgasm, Mary wishes to create a close union with a lover. Furthermore, Molly's sexuality is firmly constructed as heterosexual. Indeed, her lack of orgasmic pleasure may very well stem from her privileging male sexual pleasure in her fantasies. She imagines sexual contact with most men she thinks of—a young boy, Blazes Boylan, a priest, Stephen Dedalus—which suggests an obsession with sex and an indiscriminate taste in men. Yet, the sexual acts she imagines performing bring more pleasure to these men than to her. For example, she tells us she allows Bloom to kiss her bottom and she fantasizes about fellatio with Stephen Dedalus. Indeed, her fantasies of great conquests and also her insistence on orgasm seem to be derived from a masculine rather than a feminine perspective. Further, she says, "I wished he was here or somebody to let myself go with and come again like that I feel all fire inside me," thus suggesting the only way she can achieve orgasm is during sex with man.[37] Again, such an interpretation demonstrates a misunderstanding of female desire. In fact, Molly's sexual desire seems to be founded on penetration, which she prefers to the point of masturbating with a banana and wishing she is a man so that she can penetrate a woman. Hence, while Joyce is aiming to free female sexuality, he is framing it heterosexually and controlling desire by limiting it to orgasm by penetration. As Henderson suggests, Molly speaks her desire with "her master's voice" and thus reproduces his anxiety, his hysteria.[38] Molly Bloom has a one-track mind; that is, her sexual fantasies are by no means as polymorphous as Mary Hooligan's.

Mary's string of lovers is also indiscriminate. She describes them as "a motley crew, all shades, dimensions, breeds, ilks, national characteristics, inflammatingness, and penetratingness. Some randy, many conventional, one decrepit" (23). Yet we know that at present, she has few sexual partners and even suggests that she prefers to be alone. Mary, unlike Molly, does not fantasize about most of the men she comes into contact with, and her goal in sex is not orgasm but union. For example, with her most recent lover, Nick, she says, "I would like to think that our bloodstreams danced, bounced, bounded together, I would like to think our sensibilities met. Is that possible? Melted into each other" (24). Her attitude toward Nick suggests that Mary wants more than sex and more than a romantic relationship. Indeed, her narrative is propelled by her unfulfilled desire. It seems that Mary craves an emotional and physical union, an uncanny connection, a phantasmatic desire for the primary love object, the maternal body; perhaps for this reason, Mary experiments with lesbian sex.

Mary explores lesbianism during her affair with Nick and his wife. Also, in an unspecified relationship, Mary writes letters to a female lover. She says: "I have written some nauseating letters—'You touched my heart, you touched my cunt, I touched yours,' and so on and so forth. Devouring, cloying, calumnious. All of those missives I have kept in reserve, because to act as nonsensical as that, without presently dying, would be the most clownish of my many clownish actions" (6). At this point in the narrative, the distinction between memory and fantasy breaks down. It is not clear whether her letters are in response to a consummated relationship or whether she is imagining herself with a female lover. Mary remembers her lesbian affairs through letters, thus making sure that her lesbianism remains theoretical rather than practical. Such a stance protects her from social recrimination.

Her desire for a boundless union and the manifestation of hysterical tendencies in her narrative can be traced back to her mother, Lil, who has recently died after a long illness during which Mary nursed her. In light of this recent role, it is possible that Mary's insomnia, a symptom of her hysteria, can be attributed to the difficulties involved when nursing a sick parent, a circumstance that Jennifer L. Pierce investigates.[39] While Mary does not articulate her bereavement, she is clearly suffering; for example, she writes a letter to her mother and posts it before she remembers that her mother is dead. Such an act could represent either a gap in her memory or a fantasy of her mother's recovery. Significantly, she writes to ask her mother the color of her womb, since Mary believes she has memories from the time before she was born, when she was part of her mother's body. It is unlikely that Mary has such a memory but it is possible that she fantasizes about being still fused with her mother, an image that persists in the appearance of her mother's ghost.

Mary has seen an apparition of her mother that she believes will watch over her: "Lil had the audacity to appear there one night, swaddled in linen no less, and with a rosary swinging from her waist. . . . Some goddamn dreg of love welled up in me. . . . To tell you the truth, her visitation gave me the willies. . . . She got into the bed. . . . She arched and tilted and bowed her body so that she fitted exactly into mine, my tumescence and my curves, her tumescence and her curves, and it felt as if we were being welded together, or at least molded together. . . . She was going to be trailing me for the rest of my life" (42–43). It is clear from her description of Lil's apparition that Mary's emotional needs derive from the recent loss of her mother. Indeed, the fusion she describes has sexual pertinence, given her choice of words. "Tumescence" refers narratively and sexually to climax or a response to sexual stimulation, thus suggesting that she also desires to sleep with a woman in this fashion. Sharon Willis suggests that the hysteric's symptoms pose the question of desire for or identification with the maternal body.[40] Mary Hooligan seems to answer both. She both desires and fears the maternal body; her desire oscillates in its object; her sexual impulses

are nondifferentially oriented and multisexual. Furthermore, her identification with her mother is uncanny in that she both desires and fears
her mother's ghost, whose apparitional presence mimics the traces of
lesbian desire that usually exist in the margins but which Mary has
brought out of hiding and into the light.

Her identification with Lil is evidenced when, shortly after her
mother's death, Mary wears her mother's astrakhan coat. While she
puts on the coat merely to go for a walk, it is precisely at the time her
father asks her to stay and take care of him. Furthermore, Mary has already told us that there is a striking resemblance between herself and
Lil, so by wearing the coat so shortly after her mother's death, Mary is
symbolically trying on her mother's identity in order to decide whether
she will care for her father. Inevitably, she leaves her father rather than
stay with him and lock herself into a caretaking role. She assumes this
role in a different guise when Tig and Jonathan hire her.

Clothing and social and sexual identities are inextricably linked. As
Rabine attests, clothing indicates sexual identity, particularly the sexual
identities of women, and functions in the same way as a language.[41]
Brennan goes further by saying, "Indeed, fashion, like hysterical symptoms, confines the body of woman to a surface text."[42] As a surface text,
Mary wears clothes inappropriate to the occasions in which she finds
herself: lamé in the morning to walk home after a night of sex with Nick
and his wife, a Snow White costume on the night she has her first sexual encounter, and a satin dress for a walk in the park. Superficially,
Mary is breaking conventions and displaying her hysterical symptoms
by dressing in a manner that does not match the social circumstances.
Yet these outfits are at once disguises of and explorations into her own
identity and also signal her nonconformity, her refusal of fashion's ca-
pacity to reduce her to textuality. Significantly, Mary borrows many of
her incongruous clothes; for example, just as she wore her mother's,
she wears Tig's coat in order to attract a businessman. By borrowing
Tig's clothing, Mary attempts to adopt Tig's identity, either because she
feels that she cannot attract another successful man with her own personality or because she needs the protection of an assumed guise. It is
also possible that she is masquerading and flaunting her transgression.

Clothing is more than a disguise; in her married life it becomes a
weapon. She uses the purchase of a scarf to defy her dominating husband, Dr. Flaggler, whom she has been trying to leave. He ridicules her
attempts to extricate herself from the marriage by saying "You are not
going to escape me, not now, not ever, you are not going out of my

sight, you poor zealous wretch, you cannot make a life for yourself without me, it is beyond you, unattainable" (80). In response to Dr. Flaggler's deprecating attitude, Mary deliberately buys and puts on a scarf that she knows he dislikes. In fact, she wears it in an exaggerated fashion, "I wound it around my neck, made a double knot, followed by a nonsensical bow," to annoy her husband as well as demonstrate to him that his critical judgment of her is irrelevant (81). It also suggests that she has diminished his power since she buys the scarf herself and adorns herself with it. Instead of representing her husband's social and economic standing, the scarf marks her own. The variety of outfits Mary wears is a further indication of the fragmentation of her personality. Indeed, in her narrative, clothing functions in the same manner as a mirror. She says, "Mirrors are not for seeing by, mirrors are for wondering at, and wondering into," for speculation rather than specularization (3). Similarly, while on the surface clothes make a spectacle of Mary, she resists being framed as such and uses clothing to publicize her speculative self.

Mary is no longer obligated to wear "sensible" clothing; she has no domestic duties and no one to please or shame but herself. Hence, her wardrobe, like her sexuality, is multifaceted and both are utilized in her subjective experimentation. Conversely, Molly Bloom's interest in fashion is singularly motivated. She wishes to have new attire in order to attract her lover; before she married Leopold Bloom, Molly wooed him with a pair of her underwear, and she meets Boylan through mislaying her suede gloves. Molly thinks that without decent clothes, she will be spurned by men and women will have little respect for her because she is unattractive. Fashion in this way becomes a passport to social acceptance by both sexes. It is also compensation for her body: while she dislikes her body, she can enjoy the clothing that hides it. What is most disturbing about Molly's attitude toward both fashion and sex, however, is not that they are interconnected but that one can buy the other. In fact, Molly intends to persuade Bloom to buy her new underwear by arousing his desire: "Ill drag open my drawers and bulge it right out in his face as large as life he can stick his tongue 7 miles up my hole as hes there my brown part then Ill tell him I want £1 or perhaps 30/- Ill tell him I want to buy underclothes . . . then Ill wipe him off me just like a business his omission and then Ill go out."[43] Even though Molly is married to Bloom, she is effectively prostituting herself to get money for the new underwear she needs for her affair; and while Bloom is also guilty of infidelity, her manipulation is by no means justified by her husband's adultery. Desire and money constitute a transaction that leads to clothing. Molly does wish to use clothes to disguise her age and what she considers her physical imperfections, again for the purpose of making herself sexually desirable. However, underwear, like sex, is a means to an end, and, therefore, Molly's fashions confine her to surface text.

Hysterical Narratives

Beizer claims that "the path from voice to uterus is prepared by the clinicians, who repeatedly signal affinities between the female voice and sex organs."[44] Hysterical narrative is influenced by the body's symptoms conflated with the psychological causes underlying the woman's condition. The surface, and indeed the undersurface, of the hysterical body are considered texts. Freud and Breuer called hysterical narrative "small fragments of the sorrowful tale" that are disorganized, non-chronological, and are controlled primarily by memory and moodiness. The hysteric's lack of linearity as she embarks on an "intense reliving of her past" is exacerbated by the story's lack of closure; these narrative elements demonstrate her fragmented identity.[45] Her emotional instability is found in her lack of decorum, as Beizer explains, "Hysterics laugh or cry indiscriminately, sing or speak nonsense words, make animal noises, and give free rein to unseemly bodily sounds."[46] Freud's role in analysis was to reconstruct the narrative according to a traditional structure by analyzing the sounds and gaps and interpreting the silences. In fact, he claimed his role as translator by saying that "the study of hysteria must read like a novel," thereby implicitly suggesting that he would transform the hysteric's meanderings into a coherent form.[47] In this respect, Marcus believes that "the [hysteric's] cure is a chronological story."[48] Both Molly Bloom and Mary Hooligan resist chronology as a necessary frame; however, while Mary controls the storytelling function, Molly does not and is, in essence, framed by Joyce's representation of female subjectivity.

Mary Hooligan derives her monologue from recollections, and its structure follows the meanderings she assigns to her uterus. While Deborah White points out that "the body replaces language as though insisting on the analogy between them," Mary's narrative both replaces and comments on her body.[49] Unlike the hysteric, Mary has constructed her narrative as fragmented; while she is struggling to remember herself, her memories are by no means repressed and she needs no (male) analyst to frame her story by making sense of her symptoms. Instead of being a disorder requiring a medical audience in order to arrive at a cure, Mary's hysteria is a drive toward a critique and redefinition of her place in society. She displays a variety of voices—literary, poetic, archaic, highbrow, colloquial, comic—and employs a number of narrative techniques—reverse chronology, unconventional syntax, orders, lists, sense, nonsense—that undermine the social order and rebel against its framing of her.

Molly Bloom's soliloquy is similarly fragmented as she skips through a variety of thoughts, some of which are memories, translated into a fluid stream-of-consciousness narrative. However, her narrative is disembodied and singular in tone. She describes her body as a hindrance, and her tone of pleasure seeking and complaint remains constant throughout. Furthermore, when one reads O'Brien's novel alongside Joyce's Penelope episode, it seems that Joyce does not employ this radical style in order to question and critique women's social and sexual identities. For, unlike Mary Hooligan's identity, Molly Bloom's is never put on trial. Despite her frankness in describing the plight of women, she does not challenge the validity of her social roles of wife, mother, and lover and, in fact, celebrates her union with Bloom at the narrative's conclusion. Her story can be read as hysterical because of its nonlinear style and erasure of punctuation as well as because Molly, as Veith writes of hysterics, "forgets all rules of modesty and propriety."[50] Yet she remains framed by the roles she complains of and also by the more negative definitions of woman's irrationality, which are implicit in the narrative structure.

Mary Hooligan utilizes memories of her social roles in order to free herself from their limitations. Indeed, her acceptance of the feminine role expected of an Irish woman has resulted in dissatisfaction. She says of her past: "Half a lifetime, felt seen, heard, not fully felt, most meagerly seen, scarcely heard at all, and still in me" (3). Describing what she believes is the first half of her life, she shows her reader the process of her self-evaluation. She corrects her perceptions of her life so far to realize that her experience has been mediated by gender roles she has internalized to the point of feeling she has not really lived or has been living only by standards not her own. The Law of the Father, whether enforced by Church, state, biological father, or husband is centered on rules of behavior. Mary presents her upbringing in rural Ireland as one of constant rules, orders, and demands: "Do this, Do that, Don't do this, Do it, I'll cut the tongue out of you, How bloody dare you, D'you hear? I said, Don't do it, Do it, Sing, Vocalize, Belt up, Blow your nose, Stop picking that nose, Piss, Eat you pandy, Stop making that noise, Who farted? No farting, Don't shit, you shit you" (34). The commands represent linearity and restriction. These orders have created Mary's boundaries, the punishment for transgression being physical violence or social ostracism. Indeed, the tone of this passage houses the underlying threat of punishment that accompanies such demands. In order to remove the venom from these overt statutes and veiled threats, Mary plays them against her own disjointed narrative style. In this way, her father's orders constitute part of the pastiche of her monologue. They show the boundaries as well as the socialization that she necessarily must defeat. While she is deliberately rebelling against the representative agents of control—father, mother, Dr. Flaggler, Catholic Church—in order to cultivate a new sense of individuality, she must also deprogram herself from her past socialization in order to rediscover a sexual identity in the absence of these gender roles. Hence, she recalls her memories in order to exorcize them.

In *Night*, the connections among hysteria, social/sexual experimentation, and narrative are clear. Instead of representing sickness, experimentation testifies to Mary's search for a new sense of herself as woman, a new form of subjectivity based on critiquing myths of feminine sexuality. The opening pages of the novel demonstrate Mary's refusal of the romantic tropes that confine women's identities: "One fine day in the middle of the night, two dead men got up to fight, two blindmen looking on, two cripples running for a priest, and two dummies shouting, Hurry on. That's how it is. Topsy-turvy" (3). Mary parodies the fairy-tale structure, at the outset frustrating any desire for linear progression toward a definitive conclusion. The notions of traditional storytelling are hinted at but overturned to suggest that meaning, in the sense of building toward a climax, will not be present in this text. Her opening can also be read as a critique of the Irish folk culture of storytelling as mythmaking, and the underlying myths of female passivity and silence that characterize woman's roles both in fairy tales and in real life. Indeed, fairy tales function as romances that condition women to desire marriage and motherhood. As Rowe suggests, "Subconsciously women may transfer from fairy tales into real life cultural norms which exalt passivity, dependency, and self-sacrifice as a female's cardinal virtues."[51] Hence, by refusing a chronological narrative and using a childish, nonsensical rhyme to parody meaningful narrative, Mary is both critiquing and refusing the underlying messages of conventionality that are transmitted to women. The lack of chronology is deliberate; it serves to illustrate the fragmentation of Mary's self that consequently exists after such a refusal to conform.

Similarly, Molly Bloom does not comply with conventional narrative, and she speaks female characteristics that are taboo. However, she does so without the consciousness of her narrative as a story. While Joyce is obviously deliberate in creating her fluid narrative, his character is not. In other words, she is speaking rather than telling a story, and, therefore, she is not aware of the importance of narrative structure. Instead, Joyce takes control of this for himself. Such linguistic experimentation is important to Joyce but not to Molly Bloom, which suggests that Molly is, in effect, a mouthpiece for Joyce's perceptions of women. Furthermore, by denying her the role of storyteller, Joyce is showing the narrative as a representation of Molly's psyche. O'Brien, on the other hand, allows her character the stance of storyteller so that we may attribute the narrative style to Mary's conscious awareness of her female subjectivity. In this respect, O'Brien adds an important dimension to her character, because Mary's deliberate refusal of order and coherence is attributed not to a rambling mind but to a determined effort to resist a traditional frame. And, while Molly Bloom is not framed in a traditional narrative, she is, nevertheless, controlled by a perception of femininity as flighty, irrational, premenstrual, and manipulative. In this respect, Joyce, like Freud, relegates both the narrative and the female character to surface text. Furthermore, while Mary deliberately recreates her memories as a story, albeit with a circuitous plot, Molly speaks not to fictionalize her thoughts but instead, Joyce uses her speech patterns to represent her character.

Molly is specularized by a snappy voice and a narrative structure that lacks the coherence of punctuation. She is represented by a barrage of language. Instead of manipulating grammatical and chronological conventions, Joyce does away with them altogether in order to demonstrate the relentlessness of Molly's thoughts and, therefore, the irrationality of her character. The overall effect of Molly's narrative is incessant and monologic, and it specularizes Molly as a representative of women rather than allowing her to question more implicitly the culture in which she lives. Her episode appears as a performance at the end of a novel that is carefully structured and whose subject is the father-son quest. Hence, Molly's narrative is marginal to the story of *Ulysses*. Just like Charcot, Joyce creates the theatrical environment, and Molly, like the Salpêtrière hysterics, performs her monologue in order to expose her nature.[52] Furthermore, Joyce's refusal to punctuate suggests that a woman's mind is anarchic and unordered. But if we put the punctuation into the narrative, it would read more coherently than Mary's narrative. As Anthony Burgess suggests, "Molly's syntax gets garbled, sentence is jammed into sentence, but on the whole the presentation of her thoughts is orderly, even literary . . . it was only the lack of punctuation in the 'Penelope' chapter that made its [*Ulysses*'s] first readers see frightening modernity."[53] Under the control of its creator, Molly's character is framed by a novel whose subject marginalizes women as well as by the performance Joyce exacts from her.

Mary Hooligan resists specularization. In fact, her narrative directly challenges this construction of woman as a surface text by incorporating masculinist narrative structures into her own through pastiche. Not only can the narrative techniques be contrasted, but so can the expectations placed on Mary through these narratives. As a woman, she is controlled by masculine narratives; it is this control that she deliberately evades in order to refigure and assert her feminine self. For example, Mary both incorporates and contrasts the narrative of a potential lover, the waiter. His story is representative of those that have inscribed women as passive nurturers. Instead of having sex with Mary, the waiter tells her his life: "His life story, his poverty, his growing pains, long years of apprenticeship, his culinary courses, getting double-crossed . . . having to miss the bus home each night. . . . His room was cold, his walls were damp and devoid of pictures or engravings, he had no wardrobe and only two metal hangers. . . . It was all so predictable, the rigmarole . . . his life, his tatty little life was taking shape on me as it was told" (39–40). His autobiography follows the usual linear pattern of progression, from youth to the present, with the expected milestones of schooling, death of a father, the thesis of struggle through a less-than-charmed existence. His story is predictable and structured by the desire for a conclusion. Furthermore, he expects a sympathetic response from Mary. He presumes her pity because she is a woman and should therefore nurture him. However, she undermines her own socialized inclinations and his expectations in order to avoid falling into the traditional behavior pattern. She says, "I made a serious attempt to thwart him. I flung questions at him, questions pertaining to the libido. I said, 'What is your type, do you like it straight or sausage, do you like rubber goods?' He droned on" (39). She fights his narrative desire with her own desire for sexual consummation even though her resistance will result in sexual rejection.

As a cure, through the conflation of hysterical body and hysterical narrative, Molly's soliloquy affirms heterosexual union. The climax of the episode and indeed the novel are characterized by Molly's increasing narrative and sexual excitement. While Mary Hooligan consciously disavows the romance plot with its climax in marriage, Molly Bloom celebrates the marriage proposal: "I got him to propose to me yes . . . yes that was why I liked him because I saw he understood or felt what a woman is and I knew I could always get around him . . . and I thought well as well him as another . . . and yes I said yes I will Yes."[54] By reading the conclusion of *Ulysses* as an affirmation of female sexuality in the shape of Molly's last word, critics forget what Molly is saying yes to. In reality, she is agreeing to a contract, to being the object of economic exchange, which will curb her sexual activity and put her under the control of her husband. And, while Joyce suggests that Molly maintains control through her deliberate choice of Bloom, whom she can manipulate and cuckold, in the context of O'Brien's novel, this freedom is undermined because it still relies on the traditional ending and the satisfaction of masculine desire. Indeed, in order to "bring an ideal closure to the male plot," Molly and Leopold must be reconciled in what Pearce describes as a happy ending.[55]

The Greek cure for hysteria was marriage and motherhood; Freud believed that marriage provided a healthy outlet for women's expression of sexual desire; romance plots inform the female reader that she should strive toward marriage as a way of fulfilling herself and achieving happiness. In reality, Molly is not fulfilled as a wife and mother. Yet at the moment she stops speaking, we have every indication that her life will not essentially change. The only benefit of marriage for Molly is the sense of security and definition it provides for her. In effect, Joyce's narrative allows Molly to speak her dissatisfactions but not to act. Its excess is contained by the marriage contract.

Conversely, Mary refuses a cure precisely because she does not see herself as suffering from a hysterical disorder. Effectively, her body and her narrative reenvision hysterical symptoms as necessary to feminine resistance. In this respect, her monologue is most definitely the site of excess because it does not end in containment. Instead of avowing marriage as her end, she frees herself from the memories of her domestic life by saying "*Au Revoir,* Tig, *au revoir,* Jonathan, *au revoir,* Boss and Lil and all the soulmates, go fuck yourselves. I have been saddled long enough. It is time for memory to expire" (117). She has evoked memories of her family in order to rid herself of their influences on her life.

Also, by the end of the novel she is out of a job because Jonathan and Tig are coming back to reclaim their house. In this respect, she has no identifiable role to adopt since she has disavowed her domestic responsibilities toward parents, husband, son, and employers. She even rejects the lovers who have brought her no lasting satisfaction. Through them, Mary has discovered the futility of romance; they have not brought her the emotional security she desires. She says, "Oh, shadows of love, inebriations of love, foretastes of love, trickles of love, but never yet one true love" (116). Her narrative, then, testifies to her realization that true love is a cultural construct that women are socialized to live by but which cannot exist. Hence, the novel ends as it begins, with a rejection of romance as an influential factor in her life.

Whether the location is Charcot's Salpêtrière hospital, Freud's consulting room, or the pages of Joyce's *Ulysses,* hysterical women are framed and objectified by masculine perceptions of their sexualities. These women become media through which the doctor, writer, and psychoanalyst assert their own subjectivities. Effectively, Edna O'Brien's *Night* reclaims the subversive power of hysterical narrative and female sexuality in order to dismantle the distinction between subject and object. As an artist's model, Mary is supposedly the object of the painter's gaze, just as Dora is the object of Freud's gaze and Molly Bloom is the object of Joyce's gaze. However, O'Brien's character undermines her role as artist's model and refuses to be represented and objectified.

Instead of being silently pliant, Mary participates in the artistic creation by displaying interest in the artists' perceptions of her and their subsequent representations of her. Without the aid of a camera or the Salpêtrière photographers,[56] they paint her as they see her: "They took ages over setting up their easels and appointing the light and getting the perspective. Their charcoal made different sounds, different impacts on the sheets of paper, some silken, some more like a squiggle, and there was I, avid to know how I was turning out but not able to preen or not able to smile in case of disturbing the pose" (56). Through her narrative she transforms the painters, whose perceptions she is subject to, into the object of her gaze and her narrative. In fact, Mary creates them as models for her narrative, thereby deflecting their collective gaze. Hence, Mary is the object (of the paintings) yet subject (of her own narrative) and the painting group is subject (of the paintings) yet object (of the narrative). And since Mary's narrative controls the entire scene of representation, her gaze captures the painters and controls them. Furthermore, she writes herself out of this scene by remembering her anger at being prodded, poked, and leered at. Not under hypnosis, Mary can refuse to be literally framed or, as Beizer phrases it, "caught in an unchanging identity" in a painting by leaving the studio.[57] Molly Bloom, like the Victorian hysterics, remains as a textual surface of a masculine narrative.

While the psychoanalyst interrogates the hysteric's body, the hysteric is also interrogating her own. The hysterical body challenges the interpreter not only to find its story but to revise conventional stories, and as Brooks argues, to recognize that bodies exceed and infringe the social constructions of gender and desire.[58] This is O'Brien's relation to Joyce. While he writes the female body, she interrogates his version through the act of creating her own. While Molly Bloom is contained within the father-son quest as well as the institution of marriage, Mary Hooligan exceeds these conventional boundaries. And, in exceeding the social and literary boundaries, Mary challenges the hegemony of both constitution and canon.

Indeed, her narrative mimics Joyce's dream that O'Brien cites in her biography, one where he has definitely lost his mastery over his own creation. In the dream he meets Molly at the opera and tries to explain to her his characterization of her in *Ulysses*. Here she takes on a life of her own and refuses his portrayal and his explanation of it. Indeed, again she gets the last word but this time also mastery, "and I have done with you too Mr. Joyce."[59]

Notes

1. Quoted in Claire Kahane, *Passions of the Voice: Hysteria, Narrative, and the Figure of the Speaking Woman, 1850–1915* (Baltimore: Johns Hopkins University Press, 1995), x–xi.

2. Ibid., 175.

3. Ibid., viii.

4. Toril Moi, "Representation of Patriarchy: Sexuality and Epistemology in Freud's *Dora*," in *In Dora's Case: Freud—Hysteria—Feminism*, ed. Charles Bernheimer and Claire Kahane (New York: Columbia University Press, 1985), 202.

5. Fritz Senn, "Reverberations," *James Joyce Quarterly* 3 (1966): 22.

6. Jack Fuller, "Wryly Irish," *Chicago Tribune—Books*, 27 May 1990.

7. Edna O'Brien, *James Joyce* (London: Weidenfeld & Nicolson, 1999), 1.

8. Shusha Guppy, "Edna O'Brien," in *Women Writers at Work: The Paris Review Interviews*, ed. George Plimpton, intro. Margaret Atwood (Middlesex: Penguin, 1989), 349.

9. O'Brien, "Dear Mr. Joyce," *Times Saturday Review*, 19 December 1970; Richard B. Woodward, "Edna O'Brien. Reveling in Heartbreak," *New York Times*

Magazine, 12 March 1989; Guppy, "Edna O'Brien," 345; O'Brien, "She Was the Other Ireland," *New York Times Book Review,* 19 June 1988.

10. O'Brien, *Some Irish Loving: A Selection* (Middlesex: Penguin, 1979), 148–49.

11. O'Brien, *James Joyce,* 37, 89.

12. Michael Patrick Gillespie, "(S)he Was Too Scrupulous Always: Edna O'Brien and the Comic Tradition," in *The Comic Tradition in Irish Women Writers,* ed. Theresa O'Connor (Gainesville: University Press of Florida, 1996), 110.

13. Lotus Snow, "'That Trenchant Childhood Route'? Quest in Edna O'Brien's Novels," *Éire-Ireland* 14.1 (Spring 1979): 79.

14. Christine Froula, *Modernism's Body: Sex, Culture, and Joyce* (New York: Columbia University Press, 1996), 170.

15. Gabrielle Dane conflates plagiarism, hysteria, and feminine protest in "Hysteria as Feminist Protest: Dora, Cixous, Acker," *Women's Studies* 23.3 (1994): 247. In her discussion of Kathy Acker, she suggests the connectedness of the three, because, she argues, they collectively undermine masculinist narrative by placing it at the site of excess.

16. Marilyn Randall, "Appropriate(d) Discourse: Plagiarism and Decolonization," *New Literary History* 22 (1991): 526.

17. Cheryl Herr, in "Fathers, Daughters, Anxiety, Fiction," in *Tendencies,* ed. Eve Kosofsky Sedgwick (Durham, N.C.: Duke University Press, 1993), 173–207, argues that Joyce and his daughter closely identified with each other; that Lucia's breakdowns corresponded to the times Joyce was having the most difficulty with his writing. Joyce says of Lucia that she has her own language that he mostly understands.

18. Randall, "Appropriate(d) Discourse," 530.

19. Bonnie Kime Scott, *Joyce and Feminism* (Bloomington: Indiana University Press, 1984), 157.

20. Ibid., 179; Cheryl Herr, "'Penelope' as Period Piece," in *Molly Blooms: A Polylogue on "Penelope" and Cultural Studies,* ed. Richard Pearce (Madison: University of Wisconsin Press, 1994), 70; Kimberly J. Devlin, "Pretending in 'Penelope': Masquerade, Mimicry, and Molly Bloom," in *Molly Blooms,* ed. Pearce, 83–84; Froula, *Modernism's Body,* 177.

21. Scott, *Joyce and Feminism,* 169.

22. Suzette Henke, "James Joyce and Women: The Matriarchal Muse," in *Work in Progress: Joyce Centenary Essays,* ed. Richard F. Peterson, Alan M. Cohn, and Edmund L. Epstein (Carbondale: Southern Illinois University Press, 1983), 126; Richard Pearce, "How Does Molly Bloom Look Through the Male Gaze?" in *Molly Blooms,* ed. Pearce, 40; Diana E. Henderson, "Joyce's Modernist Woman: Whose Last Word?" *Modern Fiction Studies* 35.3 (Autumn 1989): 517.

23. Elaine Unkeless, "The Conventional Molly Bloom," in *Women in Joyce,* ed. Suzette Henke and Elaine Unkeless (Urbana: University of Illinois Press, 1982), 150.

24. Kathleen McCormick, "Reproducing Molly Bloom: A Revisionist History of the Reception of 'Penelope,' 1922–1970," in *Molly Blooms,* ed. Pearce, 17–39; Annette Shandler Levitt, "The Pattern Out of the Wallpaper: Luce Irigaray and Molly Bloom," *Modern Fiction Studies* 35.3 (Autumn 1989): 507–16; Emer

UNIVERSITY OF WINCHESTER
LIBRARY

Nolan, *James Joyce and Nationalism* (London: Routledge, 1995); Margaret Mills Harper, "'Taken in Drapery': Dressing the Narrative in the *Odyssey* and 'Penelope,'" in *Molly Blooms,* ed. Pearce, 239; Carol Schloss, "Molly's Resistance to the Union: Marriage and Colonialism in Dublin, 1904," *Modern Fiction Studies* 35.3 (Autumn 1989): 536; Ewa Ziarek, "The Female Body, Technology, and Memory in 'Penelope,'" in *Molly Blooms,* ed. Pearce, 272. Nolan describes womanly writing and feminine language that constitutes *écriture féminine,* even though she does not name it as such (164).

25. Charles Bernheimer, introduction to *In Dora's Case,* ed. Bernheimer and Kahane, 7.

26. Beret E. Strong, "Foucault, Freud, and French Feminism: Theorizing Hysteria as Theorizing the Feminine," *Literature and Psychology* 35.4 (1989): 15; Bernheimer, introduction, 5.

27. Karen Morley Brennan, "Hysteria and the Scene of Feminine Representation" (Ph.D. diss., University of Arizona, 1990), 45.

28. Edna O'Brien, *Night* (1972; rpt., New York: Farrar, Straus and Giroux, 1992).

29. Janet Beizer, *Ventriloquized Bodies: Narratives of Hysteria in Nineteenth-Century France* (Ithaca, N.Y.: Cornell University Press, 1993), 41.

30. Derek Attridge, "Molly's Flow: The Writing of 'Penelope' and the Question of Women's Language," *Modern Fiction Studies* 35.3 (Autumn 1989): 561.

31. Cited in Janice Delaney, Mary Jane Lupton, and Emily Toth, *The Curse: A Cultural History of Menstruation* (1976; rev. ed., Urbana: University of Illinois Press, 1988), 83.

32. James Joyce, *Ulysses,* ed. Hans Walter Gabler, Wolfhard Steppe, and Claus Melchior (1922; New York: Random House, 1986), 632–33.

33. Qtd. in Mary Jane Lupton, *Menstruation and Psychoanalysis* (Urbana: University of Illinois Press, 1993), 5.

34. Sigmund Freud, qtd. in Strong, "Foucault, Freud, and French Feminism," 20.

35. Joyce, *Ulysses,* 640.

36. Maureen Gaffney, "Glass Slippers and Tough Bargains: Women, Men and Power," in *A Dozen Lips,* ed. Eavan Boland with Margaret Ward (Dublin: Attic Press, 1994), 244.

37. Joyce, *Ulysses,* 621.

38. Henderson, "Joyce's Modernist Woman," 525.

39. Jennifer L. Pierce, in "The Relation between Emotion Work and Hysteria: A Feminist Interpretation of Freud's *Studies on Hysteria,*" *Women's Studies* 16.3–4 (1989), points out, "All of the women [in Freud's case studies] . . . were obliged to suppress their own feelings, needs and ambitions in order to care for someone else" (265).

40. Sharon Willis, *Marguerite Duras: Writing on the Body* (Urbana: University of Illinois Press, 1987), 163.

41. Leslie W. Rabine, "A Woman's Two Bodies: Fashion Magazines, Consumerism, and Feminism," in *On Fashion,* ed. Shari Benstock and Suzanne Ferriss (New Brunswick, N.J.: Rutgers University Press, 1994), 59.

42. Brennan, "Hysteria and the Scene," 71.

43. Joyce, *Ulysses*, 642.

44. Beizer, *Ventriloquized Bodies*, 44.

45. Joseph Breuer and Sigmund Freud, *Studies in Hysteria*, trans. and intro. by A. A. Brill (1895; rpt., Boston: Beacon, 1964), 3, 22.

46. Beizer, *Ventriloquized Bodies*, 43.

47. Breuer and Freud, *Studies in Hysteria*, 114.

48. Steven Marcus, qtd. in Deborah Elise White, "*Studies on Hysteria:* Case Histories and the Case against History," *Modern Language Notes* 104 (1989): 1036.

49. Ibid., 1043.

50. Ilza Veith, "Four Thousand Years of Hysteria," in *Hysterical Personality*, ed. Mardi J. Horowitz (New York: Aronson, 1977), 36.

51. Karen E. Rowe, "Feminism and Fairy Tales," *Women's Studies* 6 (1979): 237.

52. Charcot hypnotized his hysterical patients and displayed their hysterical symptoms for an audience of doctors.

53. Anthony Burgess, *Joysprick: An Introduction to the Language of James Joyce* (London: Andre Deutsch, 1973), 59.

54. Joyce, *Ulysses*, 643–44.

55. Pearce, "How Does Molly," 52–53.

56. During Charcot's lectures where his hysterics performed under hypnosis, he took full advantage of photography to capture images of hysterical seizures. In fact, Freud had one such photograph on the wall of his office.

57. Beizer, *Ventriloquized Bodies*, 220.

58. Peter Brooks, *Body Work: Objects of Desire in Modern Narrative* (Cambridge, Mass.: Harvard University Press, 1993), 244.

59. O'Brien, *James Joyce*, 169.

Edna O'Brien's "Love Objects"

REBECCA PELAN

In 1984, Edna O'Brien saw her major theme as being "loss as much as . . . love. Loss is every child's theme because by necessity the child loses its mother and its bearings . . . so my central theme is loss—loss of love, loss of self, loss of God."[1] What follows is an attempt to show that this conflation of the mother, the self, and God most often manifests itself in O'Brien's fiction in the figure of an idealized "love object"—occasionally nuns, but more often mothers or godlike men with whom the protagonist hopes for, but rarely achieves, a "pure" and unsullied sexual union—the sexual act itself often being described by O'Brien as an experience akin to religious ecstasy. Whatever form this love object takes, however, as a means of locating or transcending the self, it is consistently shown to be illusory.

However, only when O'Brien's writing is examined within modern but specifically Irish contexts can she be seen to share with many other Irish writers a common, albeit somber, view of life as meaningless unless there is some kind of god at its center. In O'Brien's case, however, there is a further, consistent interest in inscribing these love objects with eroticism and sexuality as a means of expressing individual and artistic liberty in the face of the conservative socio-political structures imposed on Irish writers of her time. Only, too, when her work is seen within these Irish contexts can we begin to appraise O'Brien's very significant contribution to a specifically Irish women's literary tradition. Written at a time when she was largely alienated by and from Ireland, the critical world, and the women's movement, O'Brien's early writing—produced between, say, 1960 and 1985—suggests that she has rarely veered from her iconoclastic mission to expose the brutality of various insidious forms of oppression, best seen in her undermining of the conventional patriarchal family and in her portrayal of how women are affected by being kept apart from themselves and each other.

Underpinning so much of O'Brien's work is a re/presentation of the effects on women of their having internalized aspects of Catholic dogma as a feature of Irish social policy, none more so—certainly in O'Brien's case—than the cult of the Virgin Mary. Although only augmented as official dogma in 1854, the Immaculate Conception, which exonerated Mary from any carnal implications, heralded the final achievement of patriarchy and Catholicism, its vehicle in Ireland. In Catholic countries where church and state remained largely autonomous, Mariolatry remained in the realm of theology. In O'Brien's postrevolutionary Ireland, however, where church and state became virtually indivisible, Mariolatry imposed on women a dilemma that is unsolvable: to follow Mary and remain pure, which involves a renunciation not only of sex but of motherhood, or to marry and bear children and, thus, be reduced to the sensuality and baseness of Eve. The church's answer to this dilemma has been to teach purity and chastity until marriage, at which time sex, for purposes of procreation only, becomes a duty devoid of sin, but a duty nonetheless.

This interpretation of sex as a purely functional feature of the relationship between men and women exacerbated the dilemma confronting Irish women who, taught from birth to aspire to the purity of Mary, found themselves unwittingly playing the role of Eve in order to secure a husband in a society that viewed spinsterhood as the most dreadful of fates. While the Cult of Mary may have suited the romantic vision of a pure and wholesome Ireland, it has been extremely damaging for Irish women, since not only is it a totally unattainable ideal, but, in Simone de Beauvoir's terms, represents "the supreme masculine victory": "For the first time in human history the mother kneels before her son; she freely accepts her inferiority . . . it is the rehabilitation of woman through the accomplishment of her defeat."[2] The traditional Irish Catholic mother becomes, then, a sacrificial figure in the image of Mary: "As a mother, she [Mary/mother] provides a human face in the Church [home]. She is a source of comfort, and protects sinners from the wrath of God [the father]. Yet hers was an essentially submissive motherhood. The power to conceive was not hers to control."[3] In much of her work, O'Brien captures this picture of the idealized mother in the hierarchical family structure, standing as mediator between the much-feared figure of the father and the child narrator: "She [the child] would be told by her father to get out, to stop hatching, to get out from under the mother's apron strings, and he would send her for a spin on the woeful brakeless bicycle . . . but always at the end of every day and at the end of every thought, and at the beginning of sleep and the precise moment of wakening, it was of her mother and for her mother she existed ("A Fanatic Heart," 257).[4]

Yet, at the same time, O'Brien reveals that the performance of the mother's duty in her fiction is not quite as submissive as church and state prescribed: "Her mother went along to her father's bedroom for a tick, to stop him bucking. The consequences of those visits were deterred by the bits of tissue paper, a protection between herself and any emission. No other child got conceived" ("A Fanatic Heart," 255).[5] And, similarly, in *A Pagan Place*, the child's mother "had to go across the landing to his room. An edict. . . . Before she went . . . she put tissue paper in the inside of her pussy. It made a crinkly noise. Even without a candle you knew what she was doing" (29).[6] As mediator between the father and the child, as well as the one figure responsible for day-to-day domestic life and, therefore, the well being of all, O'Brien's fictional mother acts as a powerful influence in the lives of her young protagonists. Akin to the Victorian "angel in the house," they take "the worst parts of the chicken, the skin, the Pope's nose, the posterior bits," while serving the men the breasts ("A Fanatic Heart," 258); they are endlessly inventive at economizing; and despite, or perhaps because of, their subservience elsewhere, they represent an awesome figure of authority in the lives of their children: "the two hardest things on earth—to disobey God and my own mother" (258).

Through the eyes of the child, O'Brien portrays the relationship between mother and child as an extension of the unity that existed before birth: "In your mother you were safe and that was the only time you couldn't get kidnapped and that was the nearest you ever were to any other human being. Between you and your mother there was only a membrane, wafer thin. Being near someone on the inside was not the same thing as being near them on the outside, even though the latter could involve hugging and kissing" (*A Pagan Place*, 28). This relationship is continued after birth to the extent that the child often sees no

distinction between the self and the mother: "Her mother's knuckles
were her knuckles, her mother's veins were her veins, her mother's lap
was a second heaven, her mother's forehead a copybook onto which
she traced A B C D, her mother's body was a recess that she would
wander inside forever and ever, a sepulcher growing deeper and
deeper" ("A Fanatic Heart," 257). In her nonfiction work *Mother Ireland*,
O'Brien combines the stereotypical picture of the Irish mother that appears in her fiction with an equally stereotypical one that existed in her
community: "Only mothers were safe to be with. Mothers were best.
Mothers worked and worried and sacrificed and had the smallest
amount on their plates when the family sat down to eat, mothers wore
aprons and slaved and mothers went to the confraternity on a Sunday
evening and whispered things to each other in the chapel grounds
about their wombs and their woes."[7]

In those of her stories ostensibly narrated by a child or young
woman, for example "The Rug" and "Irish Revel," the link between
child and mother is implicit and unquestioned: the picture of the idealized mother upon whom the child depends for care, protection, and
guidance is left intact by the naive narrator.[8] In other examples, however, O'Brien uses aspects of the narrative to reveal to the reader facets
of the mother that are not necessarily apparent to the narrator.

In "The Bachelor," for instance, the narrative is deliberately ambiguous regarding the circumstances that lead to the young narrator un-
knowingly becoming betrothed to Jack Holland, the unmarried owner
of a wine shop who is in love with the narrator's mother. The idealized
version of the mother in "The Rug" recurs in "The Bachelor" as the girl
watches her mother go through the rare and uncharacteristic ceremony
of "dolling up" for a visit from Jack: "She did not tie the string very
tightly and the effect was perfect: her pale neck, the white gauzy material, and the flowers so real that it seemed they might stir like flowers in
a garden . . . her hair, which was red-brown, glinted as she proceeded to
make sandwiches. . . . I thought then that when I grew up if I could be
as fetching as my mother I would be certain to find happiness" (57).
But, again the intrusive adult narrator acknowledges that "For some
reason I believed that the troubles of her life were an anomaly, and
never did it occur to me that some of her fatality had already grafted itself onto me and determined my disposition" (57).

The "child" narrator also witnesses Jack drawing his chair close to
her mother; his whispering of "something that must have been wanton," judging by her mother's writhing and her injured face; and his

dropping of three apple pips down the mother's low-cut blouse before abruptly leaving (58). While the narrator resents Jack "being so personal with [her] mother" (59), and reveals that there was something "untoward" about her mother having been upstairs in Jack's house looking at "gorgeous brooches" belonging to his sister Maggie, there are other events that puzzle the narrator more than the reader (60). A tense domestic situation, for example, in which the father, drunk and in possession of a revolver, is holding the bailiff at bay, sees the mother hurry away only to return with Jack and a "brown envelope containing a wad of money" for the bailiff (61). On leaving, Jack speaks to her mother, whose reply leaves the narrator baffled: "'How could I, Jack,' she said pityingly, and then she came back into the kitchen and asked God Almighty what would become of us" (62). Similarly, in delivering a note to Jack from her mother, the girl looks for signs of disappointment as he reads, "but there was none": "'Tell your mam that Jack understands all, and that Jack will wait for time's eventualities,' and I said I would and ran out of the kitchen, because I had some idea that he was going to kiss me" (63).

The death of Maggie, Jack's sister, causes the narrator to speculate that:

> "Whoever marries Jack will have Maggie's brooches."
> "Maybe he'll wait for you," [her mother] said jokingly.
> "She'll marry a doctor," said my father proudly, as he hoped that I would better their situation.
> "She'll marry Jack," my mother said, and the thought was offensive. (64)

At boarding school the narrator receives from Jack a letter containing five shillings: "I could hardly believe it. Its white crinkled paper with the heavy black lettering assured me that he had indeed sent this amount, *but I did not know why*" (66; emphasis mine). And, during a holiday home, she recalls: "It was inside the neck of my jumper and not Mama's that he dropped two toffees" (67). The suspicion, created in the reader's mind, though not in the narrator's, that the girl has been promised to Jack and has thus replaced her mother is confirmed when Jack takes the girl, now finished with convent life and thinking only of "flight" (69), to see the house he has built: "Coming back twirling the big key, he winked at me slyly, and then it happened before I had time to repel him. Jack turned the key in the door, then lifted me up in his arms, and carried me over the threshold, triumphantly shouting, 'Hallelujah . . . ours, ours, ours.' He said for long he had envisaged such a scene and only wished he had brought a ring" (70). And Jack's disappointment is confirmed later when he informs the priest, "Marriage, Father . . . is out of the question. I was betrothed for a long number of years to a certain little lady in this parish, who jilted me" (71). Though only alluded to in "The Bachelor," this theme of mothers living vicariously through their children and, as a consequence, being prepared to sell them short—quite literally in this case—is evident in a great deal of O'Brien's writing and, as we shall see, is closely related to a crisis of identity explored by O'Brien whereby her women, of both generations, seek fulfillment in persons or objects outside themselves.

In her fiction, O'Brien paints a picture of the Irish mother that is far removed from that of the noble, devoted, and hard-working figure evident in much twentieth-century Irish writing and exemplified by Sean O'Casey's Juno in *Juno and the Paycock.* By contrast, O'Brien's fictional mothers, though attracting our sympathy and pity, rarely attract our admiration, since it is they who are primarily responsible for programming daughters into a narrow-minded world of subjugation and imprisonment. O'Brien enacts through her fiction what Adrienne Rich has expressed in a theoretical context: "Many daughters live in rage at their mothers for having accepted, too readily and passively, 'whatever comes.' A mother's victimization does not merely humiliate her, it mutilates the daughter who watches her for clues as to what it means to be a woman. Like the traditional foot-bound Chinese woman, she passes on her own affliction. The mother's self-hatred and low expectations are the binding-rags for the psyche of the daughter."[9]

Yes, the "clues as to what it means to be a woman" given by O'Brien's fictional mothers to their daughters are, without exception, subservience, low expectations, and an unchallenged acceptance of the sacrificial role modeled on Mary: "Rather than providing a role model for women, Mary's image emphasized the radical disjuncture between the sacred and the sexual, between the religious hopes of women and the reality of their lives."[10]

As the principal role models in her young narrators' lives, O'Brien's mothers, at once victims yet advocates of social orthodoxy, function as the first in a long line of idealized figures in her fiction, confirming Dally's theory: "Since the pattern of later loving relationships usually follows the first relationship with the mother, people who have developed in this way tend to repeat the pattern, idealizing those people, things, causes, or institutions that they care about in later life."[11] The combination of the disjuncture in Irish society referred to by Condren and the idealization process mentioned above results in a romantic idealism in O'Brien's work, an inverted version of the ethic of courtly love in which the love object is viewed as a vision of religious significance, and while the object may alter, the symbolic adoration remains.

The love object in "Courtship," for example, is one of three brothers, all over six feet tall with dark eyes and thick curly hair whose diminutive mother transmits her pride by looking at them "as if they were a breed of gods" (97). Michael, the most sought after, is a famous hurling player whose skill is "renowned and immortalized in verses that the men carried in their pockets" and who was often carried on the shoulders of his fans while the crowds "would mill around, trying to touch his feet or his hands, just as in the Gospels the crowd milled about trying to touch Our Lord" (98). The young narrator, spending her first holiday with Michael's family, yearns for nothing more than to serve him—to make him apple fritters, fry him sausages, ply him with tea or another egg, or polish his tarnished trophies, but more than anything, "to remain in Michael's orbit and be ready at any moment should he summon me, or just bump into me and give me a sudden thrilling squeeze" (100). She dreams of being adopted by Michael's mother, so that she might become his sister and "shake hands with him, or even embrace, without any suggestion of shame or sin" (100).

Evident in "Courtship" are explicit connections to the "Nausicaa" section of James Joyce's *Ulysses,* in which Gerty MacDowell interprets Leopold Bloom's lecherous gaze in images of religious devotion: "His dark eyes fixed themselves on her again drinking in her every contour, literally worshipping at her shrine. If ever there was undisguised admiration in a man's passionate gaze it was there plain to be seen on that man's face. It is for you, Gertrude MacDowell, and you know it" (359).[12] Like the narrator of "Courtship," Gerty, too, dreams that she and her "dream husband" will be "just good friends like a big brother and sister without all that other" (362).

O'Brien's first novel, *The Country Girls,* also investigates this process of idealization in some depth. Taken in isolation, this first book of O'Brien's trilogy focuses specifically on the naivety and unpreparedness for life of Caithleen Brady, a young girl whose early worldview includes the untimely death by drowning of an adored mother, which leaves her at the mercy of a drunken father and an unmerciful friend called Baba Brennan. The object of Caithleen's adoration is a rather remote and distinguished Frenchman, known only as Mr. Gentleman, since no one can pronounce his name. Mr. Gentleman is described by the narrator as a "beautiful man who lived in the white house on the hill" (12).[13] A solicitor—distinguished, refined, married, and, therefore, unavailable—Mr. Gentleman represents to Caithleen all that is romantic and mysterious: "My new god, with a face carved out of pale marble and eyes that made me sad for every woman who hadn't known him" (57). The purchase of a lace handkerchief evokes dreams of going boating with Mr. Gentleman when Caithleen would stick the hanky into "Mama's silver bracelet, with the lace frill hanging down, temptingly, over the wrist," and romantic wishes of, "standing under a street light in the rain with my hair falling crazily about, my lips poised for the miracle of a kiss. A kiss. Nothing more. My imagination did not go beyond that. It was afraid to. Mama had protested too agonizingly all through the windy years" (141, 145).

On a superficial level, such stories could be read as little more than romantic tales of youthful infatuation. Under closer scrutiny, however, although told in the first person, the stories contain sufficient information for the reader to see beyond the rose-colored view of the narrator. Both "Courtship" and *The Country Girls* contain encounters with very real men who both protagonists find repulsive. "Courtship" also reveals not only the narrator's godlike Michael, but the very mortal playboy Michael, who has a steady girl called Moira, but who meets other girls at dances—"some Ellen, or some Dolly, or some Kate" (98)—who plague him with love letters for weeks afterward. The narrator herself witnesses the flirtation between Michael and Eileen, a local girl who now works in Dublin. Spying on the "bewitched pair," the narrator watches Michael stand a little behind Eileen, "Her pleated skirt raised so that it came unevenly above her knees . . . and her mounting excitement as she stood on tiptoe to accommodate herself to what he was doing" (104).

The lovers' meeting in the grounds of a ruined demesne coincides with the narrator joining Michael's mother in evening prayers, an endless recitation of "Our Fathers, Hail Mary's [*sic*] and Glory Bes" (104). Mouthing the prayers, the narrator thinks only of the lovers "with a curiosity that bordered on frenzy," picturing their meeting place she can smell the grass, hear the cows wheezing, and see "their two faces almost featureless in the dark, and by not being able to see, their power of touch so overwhelmingly whetted that their hands reached out, and suddenly they clove together and dared to say each other's Christian name with a hectic urgency" (104). The narrator's imaginative portrayal of the lovers in a mixture of romantic cliché and religious ecstasy contrasts sharply with a later boasting of Michael's description of his weekly rendezvous with Moira in the loft above his mother's mill: "Moira's arrival, her shyness, her chatter, then her capitulation as he [Michael] removed her coat, her dress, her underclothes and she lay there with not a stitch" (108). Again, echoes of Joyce's "Nausicaa" section are evident. Against a backdrop of the men's temperance retreat conducting the rosary, sermon, and benediction of the Most Blessed Sacrament, Gerty MacDowell, lame and full of romantic longing "could almost feel him [Leopold Bloom] draw her face to his and the first quick hot breath of his handsome lips," an illusion sharply juxtaposed with the reality of Bloom's interest in Gerty as a focus for his act of masturbation (Joyce, 363).

The necessity to deal with sex in purely religious terms is evident, too, in Caithleen who, once while being kissed by Mr. Gentleman, opens her eyes to find that the "carved, pale face was the face of an old, old man" (157). Her response is to close her eyes and think only of "his lips and his cold hands and the warm heart that was beating beneath the waistcoat and the starched white shirt" (157).

Contrary to the narrator's view of Mr. Gentleman, however, the reader is presented with an unhappily married, aging man with a penchant for young girls. He directs Caithleen not to wear lipstick when next they meet since "men prefer to kiss young girls without lipstick"; on a number of occasions his look is described as sly—"sly and loving and full of promises" when his eyes dwell on Caithleen's legs flattered by new stockings—"as if he were planning something in his mind" (54, 87). What Mr. Gentleman is planning, of course, is exactly what Harry of the same novel, Michael and Tom of "Courtship," O'Toole of "Irish Revel," and, indeed, Leopold Bloom of *Ulysses* planned, if only in his mind: the seduction of a naive, gullible girl who has been led to believe that purity in love is achievable and that sex, in real terms, is a sinful and sordid duty or, as Marina Warner suggests: "Mary's role as the embodiment of maternity reinforces a biologistic insistence on woman's function as reproducer and nurturer, while adoration of her paradoxical virginity masks a hatred of the unclean female body and a denial of female desire."[14]

As mentioned, however, the love object in O'Brien's fiction is not always a member of the opposite sex. In "Sister Imelda," for example, the object of the young narrator's adoration is a nun who, having spent four years at university in Dublin, is different from the other nuns around her. In this story, O'Brien investigates the disjuncture through a constant oscillation between the hard reality of life—"I pitied her and thought how alone she must be, cut off from her friends and conversation, with only God as her intangible spouse"—and what she sees as the purity of spirituality—"It did seem enticing to become a nun, to lead a life unspotted by sin, never to have to have babies, and to wear a ring that singled one out as the Bride of Christ" (124, 125). The narrator ultimately concludes that her version of pleasure is inextricable from pain, that they "existed side by side and were interdependent, like the two forces of an electric current" (130). The love of Sister Imelda, like the loves of the other stories, is fostered in the mind of the narrator by the shroud of mystery and unattainability surrounding the nun—mystery about her life in Dublin, about the food she eats, the way she sleeps, and the color of her hair and eyebrows, which have never been seen under the wimple.

Sister Imelda advises the narrator, shamed by her inadequacy at sport, that "humiliation was the greatest test of Christ's love, or indeed any love" (136). This causes the narrator impulsively to decide on becoming a nun so that she and Sister Imelda, though probably never able to express their feelings, "would be under the same roof, in the same cloister, in mental and spiritual conjunction all our lives" (137). This idealized love, then, also takes the form of a union between women, but, again, one of the purest kind.

In "Sister Imelda" we again meet Baba, the outrageous friend from *The Country Girls.* As a foil to the narrator, Baba offers the reader a view of life untainted by romance or religious mystery. The only girl able to stand up to a prefect, Baba sees convent life as little more than a prison that holds no joy or mystery. Her realistic, albeit cynical, view is in direct contrast to that of the narrator, who, with the utmost gravity, relates the acts of mortification during the month of the Suffering Souls in Purgatory, in which the agonized yearning for Christ is matched by the torture of the leaping flames that burn and char their limbs; Baba's response is to suggest that "saner people were locked in the lunatic asylum, which was only a mile away" (127).

But Sister Imelda represents to the narrator of the story much more than a focus of youthful infatuation. She is, rather, a replacement of the mother figure evident in so much of O'Brien's fiction: "I was happy in my prison then, happy to be near her, happy to walk behind her as she twirled her beads and bowed to the servile nun. I no longer cried for my mother, no longer counted the days on a pocket calendar until the Christmas holidays" (129). Similarly, when thinking of her mother and her home, the narrator ponders over whether Sister Imelda has "supplanted my mother, and I hoped not, because I had aimed to outstep my original world and take my place in a new and hallowed one" (130).

As a replacement love object, it is significant that Sister Imelda, in keeping with O'Brien's fictional mothers, is quite prepared to encourage the girl to enter a life of service—though religious, as opposed to domestic. Despite admitting that life as a nun is "awful" (137), Sister Imelda has no qualms in openly encouraging the narrator to emulate her, reflecting a time in Ireland's history when entering the church offered one of the few career options outside marriage and motherhood available to young women. On a more abstract level, of course, the religious option also offered Irish women a solution to the dilemma of whether to be "good" or "bad" women.

The narrator of A Pagan Place, even before learning of her sister Emma's illegitimate pregnancy, reveals how pervasive the image of "good" and "bad" women had become: "Your aunt and your mother kissed and you thought of Mary Magdalene and her sister Martha and how one was a saint and one was a sinner, and then you thought of you and Emma" (48). Given that Emma herself had been a "love child," and that "your aunt had loved her husband. She believed in love, unlike your mother who said it was a form of dope," and that the young girl witnesses her mother's illicit relationship with the local doctor, she appears to have no conception of women beyond the good/bad binary (30, 47, 38).

As in "Courtship," the narrator of A Pagan Place is ultimately seduced by her godlike idol, but here this figure is a local priest "that everyone was in love with": "You often invented situations where you were his sacristan, ironing his vestments and things, serving him but hardly ever encountering him" (37). This is a daydream not too far removed from her later "vision" in which "you were with Jesus on a mountain road and he wore a white robe and was performing miracles easily. You were his assistant, you were carrying his equipment" (169).

Father Declan's seduction of the narrator, in which penetration and loss of virginity is avoided only by her resistance, is far from a spiritual experience: "He said he could go through you like butter. He put his finger under the leg of your knickers and sought you out and said what kind and what cushy you were" (177). The narrator, after an interrogation by her mother and a beating from her father who suggests that "one prodigal in any family was enough" decides that "the thing you had to be was fervent and more fervent and most fervent," a penance implemented by gargling with salt water and eating dry sulphur, presumably in an attempt to emulate Mary and not Martha (184).

The implication that she has been responsible for her own seduction, evident in her parent's reaction, is, of course, never questioned by the narrator. Rather, there is a continually misguided binary association in her mind of saints/sinners and secular/spiritual experience: "After communion you had this funny feeling in your stomach, tickly, the same as when you used to tickle yourself, only you did nothing to bring it about . . . you thought it might be a touch of religious ecstasy. You knew that saints experienced such things" (163). This confusion of early sexual arousal with religious ecstasy, along with her construction of "good" and "bad" women leads the narrator to volunteer to serve Christ during a recruitment session at school: "She [Mother Baptista] said yes, it was a marriage to God, she admitted that most girls wished for a marriage to someone but in that union of God and woman there was something no earthly ceremony could compare with, there was constancy" (192). The life of a nun, then, represents to the narrator an opportunity to escape secular marriage and find, in its place, a marriage of the purest kind. But it also, clearly, offers her a means of avoiding damnation as a "bad" woman. O'Brien's use of irony is evident in the paradox of the title and the fact that the Catholic church, so influential in a society that at once glorifies and destroys its women, recruits volunteers by quoting the number of pagans in the world: "That outrage, that lamentable state of affairs. She [Sister Baptista] said not to shrink from it, not to turn away" (191).

While the narrator's rejection of secular service, and thus the mother, is implicit in *A Pagan Place,* the narrator of "A Rose in the Heart of New York" explicitly acknowledges the necessity of rejecting a relationship that leaves her feeling like "a gouged torso" (397). The story, one of O'Brien's longest, encompasses the early devotion between mother and child, as well as the daughter's ultimate anger at the mother—"someone she wanted to banish": "Like an overseeing spirit, the figure of the mother, who was responsible for each and every one of these facets . . . They were more than thoughts, they were the presence of this woman whom she resolved to kill. Yes, she would have to kill. She would have to take up arms and commit a murder" (391, 393).

Throughout the story, O'Brien uses opposing images of emptiness/saturation and dismemberment/stitching to reflect the associations among the child, the father, and the mother, as well as the emotional damage suffered, first, by the mother and then by the narrator herself.

The birth of the child, a nightmarish piece of fiction, in which images of carving, pieces of flesh, stitching, and gushing blood, reveal the mother as a woman whose "last bit of easiness was then torn from her, and [who] was without hope," who is "no longer a lovely body, she was a vehicle for pain and insult" and who regards her "whole life as a vast disappointment" (378, 379). "When she married she had escaped the life of a serving girl, the possible experience of living in some grim institution, but as time went on and the bottom drawer was emptied of its gifts, she saw that she was made to serve in an altogether other way" (376).

The mother being "burst apart" during childbirth and on the same bed where she had been "prized apart, again and again," feels the "blood gushing out of her like water at a weir," and is stitched "down the line of torn flesh that was gaping and coated with blood" while the father, associated throughout the story with dismemberment, waves an unappetizing "strip of pink flesh on a fork" as he seeks out a knitting needle to "skewer out [a] bit of broken cork" (376–78). The goose, left neither cooked nor uncooked, and from which the men tear off bits of breast, leaving it "wounded, like the woman upstairs who was then tightening her heart and soul, tightening inside the array of catgut stitches," links the mother of the story to the title and to an embroidery done many years before in which she had made a "statement in stitches that there was a rose in the heart of New York" (379, 398).

This image of the mother as a woman emptied of everything but with a secret stitched into her heart is, in the early part of the story, shown to fill up the emptiness with the child who "drinks them in," whose fingers, when cut, are taken into the mother's mouth and sucked "to lessen the pain and licked . . . to abolish the blood" and who, in turn, represents to the child "a gigantic sponge, a habitation in which she longed to sink forever and ever" (380, 385). The image ultimately becomes one of parasitic association, however, in which the narrator feels she has been "milked emotionally" and realizes that "stitches played such an important role in life" (399, 398). This narrator acknowledges her mother as a woman who "had a whole series of grudges, bitter grudges concerning love, happiness, and her hard impecunious fate. The angora jumpers, the court shoes, the brown and the fawn garments, the milk complexion, the auburn tresses, the little breathlessnesses, the hands worn by toil, the sore feet, these were but the trimmings, behind them lay the real person who demanded her pound of flesh from life" (396). The narrator's own "emptiness" is manifested as a hunger upon her mother's death for "something, some communique," such as "buy

yourself a jacket" or "have a night out" or "don't spend this on masses,"
as an indication that the heart was not stitched as tightly as had appeared, "but there was no such thing" (402, 404).

Yet, while O'Brien's symbolic killing of the "angel in the house" reveals an artistic freedom to carry out the fictional slaying, absolute freedom is implied to be an impossibility for her protagonists. "Staggered
by the assaults of memory," the narrator of "A Rose in the Heart of New
York," searching for "leaks" from her mother's life as a woman rather
than as a mother, confronts a palpable wall of silence: "And there was a
vaster silence beyond, as if the house itself had died or had been carefully put down to sleep" (393, 403, 404). The passing on of the mother's
affliction, in Rich's terms, is exposed in O'Brien's fiction, then, as an
endless cycle of entrapment of women by women as guardians of social
norms in which the mother, stripped of identity and power, reproduces
herself, metaphysically absorbs the identity of the child who, in turn,
defines herself through the mother, a cycle only broken by total rejection of the mother/Mary model. O'Brien suggests, however, that in
doing so there remains an emptiness that can never be filled.

More than in any other example of her fiction, O'Brien explores the
crisis of identity resulting from the mother/daughter relationship in *The
Country Girls* trilogy, which, despite a critical emphasis on the first book,
in its entirety reveals O'Brien's attempt to articulate not only the root of
the psychological damage evidenced in the figure of Caithleen Brady
but the possibility of an alternative model in the figure of Baba Brennan.

Early in *The Country Girls,* Caithleen is revealed as a young girl whose
identity is defined purely through emotional attachment to her mother,
images of whom infiltrate Caithleen's every move: the unfolded bed-
spread, the slippers kept for special visits, and the girl's letting up of the
blind incorrectly, all establish, on the first page, the woman who "knew
things before you told her" (9). The death, remarkably early in the novel,
of this all-powerful and beloved figure in Caithleen's life, inflicts upon
Caithleen a state of emotional paralysis from which she never recovers.
Having never achieved the necessary separation from the mother,
Caithleen is abruptly stranded at a level of psychological and emotional dependence from which she cannot escape: "After that I heard
nothing, because you hear nothing, nor no one, when your whole body
cries and cries for the thing it has lost. Lost. Lost. And yet I could not believe that my mother was gone; and still I knew it was true because I
had a feeling of doom and every bit of me was frozen stiff" (41). Four
years later, and now in Dublin, Caithleen has moved no further: "I was

waiting for someone to come and warm me. I think I was waiting for Mama" (170).

As discussed earlier, Caithleen's initial quest for self identification and psychological union modeled on the lost mother occurs in *The Country Girls* through the figure of Mr. Gentleman. It is repeated in *The Lonely Girl,* the second book of the trilogy, through the figure of Eugene Gaillard, whose face reminds Caithleen of "a saint's face carved out of gray stone" but whose sexual advances repel her: "I just wanted to go to sleep and wake up, finding that it was all over, the way you wake up after an operation" (185, 230). Once she realizes that her wish that "people just kissed" when in love is futile (233), Caithleen's quest for selfhood through another moves toward the possibility of spiritual fulfillment through sexual union, which also proves fruitless, since it offers only a temporary state. She laments: "I thought that being one with him in bed meant being one with him in life, but I knew now that I was mistaken, and that lovers are strangers in between times" (356).

While the contrast between the two young narrators of *The Country Girls* trilogy has attracted a good deal of critical attention, the equally important contrast between their mothers has gone virtually unnoticed. In contrast to Caithleen's mother, Baba's mother is known to her children by her (symbolically significant) first name of Martha and is described as being not motherly since she is "too beautiful and cold for that" (30): "Martha was what villagers called fast. Most nights she went down to the Greyhound Hotel, dressed in a tight black suit with nothing under the jacket, only a brassiere . . . pale face, painted nails, blue-black pile of hair, Madonna face, perched on a high stool" (31).

Unlike Caithleen's "Mama," Martha divides food evenly among herself and her children, enjoys depriving her husband of pleasures, and advises her children to "get out of this dive—be something—somebody" (31). By no means does O'Brien suggest in the trilogy that Baba's sense of self is the ideal, but she does reveal her as a young girl and, finally, as a woman who, unlike Caithleen, relies on herself for her own survival. Baba married for money; her cynical and realistic approach is contrasted to Caithleen's romantic idealism, toward not only life in general but also motherhood specifically. Baba's willful daughter, Tracy, "vomited the milk I gave her, rejected me from day one, preferred cow's milk, solids, anything. She left home before she was thirteen, couldn't stand us" (515). In contrast, Caithleen's mistake is described as "the old umbilical love. She wanted to twine fingers with her son, Cash, throughout eternity" (515).

Caithleen's ultimate realization in *Girls in Their Married Bliss,* the final book of the trilogy, that the process of idealization and search for identity—whether through the mother, a man, or a child—is an illusion, leads to her ultimate disillusion and self-destruction. Having temporarily lost her son to his father who "will not allow [her] to destroy [the son's] future life, to turn him into one of the mother-smothered, emotionally sick people, [her] favourite kind" (504). Caithleen's disillusionment manifests itself in anger against "that woman . . . a self-appointed martyr. A blackmailer. Stitching the cord back on. Smothering her one child in loathsome, sponge-soft, pamper love" (476–77). This elucidates, as does most of O'Brien's work, Dally's suggestion that "since idealization is based on illusion, there is always the danger of disillusion."[15]

In 1986, O'Brien wrote the epilogue for a republication of the combined trilogy. Narrated by Baba as she awaits the arrival of Caithleen's remains at Waterloo Station, the epilogue skillfully combines all the elements of tragedy and comedy for which *The Country Girls* was critically acclaimed: "Even now I expect a courier to whiz in on a scooter to say it's been a mistake; I'm crazy, I'm even thinking of the Resurrection and the stone pushed away, I want to lift her up and see the life and the blood coming back into her cheeks. I want time to be put back, I want it to be yesterday, to undo the unwanted crime that has been done. Useless. Nothing for it but fucking hymns" (531).

In the epilogue, which reveals Baba as an embittered and battle-scarred survivor, the subject of mothers is a focal point in which Caithleen's (now known as Kate) and Baba's roles as mothers are shown as perpetuations of their respective roles as daughters. Kate, like her mother before her, leaves behind a question regarding her death by drowning: "Alone and covert as always, not knowing whether it was deliberate or whether she just wanted to put an end to the fucking torment she was in. Probably realized that she had missed the boat, bid adieu to the aureole of womanhood and all that. No more cotillions. Her letter to me says nothing . . . a blind really, so that no one would know, so that her son wouldn't know, self-emulation to the fucking end" (524).

By contrast, Baba, having recalled that when she was four years old, during a bout of scarlet fever, her mother had sent her away rather than look after her, reveals no illusion about her responsibility either as daughter or mother: "I don't hold it against her. I don't expect parents to fit you out with anything other than a birth certificate and an occasional pair of new shoes" (386).

Viewed in its entirety, *The Country Girls Trilogy,* then, is much more than a superficial tragicomedy that follows the lives of two young Irish girls from innocence to experience. It is, rather, a bildungsroman in which the search for women's selfhood is thwarted by elements beyond their control. Caithleen, emotionally retarded, spends her life searching in vain for a replacement of her first love object—the idealized mother figure—without which her identity is nonexistent, while Baba, rejected in quite a different way, defines her selfhood in terms of difference of degree rather than kind: "I thought, We're lonely buggers, we need a bit of a romp so as not to feel that we're walking, talking skeletons" (515).

Increasingly in her fiction, a "bit of a romp" becomes the central way many of O'Brien's protagonists seek a sense of self beyond the existence of a love object. But stories such as "The Love Object" and "Paradise," as well as the novels *August Is a Wicked Month, Casualties of Peace,* and *Johnny I Hardly Knew You,* which focus on women whose sexuality is foregrounded, equally reveal features familiar to all of O'Brien's writing, including the ultimate disillusionment in the search for selfhood; an acute awareness of writing within an existing, and predominantly male, literary tradition; and a use of irony.

O'Brien's titles, in particular, have always revealed something of the ironic playfulness with which she approaches her material. In "The Love Object," for instance, this irony has a comedic element, since what we, as readers, know of the narrator's lover—the "love object" himself—is that he is elderly, has blue, deceitful eyes, khaki hair, a religious/inner smile, is currently married to his third wife, and is a famous lawyer with ugly pink legs and no waist. Hardly Mr. Perfect, but remarkably reminiscent of Mr. Gentleman of *The Country Girls,* in relation to whom the narrative, similarly, reveals sufficient details to permit the reader a view of him significantly different from Caithleen's romantic illusion.

This iconoclastic tendency in her fiction led critics like Anatole Broyard to view O'Brien as a "marvelous diminisher of men. Nobody sees the comedy of masculinity, as we define it now, better than she does."[16] Yet, more often than not, criticism of O'Brien assumes an implicit sympathy between the author and her protagonists' experiences that, in turn, assumes the complicity of the reader. On the contrary, however, a story such as "The Love Object," one of O'Brien's psychological portrayals in which few external details or events distract the reader from the mind of the first-person narrator, ultimately places us in as restrictive and claustrophobic a frame of mind as the narrator herself.[17] The narrator remembers: "It was like being shut off . . . a little animal locked away. I thought very distinctly of a ferret . . . in a wooden box, when I was a child, and of another ferret being brought to mate with it once. . . . I thought of white ferrets with their little pink nostrils in the same breath as I thought of him sliding a door back and slipping into my box from time to time. His skin had a lot of pink in it" (158).

Unlike Caithleen of *The Country Girls* and Willa of *Casualties of Peace*—whose identity crises, through immersion in an idealized other, lead to their ultimate destruction (literally, since neither survives the fiction)—Martha of "The Love Object" survives the pain of rejection and the temptation of suicide to "mend . . . with a vengeance" (169). Her recurring nightmare, in which she is "being put to death by a man" but from which she awakens "calmer than [she] had been for months," becomes an inverted "dream within a dream" in which the lovers and murderers are interchangeable and are identified only as "Him" or "the Other One" (149, 153). Her panic on waking signals Martha's progression toward a reconciliation of the self. Her feelings of foolishness and inadequacy at not being able to tie her lover's bow are followed by those of hatred and a realistic view of his physical unattractiveness. Unlike Caithleen, then, who never finds a sense of self, Martha acknowledges that what she has always feared is "imprisonment, the nun's cell, the hospital bed, the places where one faced the self without distraction, without the crutches of other people" (171). Her ultimate arrival at a "normal" state is one in which she sees in life the romantic and the real—"the moon, trees, fresh spit upon the pavement" (171).

This attempt at reconciliation within the self is also evident in *August Is a Wicked Month* in which Ellen, a woman who has been "brought up to believe in punishment," is almost defeated by her young son's death by mutilation, and by her own contraction of a sexually transmitted disease as a result of her longing to be "free and young and naked with all the men in the world making love to her at once" (27).[18] But Ellen's survival, like Martha's, depends on a confrontation with reality that, by necessity, destroys the illusory, romantic view of life and replaces it with a more balanced one in which "if the days were never quite so lustrous-bright again, equally so the nights would not be as black" (168).

The emphasis in O'Brien's early fiction on daughters who exist as part of an intense and strictly role-defined family is inverted in much of her later writing, whereby her female protagonists, most often separated or divorced (and almost always lapsed Irish Catholics), do not have custody of their children—who are usually boys. This exposes a marked contrast between the stories in which the mother holds control of future generations and those in which control is removed from the women altogether. Similarly, the killing off of young men in her fiction—the son in *August Is a Wicked Month* and the lover in *Johnny I Hardly Knew You*—implies, perhaps, an interference with the future (symbolized, again, by the youth) as an essential element in the reconciliation of her female protagonists' selfhood.

O'Brien's interest has always been in women who are active and extraordinary rather than passive and average, though she also presents the effects or results of passivity on the part of women. Similarly, there seems little accuracy or point in the critical accusations that O'Brien never allows her later protagonists to seek fulfillment in avenues other than sex: Martha of "The Love Object" is a television announcer, Ellen of *August Is a Wicked Month* is a clerical worker, Willa of *Casualties of Peace* is an artist in glass, and the protagonist of *Johnny I Hardly Knew You* is a restorer of fine art. The point is not that they never seek fulfillment in these other areas of their lives but that O'Brien represents them as women who don't see fulfillment available to them by means other than as "looking glasses possessing the magic and delicious power of reflecting the figure of man at twice its natural size."[19] As means of fictionally representing alternative modes of finding themselves, O'Brien's methods seem extreme, but in their extremity, they expose the extent to which O'Brien's own internalization of her society's religious and social orthodoxies have colored her imaginative vision.

Notes

1. Edna O'Brien, "The Art of Fiction No. 82: Interviewed by Shusha Guppy," *Paris Review* 92 (1984): 38.

2. Simone de Beauvoir, *The Second Sex* (Harmondsworth: Penguin, 1983), 193.

3. Jenny Beale, *Women in Ireland: Voices of Change* (Houndsmills: Macmillan, 1986), 51, my emphasis.

4. All citations to "A Fanatic Heart," "The Rug," "Irish Revel," "The Bachelor," "Courtship," "Sister Imelda," and "A Rose in the Heart of New York," are to Edna O'Brien, *A Fanatic Heart* (Harmondsworth: Penguin, 1985).

5. Inventive forms of contraception represent just one aspect of life which contravenes the teachings of the church in O'Brien's fiction: self-abortion is undertaken by the doctor's maid in *A Pagan Place*, while in stories of illegitimate pregnancies, such as "Savages," abortionists are hinted at, usually in the form of unknown visitors to the house; lesbianism is the subject of "The Mouth of the Cave" and is also alluded to in "Sister Imelda"; while the sterilization of Caithleen in *The Country Girls*, as well as the numerous illegitimate pregnancies and illicit love affairs all contributed at one time to make O'Brien's work "obscene" in the eyes of the Irish censors.

6. All citations to *A Pagan Place* are to Edna O'Brien, *A Pagan Place* (Harmondsworth: Penguin, 1971).

7. Edna O'Brien, *Mother Ireland* (Harmondsworth: Penguin, 1976), 50.

8. "The Rug" does still contain narrative features that make clear the adult narrator's distance from the child of the stories: "I've since learned that it is the smell of linseed oil" (199).

9. Adrienne Rich, *Of Woman Born: Motherhood as Experience and Institution* (London: Virago, 1977), 243.

10. Mary Condren, *The Serpent and the Goddess: Women, Religion, and Power in Celtic Ireland* (San Francisco: Harper & Row, 1989), 171.

11. Ann Dally, *Inventing Motherhood: The Consequences of an Ideal* (London: Burnett Books, 1982), 94.

12. All citations to the *Ulysses* are to James Joyce, *Ulysses* (Harmondsworth: Penguin, 1983).

13. All citations to *The Country Girls, The Lonely Girl,* and *Girls in Their Married Bliss* are to Edna O'Brien, *The Country Girls Trilogy and Epilogue* (New York: Farrar, Straus & Giroux, 1986).

14. Marina Warner, *Alone of All Her Sex: The Myth and Cult of the Virgin Mary* (New York: Vintage, 1983), 77.

15. Dally, *Inventing Motherhood,* 95.

16. Anatole Broyard, "The Existentialist in Bed," *New Yorker,* 26 September 1974, 12.

17. All citations to "The Love Object" are to Edna O'Brien, *The Love Object* (Harmondsworth: Penguin, 1970).

18. All citations to *August Is a Wicked Month* are to Edna O'Brien, *August Is a Wicked Month* (Harmondsworth: Penguin, 1966).

19. Virginia Woolf, *A Room of One's Own and Three Guineas* (London: Chatto & Windus, 1984), 34–35.

Edna O'Brien and the Lives of James Joyce

MICHAEL PATRICK GILLESPIE

As if writing about Edna O'Brien writing about James Joyce were not sufficiently disjunctive, one finds the topic of such an examination comes imbedded in an imaginative context that requires immediate digression to comprehend. O'Brien's account of Joyce's life emerges against the backdrop of a literary scene crowded with memoirs, collections of letters, and several competing biographies. Before attempting to come to grips with her *James Joyce*, it is useful to survey the tradition and the work that preceded her efforts.[1]

Every biographer has an agenda. Plato's *Republic* does more than articulate an ideal society: it constructs the Socrates that Plato wished to preserve. Hagiographers of the early Church represented various saints as embodiments of the beliefs that the writers felt distinguished the new religion from those surrounding it. Pietro Arentino, the Renaissance author and blackmailer, probably made more money from what people paid him to ensure that he did not write about their lives than he did from the work that he published. Beginning in the eighteenth century with Samuel Johnson's *Lives of the Poets* and James Boswell's *The Life of Dr. Johnson*, biographers have tried to produce multidimensional and even contradictory views of their subjects. However, implementing that scheme has become increasingly complex as the tendency of biographers to project a range of human strengths and weaknesses onto their representations has made the writing a more personalized and ambivalent task.[2]

From the early twentieth century onward, that task has become increasingly complex, even contradictory. (As Merlin Holland, grandson of Oscar Wilde, remarked at a Wilde conference in Monaco in 1993, "Sigmund Freud has a great deal to answer for.") As a result, one reads biographies with the same interpretive skepticism that one brings to (other) works of fiction.

Accounts of the various lives of James Joyce that have appeared over the last eight decades amply illustrate this condition. When it appeared in 1924, Joyce's first biography, *James Joyce: His First Forty Years*, was as much the product of Joyce's art as of Herbert Gorman's, the American journalist who undertook the project; through extensive interviews and selected editing Joyce crafted Gorman's narrative into the picture of himself that he wished to appear.[3] Prior to Gorman's publication of an expanded version seventeen years later, *James Joyce: A Definitive Biography*, Joyce's participation in the production was even greater.[4] A letter of 6 June 1939 written for Joyce to Gorman by Joyce's friend Paul Léon makes the extent of that involvement quite clear. "Mr Joyce . . . states that he could not authorize the publication of your biography of him without having in his possession for perusal and comparison the entire set of the typescript and of course the subsequent proofs."[5]

Joyce had far less control, however, over most accounts of his life that appeared in print. As early as the mid-1930s, a number of people who knew Joyce at one time or another took advantage of that association and his notoriety to get their own work in print. Dr. Oliver St. John Gogarty—who during his lifetime gained some measure of renown as a surgeon, politician, and raconteur—the model for Buck Mulligan in *Ulysses* and a man determined to counter the portrait of himself found in those pages, brought out his own account of life with Joyce in Dublin at the turn of the century, *As I Was Going Down Sackville Street*. Although for the rest of his life, Gogarty, a Dubliner with literary ambitions, would fiercely deny the link between himself and Buck Mulligan and demand that his writing be taken seriously on its own terms, he went on to exploit the benefits of his Joyce connection in a series of publications that increasingly reflected his determination to reconfigure public conceptions of both himself and Joyce.[6]

Not all who wrote memoirs proved to be so self-serving. Throughout the 1940s a series of accounts written by friends who had known Joyce during his Paris days sought to represent the warmth, the genius, and the affection that they felt characterized his nature. Paul Léon and later his wife, Lucie Noel, celebrated their close ties with the Joyces.[7] Some still sought to capitalize on Joyce's name, and we see this in Leon Edel, who traded on a brief meeting and published a short work that reveals far more about its author than about the subject.[8] From this period, however, it is more likely to encounter the work of friends seeking to preserve the memory of a man for whom they felt great affection. One sees this perfectly expressed in *A James Joyce Yearbook,* edited by Maria Jolas, one of the family's closest Paris friends, a book that sought to capture the creative and emotional ambiance of Joyce's world.[9]

Whatever the motivation, by the 1950s a cottage industry developed as friends, acquaintances, and adversaries attempted to present their views on Joyce, cash in on the public interest in him, or simply rebut impressions that grew out of Joyce's fiction and the memoirs of others. In 1953 J. F. Byrne, the model for Cranly in *A Portrait of the Artist as a Young Man,* published a recollection of Joyce that also prominently features Byrne's theories on cryptograms.[10] Padraic and Mary Colm brought out a book of recollections of Joyce during the years that he lived in Paris.[11] And most tellingly, Joyce's brother, Stanislaus, published *My Brother's Keeper,* an account of their lives growing up in Dublin that clearly featured a view of James that Stanislaus would perpetuate in the work of Richard Ellmann.[12]

When in 1959 Richard Ellmann published his life of James Joyce, he seemed self-consciously to be working out of the context laid down in the memoirs of Joyce's friends and associates. Ellmann began his study with a broad articulation of his agenda, sententiously telling us that "we are still learning to be Joyce's contemporaries."[13] In the biography that follows, for all its flaws one of the most beautifully written works on Joyce's life currently available, Ellmann proceeds to sketch what in his view it means to be one of "Joyce's contemporaries." He does so by telling the story of Joyce's life based primarily upon interviews with and published accounts rendered by those who knew him first hand, in Dublin, Trieste, Zurich, and Paris. Most particularly Ellmann's version of Joyce's life turns upon the views of Joyce's brother Stanislaus, who grew up with him in Dublin and lived with Joyce and his family for nearly a decade in Trieste. Ellmann's book enjoyed instant acclaim and continues to be the reference of choice for individuals interested in Joyce's life.

That is not to say that the Ellmann biography is without its problems. Twenty-three years after its initial appearance, Ellmann marked
the centenary of Joyce's birth with a "revised edition." The fact that
little in the biography changed, repeating the opening line of the book's
introduction—"we are still learning to be Joyce's contemporaries"—
implies, unfairly I believe, scholarly paralysis.[14]

Perhaps Ellmann was concerned with helping us understand how to
be a particular kind of contemporary of Joyce. As noted above, Ellmann
got from Joyce's brother Stanislaus the lion's share of the material upon
which he drew in writing the biography. Recent scholarly studies, involving more careful examinations of that information than perhaps
Ellmann undertook, have noted the biases and distortions that consequently crept into the work.[15] This work does not so much discredit Ellmann's efforts as put them in perspective. It provides a timely reminder
of the way agendas inform accounts of individuals' lives. While we
should not dismiss these chronicles, we do well to remember that they
grow out of specific judgments.

Subsequent works on Joyce have either tactfully addressed deficien-
cies in Ellmann's work or they have quietly expanded areas left uncon-
sidered. One finds one of the most clear-sighted assessments of this
trend in an essay written by Ronald Bush in the early 1990s. With the
consummate humanity that characterizes all of Bush's work, it evalu-
ates the significant impact of Ellmann's writing while at the same time
offering a judicious assessment of its limitations and of the work that
remains to be completed.[16]

While the works mentioned above achieved varying levels of success
and reflected a range of abilities, in every case the overall aim of each
was relatively easy to discern. Scholars were writing about Joyce as the
subject of literary criticism or at least as the producer of material that became the subject of literary criticism. Friends, acquaintances, and family
members sought to protect or undermine Joyce's public persona or to
safeguard or rehabilitate their own. And some simply wanted to see
their own ideas in print and knew that linking them to Joyce's name
greatly increased the chance of publication. All of these are perfectly
understandable human motivations, but none quite touches on the impulse that will cause someone like Edna O'Brien to write about James
Joyce.

Edna O'Brien is above all else an Irish writer, and understanding her
work on Joyce also demands an awareness of the impact of Joyce on

any contemporary Irish writer. When I reviewed O'Brien's account of the life of James Joyce in the *James Joyce Quarterly*, I set out to examine her book in the same manner that I would assess any other literary biography.[17] I now can see that I made two mistakes in following such an approach. I commented on *James Joyce* from the perspective of a literary critic, demanding that O'Brien's work conform to the same somewhat stuffy academic protocols that I found in my own writings and in that of colleagues. I would certainly be justified taking such an approach if this were a work intended as a scholarly study, but in retrospect *James Joyce* now appears to me to be every bit as artistic in its aims as any of O'Brien's other writings.

I also treated O'Brien's book as an account of the life of James Joyce. In fact it now strikes me as much more useful to see it as a book about the art of Edna O'Brien. No author as committed to her craft as O'Brien is could contemplate the events in Joyce's life that shaped his consciousness without thinking of analogous experiences in her own. No author as committed to her craft as O'Brien is could write about Joyce's life without, consciously or not, referencing her own, bringing her own values into that account. And finally, no author as committed to her craft as O'Brien is could assess the character elements that made Joyce a great writer without touching upon those that give force to her own work.

This certainly is not a new revelation. Irish writers (with the exception of begrudgers, *pace* Dr. Gogarty) who have commented on Joyce's life take up a very different task either from that assumed by literary critics or that taken on by personal associates. More often than not, Irish writers who choose to comment upon Joyce's life are in fact taking the opportunity to consider their own.[18] With or without the help of Harold Bloom, they examine their anxieties of influence. They consider similarities and differences between their publishing world and Joyce's. And, more often than not, they talk about how difficult it is to create literary art in an imaginative context still dominated by Joyce's ghost.[19]

Were that all that one could say that Edna O'Brien has done in her biography of James Joyce, however, there would be little reason, outside of the motivations of an analysand, to explore its implications. Indeed, to assume that those achievements completely encompass her aims is to miss important features of *James Joyce*. While O'Brien's study doubtless struggles with the impact of what Joyce has already written, it offers a much more significant commentary on how one goes about understanding her work. O'Brien has used Joyce's life as a sounding board for amplifying her aesthetic values and for highlighting the imaginative goals that shape her fiction. Thus, in writing about Joyce, O'Brien offers useful guidelines for approaching her own work.

Having just sneered at the psychoanalytic approach to literary criticism, I should clarify the point that I am making about what I claim to derive from reading O'Brien's life of Joyce. I am not trying to link some form of authorial intentionality to interpretations of O'Brien's canon; in my view, it would be presumptuous and intrusive to attempt to read *James Joyce* as a gloss on the nature of Edna O'Brien. At the same time, I do feel that having some sense of the extratextual features that shape creative efforts of an artist provide useful interpretive reference points. These elements, often masked in her fiction, come to the foreground in her biography of Joyce, and in that regard, the biography has heightened my awareness of how I understand the rest of her work.

Some general features of O'Brien's biography help to set it apart, for me at least, from other works on Joyce and indeed from O'Brien's fiction. Unlike many other Irish authors' writing about Joyce, O'Brien's approach is neither reverential nor resentful. Rather, she shows wonderful self-confidence and a deep generosity of spirit. Joyce stands out as an artist for whose works she feels great admiration and for whose life she feels great sympathy. In neither instance, however, do these feelings deflect her professional assessments. O'Brien understands Joyce's frailties without excusing them, and she celebrates his imaginative power without begrudging it. In short, she takes a very atypical Irish view of the man.

Although O'Brien wears her knowledge lightly (to the point of appending a deceptively short bibliography to her account of the life), a careful reading of her prose shows that she put a great deal of scholarly effort into this study. Numerous offhand intertextual references to a number of interpretive and biographical works offer ample testament to the seriousness with which she approached her task. The recurrence of deft puns and sly quotations referencing Joyce's own writing make it quite clear that she has read and reread his canon. In short, *James Joyce* demonstrates not simply an admiration of its topic but a deep respect for the craft of writing.

It stands as a timely corrective, to me at least, to the impressions gained from the Sunday supplement interviews that O'Brien has given over the years.[20] The antic disposition that inspired her observations in those venues may be a valid aspect of her nature. Nonetheless, it remains only a part of the complex artistic consciousness that creates her fiction. When considering the craft of writing for an audience interested in the topic, as evidenced by her Joyce biography, she takes the role of the writer and the formation of writing far more seriously than these offhanded exchanges might lead us to believe.

For me, however, even more important are the conclusions that I draw from reading *James Joyce* about O'Brien's particular aesthetic and artistic values. In comparison with other accounts of Joyce's life, it is a short book, less than 180 pages. Consequently, the specific elements that O'Brien chooses to emphasize, and, equally, the particular aspects that she chooses to omit, take on a significance conferred by the need for careful selectivity.

Early on in the biography, for example, O'Brien acknowledges the importance of creative antecedents. In a fairly conventional way, she invokes the influence of Ibsen, Carlyle, Cardinal Newman, and Macaulay on the artistic sensibilities of Joyce as a young man (11–12). She references his critiques of Hardy and Wilde (58). And she sets him in context with novelists from Dickens to Proust (59). This all seems fairly conventional, yet even that orients me toward O'Brien's sense of a writer's place within the literary tradition.

On a more subtle level, and to my mind more revealing, she demonstrates the infectious quality of fine writing on other artists. With a delightful panache, O'Brien integrates lines from Joyce's writing into her description of her subject. In an unattributed quotation, for example, she has Joyce replying to a creditor: "molecules change, other I borrowed money, I other I now" (24). One encounters the same lines in the Scylla and Charybdis episode of *Ulysses* as Stephen Dedalus mentally forgives his own debt to George Russell. "Wait. Five months. Molecules all change. I am other I now. Other I got pound" (9.205–6).[21] Immediately following that remark, O'Brien describes the effect of alcohol upon the creative powers of the young Joyce: "Only the sacred pint could unbind his tongue" (25). In the Telemachus chapter, Buck Mulligan applies the same condition to producing witticisms from Dedalus: "The sacred pint alone can unbind the tongue of Dedalus" (1.565).

Perhaps most delightfully, she opens the biography in the following manner: "Once upon a time there was a man coming down a road in Dublin and he gave himself the name of Dedalus the sorcerer, constructor of labyrinths and maker of wings for Icarus who flew so close to the sun that he fell" (1). The passage unabashedly mimics the famous opening of *A Portrait of the Artist as a Young Man:* "Once upon a time and a very good time it was there was a moocow coming down along the road and this moocow that was coming down along the road met a nicens little boy named baby tuckoo."[22] The wit of the opening turns upon O'Brien's trust that her readers will make the connection with Joyce's famous first paragraph, but the passage has for me a much greater significance. In a wonderfully flamboyant fashion O'Brien acknowledges the way Joyce's prose can permeate the imaginations and the creations of any artist, and she articulates an unabashedly enthusiastic willingness to mimic that style in her own work. This gentle parody that embraces rather than flees from evocations of Joyce's style shows a refreshing artistic self-confidence evident in the writings of few other contemporary Irish authors.

O'Brien also attests to an understanding of the cold ruthlessness of a writer. In describing Joyce's calculated examination of love letters written to his mother by his father, O'Brien underscores the imperative that any author feels to exempt no experience, no matter how personal, from incorporation into the artistic process or to exclude any event, no matter how sentimentally powerful, that does not meet rigorous imaginative standards: "Among his mother's girlish mementos were the early love letters John [Joyce] had written to her. Joyce took them into the garden where he could read them at his leisure to see if they were of any use for his future writings. Deciding they were not, he and Stanislaus burned them" (21).

At the same time, O'Brien knows that family and friends form a crucial buffer between the artist and the world. She quotes criticism that Stanislaus Joyce made of his brother's *Ulysses,* noting with the understatement that suggests to me that it comes from personal experience that "[Stanislaus's] little cavils were unfortunate" (125). Just a few pages later, O'Brien underscores the importance of familial support to Joyce: "His fear of dogs and thunder are no secrets to us, his fear of madness he both admitted and repudiated, but his fear of aloneness he kept to himself. His family were a bulwark against it" (128).

It is both churlish and pointless to ask how, if Joyce kept this fear of isolation to himself, O'Brien would know of it. Instead, what strikes me are the implications that one might draw from this passage about O'Brien's own imaginative state. The very intimate nature of the observation underscores its tone of fellow feeling. Despite her well-deserved reputation for independence and tough-mindedness, this observation about isolation offers a much clearer sense of O'Brien's vulnerability than I had before reading it.

This conclusion may seem farfetched to some, but the tendency in O'Brien's biography to recur to the bonds of family and friends makes the point quite strongly for me. Indeed, the long account of Lucia Joyce's descent into madness (152–59), at least relatively so in a book of less than 180 pages, strikes me as telling. While the father-daughter ties were clearly important to Joyce, so were many other issues to which O'Brien gives far less space. Her probing yet sympathetic examination of this aspect of Joyce's life invites one to see it as a privileged element in her own.

O'Brien's treatment of Ireland in her biography of Joyce foregrounds even more provocative issues. Time and again, she has articulated a clear vision of the many problems that confront Irish society, and she has proven quick to attack what she sees as half-hearted or narrow-minded responses.[23] While her impatience with Irish provinciality stands as evident from these remarks, the representation of Irish society in *James Joyce* shows a far more complex attitude than the rancor of a disillusioned expatriate.

She begins a description of Joyce's world pulling no punches and using no equivocations to elicit the atmosphere in which he grew to manhood: "Joyce's birthright was a plaster virgin in Fairview, perched fowl-wise on a pole, the smell of rotting vegetables and a confraternity of rotting souls. To call this man angry is too temperate a word, he was volcanic. No one who has not lived in such straitened and hideous circumstances can understand the battering of that upbringing" (15). Even a casual reader of *The Country Girls* trilogy can see analogues between the life she describes Joyce as living and that from which its characters Baba and Kate emerged.

O'Brien sees the caustic effect of Ireland, and more specifically of Dublin, as reflected well beyond the strained economic circumstances of a materially impoverished childhood. She understands all too well the begrudging mentality of her countrymen and the vulnerability of the native Irish to its barbs. Speaking of Joyce's experiences during last visits to his homeland, she characterizes his reception as follows: "Dublin was waiting to discharge more wrongs on his already scalding psyche and the three visits which he made between 1909 and 1912 led to such emotional havoc that he broke with his native city forever" (63). Richard Ellmann and others have retold the story of Joyce's final trips to Ireland to the point of making them familiar to anyone with an interest in Joyce, but rarely has their impact been characterized so economically with such deft and biting insight.

At the same time, as O'Brien recognizes with superb sensitivity, the Ireland of Joyce's youth had an unshakeable hold upon his imagination and, if truth be told, upon his affections:

Asked by a visitor [to Paris] about a street in Dublin thirty years after he had left it, [Joyce] paused, then went on to describe the cobblestones with the sound of the horses' hoofs, the sound of footsteps and their different echoes, then the smells, must and otherwise, the smell of fresh and dried horse manure, or "horse apples" as the locals called them, the play of light at different times of day. It must have been agony for Joyce to be separated from the city he loved so and not to be able to walk about it or to walk along the strand with the tide out, lozenges of sand, water lapping and sidling, dim sun-drenched sea. That landscape was the first enthrallment to his young and highly charged being. And he never forgot it, never really left it, regardless of exile. (168)

More than capturing the poignancy of Joyce's separation from his native land, this lyrical description of the suffering enforced by separation testifies to O'Brien's abiding love for her country if not for its social institutions, which gave her as much pain as they did James Joyce.

Indeed, O'Brien captures both the pain and the necessity of exile for a writer determined to grow beyond the claustrophobic imaginative atmosphere of Ireland. She describes Joyce's first experiences as a would-be medical student alone in Paris. "His letters [to his mother] veer from arrogance to self-pity" (17). She touches upon the exhilaration that he first must have felt when he and Nora eloped to the Continent, noting wryly that Nora was not likely to share that exuberance (44). And she records how Joyce vacillated, at least in the early years, between remaining abroad and returning home (47). All this serves as a timely reminder to O'Brien's readers of the emotional shifts that she also endured as she struggled to break the hold of Ireland even as she strove to maintain her connections.

Most striking of all is O'Brien's treatment of faith and religion. Like Joyce, she has a sophisticated sense of each, and so she does not make the mistake of collapsing the two in her assessment of the role of Catholicism on the psyche of an Irish writer. Superficial readings have made much of Joyce's representations of the rigidity of the Irish Church. Nonetheless, his shadings of difference between aspects of Catholicism in Irish life are so vast and so complex as to leave open to ridicule anyone too quick to generalize on the topic. Fortunately, O'Brien is far too sophisticated to fall into such a trap.

Before proceeding, it would be well to consider the distinction Hugh Kenner made regarding the religious faith of Stephen Dedalus. Speaking of Stephen's decision to leave the Church, Kenner notes that Stephen expresses his defiance through the term *non serviam* (I will not serve) rather than *non credo* (I do not believe).[24] The distinction is an important one. By what he says, Stephen clearly rejects the authority of the Irish Catholic Church. At the same time, by what he chooses not to say, Stephen leaves his own faith an open question.

One might take the matter a step farther. In rejecting Catholicism, Stephen assumes the pose of a heroic rebel. The implication is that he is willing to risk his soul for art. Such a gesture, with its everlasting consequences, cannot fail to command respect. At the same time, it only ranks as a courageous move if one accepts belief in a God who has the power to damn that soul for eternity. Without that belief, the gesture becomes the buffoonery of comic opera proportions.

O'Brien, with her own abiding understanding of faith and Catholicism, deftly articulates how these views operate on Joyce's psyche. She gives a fine gloss of the notoriously sexually explicit letters that Joyce wrote to Nora while he was in Ireland between 1909 and 1912. "The voyeur in him had at last been unleashed and in his own city, amongst his own kin and in the country which he believed had repressed him and upon which he wished to pour the glorious and unabated bucket of sexual slime. The letters were for Nora, of course, but they were also for Joyce, to convince himself that he was free of every vestige of Roman Catholic guilt. But was he?" (74–75).

In 1928 H. G. Wells, who would not have known of these letters, wrote to Joyce: "You really believe in chastity, purity, and the personal God and that is why you are always breaking out in cries of cunt, shit, and hell." Wells may have been right, but Joyce committed his most secret impulses to paper both as testament and liberation (74–75). As she does throughout the biography, O'Brien here shows a clear sense of the conflicted feelings that Ireland and Irish institutions arouse in the writer determined to break from them yet dependent upon them for inspiration.

As one might expect, O'Brien's study of Joyce shows particular sensitivity to the roles women played in his life and to the differing demands Joyce's society placed upon theirs. O'Brien sees Joyce as endeavoring to subsume Nora during their courtship: "He tried to be her, to know her as in her convent days when the Sisters of Mercy prepared her for First Holy Communion, her scallywagging days when she made a date with an older man and then later with a girlfriend hid in a church and devoured the chocolates the man had given her" (37–38). She notes the sympathy of his representations of women: "In his early fiction the women were sacrificial creatures modeled on the women around him, the mothers and the sisters socially and economically beholden to the men whom they served. Worn out with childbearing, child rearing, and the washing of corpses, they believed that they were securing divine mercy for the next world" (90). At the same time, O'Brien has no illusion as to the impact of Joyce, or any other writer, on the life of the person who shares his: "Writers are a scourge to those they cohabit with" (103).

Nonetheless, women, as lovers, relations, or friends, form an important buffer against the world that, through jealousy, pettiness, or pure contrariness, remains alert for the opportunity to exploit the artist's weaknesses. In a painful chapter on the efforts of Dublin acquaintances to undermine Joyce's faith in Nora (63–68), O'Brien emphasizes the crucial nature of the support Joyce derived from the woman who had eloped with him from Dublin. At the same time, O'Brien devotes equal space to Joyce's experiments with other women and with the possibility of Nora becoming involved with other men (85–92). At the heart of these gestures is an understanding of the cold-blooded need for experience that impels the artist to push the limits of personal life into the realm of the professional.

Just as O'Brien's biography of Joyce says much about her, these brief remarks on *James Joyce* doubtless say more about me than I realize. Like every act of reading, my assessment of Edna O'Brien's biography of James Joyce rests upon personal assumptions and grows out of a series of subjective associations. The emphases that I place upon various elements in *James Joyce* may seem distorted, obsessive, and wrong-headed to any other reader. That may well be the case, but given the aim of this essay such a view does not trouble me.

What I hope that I have demonstrated in the analysis that I offer here is not that I have created a definitive account of O'Brien's aesthetic views. Quite the contrary, my goal has been to show the subjectivity and transitory nature inherent in every reading. *James Joyce* has done little to enhance my comprehension of that author or his works, for the story O'Brien tells is too familiar to be revelatory and the approach that she takes is too idiosyncratic to have broad application. At the same time, seeing the way that O'Brien writes about Joyce has made me aware of aspects of her own imaginative world that had previously escaped me. This, in turn, changes the way I will see her writing whenever I next encounter it.

To come away from this analysis with a checklist for reading Edna O'Brien would surely miss the point of her biography and of my essay. However, it is most appropriate to see in the way that she writes about another author elements significant in her own work. Indeed, it is hard to imagine how one could be more revelatory than when one critiques the work of a peer.

Notes

1. Edna O'Brien, *James Joyce* (London: Weidenfeld & Nicolson, 1999). When this volume first appeared, a number of critics took issue with factual flaws and typographical errors that marred its narrative. Thus, it quickly was followed by an American edition, published in the same year by Penguin, which corrected these flaws. The page references for all quotations are from the Penguin edition.

2. For a detailed examination of the advent of modern biography in the way that Boswell constructed our sense of Samuel Johnson, see Adam Sisman's *Boswell's Presumptuous Task: The Making of the Life of Dr. Johnson* (New York: Farrar, Straus & Giroux, 2001).

3. Herbert S. Gorman, *James Joyce: His First Forty Years* (New York: B. W. Huebsch, 1924).

4. Herbert S. Gorman, *James Joyce: A Definitive Biography* (1941; rpt. London: John Lane, Bodley Head, 1949).

5. James Joyce, *The Letters of James Joyce,* ed. Richard Ellmann (New York: Viking Press, 1966), 3: 443; see also 93, 132, 142–43n, 209, 225–226, 398–99, 426, 445, and 447.

6. Oliver St. John Gogarty's works include *As I Was Going Down Sackville Street* (London: Rich and Cowan, 1937); *It Isn't This Time of Year at All: An Unpremeditated Autobiography* (Garden City: Doubleday, 1954); "James Joyce: A Portrait of the Artist," in *Mourning Becomes Mrs. Spendlove and Other Portraits, Grave and Gay* (New York: Creative Age, 1948); "The Joyce I Knew," *Saturday Review of Literature* 23 (25 January 1941); "They Think They Know Joyce," *Saturday Review of Literature* 33 (18 March 1950): 8–9 and 35–37; "The Tower: Fact and Fiction," *Irish Times* (Dublin), 16 June 1962.

7. Paul Léon, "In Memory of James Joyce," *Poésie* 5 (1942): 35. Lucie Noel, *James Joyce and Paul Léon: The Story of a Friendship* (New York: Gotham Book Mart, 1950).

8. Leon Edel, *James Joyce: The Last Journey* (New York: Gotham Book Mart, 1947).

9. Maria Jolas, ed., *A James Joyce Yearbook* (Paris: Transition Press, 1949).

10. J. F. Byrne, *Silent Years: An Autobiography with Memoirs of James Joyce and Our Ireland* (New York: Farrar, Strauss and Young, 1953).

11. Padraic Colm and Mary Colm, *Our Friend James Joyce* (Garden City, N.Y.: Doubleday, 1958).

12. Stanislaus Joyce, *My Brother's Keeper: James Joyce's Early Years* (New York: Viking Press, 1958).

13. Richard Ellmann, *James Joyce* (New York: Oxford University Press, 1959), 1.

14. Richard Ellmann, *James Joyce,* rev. ed. (New York: Oxford University Press, 1982), 3.

15. A very good summary of such critiques can be found in Ira Nadel's "The Incomplete Joyce," *Joyce Studies Annual* (1991): 86–100.

16. Ronald Bush, "Family Portraits and How They Grow," *James Joyce Quarterly* 31 (Summer 1994): 581–96. Bush specifically examines Morris Beja's *James Joyce: A Literary Life* (Columbus: Ohio State University Press, 1992) and Peter Costello's *James Joyce: The Years of Growth, 1882–1915* (London: Kyle Cathie, 1992). He also, however, offers a thoughtful examination of the challenges facing anyone writing about Joyce and a careful account of what Ellmann's work has left undone.

17. Michael Patrick Gillespie, review of Edna O'Brien's *James Joyce, James Joyce Quarterly* 36 (Spring 1999): 696–701.

18. See for example, *A Bash in the Tunnel: James Joyce by the Irish,* ed. John Ryan (London: Clifton Books, 1970).

19. See Seamus Heaney, "Station Island," in *Selected Poems (1966–1987)* (New York: Farrar, Straus and Giroux, 1990).

20. "Passion's Progress," *The Atlantic Online,* 20 April 2000, www.theatlantic .com (accessed 9 January 2002); "Ireland's Wayward Writer, Still Raising Eyebrows," *New York Times,* 23 December 1999; "Public Lives: Doing the Real Thing," *Guardian* (London), 16 September 1992.

21. James Joyce, *Ulysses,* ed. Hans Walter Gabler (New York: Random House, 1986). All citations are from this edition, using the chapter/line format suggested by Gabler.

22. James Joyce, *A Portrait of the Artist as a Young Man* (New York: Penguin, 1968), 7.

23. See, for example, "The Books Interview," *Independent* (London), 12 June 1999.

24. Hugh Kenner, *Dublin's Joyce* (Boston: Beacon Press, 1962), 127.

Godot Land and Its Ghosts

The Uncanny Genre and Gender of Edna O'Brien's "Sister Imelda"

WANDA BALZANO

Here we advance a bifid reading, between literature and psychoanalysis, with a double attention to what is produced and what is concealed in the unfolding of the text, sometimes led by Freud, sometimes doubling him in a way which appears to us less like a discourse than like a strange theoretical novel: there is something savage [*sauvage*] in the *Unheimliche*, a breath [*souffle*], a provocative spirit that at times catches the author himself unprepared, anticipates and contains him.

> Hélène Cixous, "Fiction and Its Ghosts: A Reading of Freud's *Unheimliche*"

Writing is a vocation, like being a nun or a priest. I work at my writing as an athlete does at his training, taking it very seriously. Whether a novel is autobiographical or not does not matter. What is important is the truth in it and the way that truth is expressed.

> Edna O'Brien, "The Art of Fiction"

The Genre

But the storyteller has a peculiarly directive power over us; by means of the moods he can put us into, he is able to guide the current of our emotions, to dam it up in one direction and make it flow in another, and he often obtains a great variety of effects from the same material. All this is nothing new, and has doubtless long since been fully taken into account by students of aesthetics.

Sigmund Freud, *The "Uncanny"*

For a short story such as Edna O'Brien's "Sister Imelda" the meanings of the text are as plural as are the traces followed by any patient reader of detective stories such as those by Italo Calvino.[1] Dealing with the development of a young woman, the short story could easily belong to that category of the literature of education that is called bildungsroman, or it could belong to the wider sentimental genre, its main concern being "love's ending, particularly love that has never been fully realised" (158).[2] Set in a convent, with a nun as its title figure, it could be registered as a form of religious literature, with either devotional or claustrophobic undertones—at times bordering, hyperbolically, on the somewhat analogous trend of prison literature. The convent, from the start described "with its high stone wall and green iron gates enfolding [the boarders], seeming more of a prison than ever," causes its inmates to be "dreaming of [their] final escape, which would be in a year" (137). In the narrator's more than explicit subsequent words, "convents were dungeons and no doubt about it" (148).

The short story could also be read in the mode of a feminist parable, placing the emphasis either on the effective criticism of easily recognizable patriarchal codes and structures through the resentment of and resistance to manmade rules, or on the dejection of that very ideal of female freedom advocated in the narrative. If viewed from the perspective of the characters' (nuns and boarders) separation from their native abode—separation from the mother, banishment from the childhood home, and a certain displacement from the past—then it is possible to allegorically associate this short story with the narrative of exile. The narrator's resolve to "outstep [her] original world and take [her] place in a new and hallowed one" is quite clear throughout the story (143). The condition of being elsewhere, as an exile, an expatriate, or an internal émigré is of particular importance for Edna O'Brien, who moved to London in 1959, with the realization that she "would have had to leave Ireland in order to write about it. Because one needs the formality and the perspective that distance gives in order to write calmly about a place. Ireland is a wonderful incubator and . . . I would rather be from Ireland or Russia as a writer than from any other country. To live there and actually write is quite difficult; it's not simply the question of censorship."[3]

For most writers-in-exile, including Joyce, recollections of childhood are a literary food source and have been hoarded, squirrel-wise, against the winter; it does not appear to matter whether the childhood was happy. "Sister Imelda" could therefore be said to belong to the autobiographical genre insofar as it contains the recollections of Edna O'Brien's own convent-school background. It must be pointed out, however, that *Mother Ireland,* a work of nonfiction dealing with her memories of growing up in rural Ireland, more legitimately belongs to this category. Maureen L. Grogan's parallel reading of "Sister Imelda" and chapter 5 of *Mother Ireland* in fact aims to separate the two categories of fiction and autobiography. She states that "the real problem with all this focus on O'Brien's so-called 'emotional' style and the continuing praise of her descriptive powers is that it has often deflected attention from her finely crafted narrative style," and that the author, "although strongly reliant on the power of personal memory in creating her intense and evocative fiction, does alter, rearrange, and create entirely new stories as she distances herself from these childhood 'ghosts.'"[4]

In a minor way the story could also be classified as a psychological thriller or a detective story. One of the latter genre's favourite semantic elements is the tension between science and conjecture in the pursuit of knowledge. The creation of an appropriate atmosphere and the quest for the "truth" are essential ingredients of the genre, where the truth-seeker emphasizes a need to decipher, to make sense of what is perplexing, to render known what appears hidden, silent, impenetrable. The search for clues and details of Sister Imelda's mysterious life is a constant obsession in the story: "Excitement and curiosity impelled us to follow her and try to see what she looked like, but she thwarted us by walking with head bent and eyelids down. . . . Some days when her eyes were flashing she looked almost profane and made me wonder what events inside the precincts of the convent caused her to be suddenly so excited" (137–38).

Furthermore, the preoccupation with guilt and shame throughout the narrative labels it as psychoanalytically inspired literature, which stresses the importance of the family saga or ethnic diversity, making ample use of what guilt and blame arise from familial or ethnic backgrounds. In what we could call a neuro-narrative, the inner landscapes of the brain reflect the narrator's contemporary locus of self-discovery. The story, in short, draws an example of what in Ireland forms a genre per se, and a rich one. It is the Catholic, colonial, and patriarchal pedi-gree that Edna O'Brien, who has called herself "only a guilt-ridden Irish woman," suggestively describes in *Mother Ireland:* "The children inherit a trinity of guilts (a Shamrock): the guilt for Christ's Passion and Crucifixion, the guilt for the plundered land, and the furtive guilt for the mother frequently defiled by the insatiable father."[5]

However, more interestingly perhaps, against the background of a gloomy and isolated interior, under "a sky that was scarcely ever with-out the promise of rain or a downpour" (139), the story shows a taste for the mysterious, the grotesque, and the supernatural in depicting an anomalous relationship between a nun and one of the girls boarding in the convent. Against the claims of lesbian literature advanced in the course of an interview conducted by Sandra Manoogian Pearce, Edna O'Brien defends her story by stating that "almost every girl who goes to a convent falls in love with a nun and wants to be a nun."[6] For this rea-son, she feels quite free and innocent to write in "Sister Imelda": "It was as if every girl was in love with [the nun]" (142). Although she suggests that a similar attraction could easily develop between any teacher and student, she also does admit that it is the fear and excitement of this latent bisexuality that "thrills and terrifies us."[7]

A trait common to both Fantastic and Gothic literature, this fascina-tion with something *sauvage,* uncanny, is the sign of a provocative chal-lenge that takes the author herself by surprise, simultaneously surpass-ing and containing her, in the same way as Freud, according to Hélène Cixous, is challenged by *Das Unheimliche* (1919). Cixous illustrates how Freud, in writing his famous essay, is seduced by the secret of the envi-able power of the creator, by "'the freedoms of the author, the privileges of fiction to evoke and inhibit' the emotions or the ghosts of the reader, the power to lift or lower the bar of censure." On the one hand, Freud's very style, swaying between realistic tale and analytic deviance, could be said to produce a fictional creation, on the other, perhaps any fic-tional creation is per se uncanny. As Cixous puts it, "A reserve of repres-sion, fiction is in the end what resists analysis while at the same time at-tracting it." Freud, in his text "which appears to us less like a discourse than like a strange theoretical novel," tries to lead the fantastic back to the rational (the *Unheimliche* to the *Heimliche*).[8] In doing that, he is en-gulfed by hesitation, a feature that in Todorov's opinion is the quintes-sence of the Fantastic genre and which, in Freud's case, becomes his own pleasure principle, his own double.[9] One could say, inversely, that in Edna O'Brien's short story, which appears to us like another strange theoretical piece of fiction, the author moves from a different perspective but reaches the same end as she attempts to bring the rational back to the fantastic, the realistic tale of her convent days in *Mother Ireland* to the analytic deviance of "Sister Imelda," and the *Heimliche* to the *Unheimliche*. In this sense, here too "Hesitation" becomes Edna O'Brien's own double, and writing, as the author's phantasmal appearance, produces in this doubling an uncanny pleasure.

Already the writer's Irishness, according to Donald Morse, opens to a world that is essentially fantastic: "Irish writers and artists have always found the fantastic congenial and, even, necessary for their art. Early on they realised that 'there is an elegant efficiency to fantasies' that enables a writer to express ideas, emotions, and insights not available through mimesis. Thus for the Irish, the road to insight often lay not through literalism, rationalism, or logic but through the marvelous and the fantastic."[10] Even in Edna O'Brien's own opinion, her Irishness is a sometimes awkwardly prescribed inheritance and guarantee of ghostliness: "You are Irish you say lightly, and allocated to you are the tendencies to be wild, wanton, drunk, superstitious, unreliable, backward, toadying and prone to fits, whereas you know that in fact a whole entourage of ghosts resides in you, ghosts with whom the inner rapport is as frequent, as perplexing, as defiant as with any of the living. . . . This is Godot land."[11]

Toward the Uncanny

Thus *heimlich* is a word the meaning of which develops in the direction of ambivalence, until it finally coincides with its opposite, *unheimlich*.

> Sigmund Freud, *The "Uncanny"*

Freud's definition of the "uncanny" corresponds to that anxiety aroused through the encounter with something that is experienced as at once foreign and familiar, distant and close, altogether estranged, unknown, and yet at the same time strangely recognizable and known. According to Freud,

What interests us most . . . is to find that among its different shades of meaning the word *"heimlich"* exhibits one that is identical with its opposite, *"unheimlich."* What is *heimlich* thus comes to be *unheimlich*. . . . In general we are reminded that the word *"heimlich"* is not unambiguous, but belongs to two sets of ideas. . . . [O]n the one hand it means what is familiar and agreeable, and on the other, what is concealed and kept out of sight. *"Unheimlich"* is customarily used . . . as the contrary only of the first signification of *"heimlich,"* and not of the second.[12]

The meaning of *heimlich,* therefore, becomes more and more ambivalent until it finally coincides with its opposite, *unheimlich.* In short, the uncanny is something disturbing that leads back to what has long been familiar. The apparently uncomplicated plot of Edna O'Brien's short story revolving around a close relationship between a girl and a nun, set in postwar Ireland and cadenced by the boarding school's daily routine, encompasses such a reading. Appearing at first in a miscellaneous collection forebodingly entitled *Winter's Tales* (1963), "Sister Imelda" reappeared, ghostlike, throughout the pages of *Mother Ireland* (1976) and later in the author's own collection of childhood stories entitled *Returning* (1982). "Sister Imelda," like a *revenant,* like one that comes back after an absence, *returns* (both as reproposed fiction and as the nun, who at the end of the story comes back to haunt the narrator's—and the author's—conscience). Since the beginning, in fact, Sister Imelda is surrounded by a mysterious aura. Revealing an impervious nature to the convent boarders, "she thwarted [them] by walking with head bent and eyelids down" in what is a sign not only of modesty but also of obliqueness and concealment (137). Hers is an unconventional image, at times inspiring a ghastly energy and an ungodly vulgarity: "Her pale, slightly long face I saw as formidable but her eyes were different, being blueblack and full of verve. Her lips were very purple as if she had put puce pencil on them. They were the lips of a woman who might sing in cabaret and unconsciously she had formed the habit of turning them inwards as if she too was aware of their provocativeness. . . . She might have been a girl going to a dance except for her habit" (137–38).

Sister Imelda's demeanor is recognized by the pupils in the convent school as unorthodox: "Her spell in the outside world made her different from the other nuns, there was more bounce in her walk, more excitement in the way she tackled teaching" (138). Her conduct is almost blasphemous, as when "she uttered the phrase 'Praise be the Incarnate *World'*" rather than "Praise be the Incarnate *Word*" (138). She is animated by a wanton deportment: "There was something reckless about her pose, something defiant. It seemed as if any minute she would take out a cigarette case, snap it open and then archly offer me one" (143). Like the devil of popular belief, she knows many languages, having studied them at university. She teaches geometry, which studies the configuration of the earth as opposed to more transcendental subjects like theology or philosophy. Her mutable gaze is specifically defined, by contrast, against the immutable one of God: "She read how God dwelt in light unapproachable, and how with Him there was *neither change nor shadow of alteration.* It was amazing how her looks *changed*" (138, my emphasis). Sister Imelda's impulsiveness and lack of self-control fuel allegations of her fierce temper: "It was also rumoured that she possessed a fierce temper and that while a postulant she had hit a girl so badly with her leather strap that the girl had to be put to bed because of wounds" (139). Her flashing dark eyes, sometimes reddened "as if she was getting a sty," are possibly hints of a *Sty*gian nature: "Some days when her eyes were flashing she looked almost profane," and, "Her dark eyes yielded such vehemence that I prayed she would never have occasion to punish me" (139, 138, 140). Even the apparently hallowed image of her obscure sacrifices—presumably the cause of the swelling of the eyes—suggests some mysterious, terrible presentiment: "One of her eyelids was red and swollen as if she was getting a sty. I reckoned that she over-mortified herself by not eating at all. I saw in her some terrible premonition of sacrifice which I would have to emulate. Then in direct contrast she absently held the stick of chalk between her first and second fingers the very same as if it were a cigarette" (139).

Sister Imelda's supposed familiarity with cigarettes, or, more broadly, with fire, which also emerges during the practice of her other expertise, cookery, equally develops in the direction of ambivalence, evoking, on the one hand, a world of ordinary habits and, on the other, a world of infernal glare. Fire is the element that gives warmth and light but is also that which brings pain and death. In Bachelard's *The Psychoanalysis of Fire,* "Among all phenomena, it is really the only one to which there can be so definitely attributed the opposing values of good and evil. It shines in Paradise. It burns in Hell. It is gentleness and torture. It is cookery and it is apocalypse."[13] In short, to use Freud's terminology, fire is uncanny. When cooking or more or less unconsciously simulating the act of smoking, Sister Imelda appears to be right in her element and perfectly at ease, dwelling Satan-like "in light approachable." The image of her spitting on the hot stove with the subsequent sizzling conjures up for the reader the equivocal paradigm of her actions: "She must have liked cookery class because she beamed and called to someone, anyone, to get up a blazing fire. Then she went across to the cast-iron stove and spat on it to test its temperature. It was hot because her spit rose up and sizzled" (142–43). At last, the flashlamp she is given at Easter as a token of love and friendship by the girl narrator positively identifies her as a Luciferian creature, "a light bearer." A *mater reverenda,* a figure to be *revered,* that is to be "regarded with devotion" but also "with awe," she appears to be surrounded by a brimstone halo.[14]

Notwithstanding the disapproval of convent rule for any morbid type of earthly attachment, a visceral, secret bond gradually develops between the nun and the girl, urged by a mutual attraction that goes beyond the limits imposed by the rule. They manage to steal some moments of friendly intimacy together, as when Sister Imelda invites the girl to join her after cookery class. It is now that the enigmatic nun emerges as a true agent of temptation; like the serpent in Genesis, she is the temptress who fosters transgression. She brands the proscribed territory by "crossing" the kitchen and offers the girl the forbidden fruit in the extravagant shape of two jam tarts marked by the criss-cross sign of prohibition:

> "I bet you have a sweet tooth," she said and then she got up, crossed the kitchen and from under a wonderful shining silver cloche she produced two jam tarts with a criss-cross design on them, where the pastry was latticed over the dark jam. They were still warm.
> "What will I do with them?" I asked.
> "Eat them, you goose," she said and she watched me eat as if she herself derived some peculiar pleasure from it . . . and inherent in the pleasure was the terrible sense of danger. (143)

Again, something so disturbing as to arouse the sense of danger springs from the heart of its opposite, of what is agreeable, pleasurable. In the narrator's own view, it is clear that her "version of pleasure was inextricable from pain and they existed side by side and were interdependent like the two forces of an electric current" (143).

The Token of Repression

> This *unheimlich* place, however, is the entrance to the former *Heim* [home] of all human beings, to the place where each one of us lived once upon a time and in the beginning. There is a joking saying that "Love is home-sickness"; and whenever a man dreams of a place or a country and says to himself, while he is still dreaming: "this place is familiar to me, I've been here before," we may interpret the place as being his mother's genitals or her body. In this case too, then, the *unheimlich* is what was once *heimisch*, familiar; the prefix "*un*" ["un-"] is the token of repression.
>
> Sigmund Freud, *The "Uncanny"*

"The prefix '*un*' is the token of repression," Freud said. We add: All the analysis of the *Unheimliche* is in itself a '*un*,' a token of repression and the dangerous vibration of the *Heim-liche*. *Unheimliche* is nothing but the other face of the repetition of the *Heimliche;* this repetition has two faces: what is released and what is repressed.

> Hélène Cixous, "Fiction and Its Ghosts: A Reading of Freud's *Unheimliche*"

Sister Imelda and the girl *are* the forces of pain and pleasure, existing side by side. They are the two inseparable faces of the same coin: two in one, like soul and body. Sister Imelda, being herself uncanny, also brings to light the uncanny aspect of the life of her young disciple—her home. Through her own baking she brings back to her pupil the memory of home, which the girl had aimed to "outstep," to repress: "The wonderful smell of baking . . . brought back to me my own home, my mother testing orange cakes with a knitting needle and letting me lick the line of half-baked dough down the length of the needle. I wondered if she had supplanted my mother and I hoped not, because I had aimed to outstep my original world and take my place in a new and hallowed one" (143). In both characters' lives the maternal is repressed in different degrees. The nun voluntarily embraces an unmarried, childless, desexualized life; the girl, during her boarding at the convent, and through the development of a special relationship with Sister Imelda, rejects the matrimonial burden of her mother's life, that subservient condition sanctioned by article 41.2 of the Bunreacht na hÉireann[15] (the Irish Constitution):

I . . . thought of my mother at home on the farm mixing hen food, thought of my father, losing his temper perhaps and stamping on the kitchen floor with nailed boots. (153)

I was happy in my prison then, happy to be near her, happy to walk behind her as she twirled her beads and bowed to the servile nun. I no longer cried for my mother, no longer counted the days on a pocket calendar, until the Christmas holidays. (142)

I . . . hated the thought of my mother standing in the doorway in her good dress, welcoming me home at last. I would have become a nun that minute if I could. (155)

The ideology of Catholicism dominates the girl as well as the nun. The nun more readily conforms to the model of the desexualized Virgin; the girl seeks fulfillment of desire in a new and hallowed world outside the family (outside the marriage and motherhood she knows). As Lorna Rooks-Hughes has argued apropos of O'Brien's work, "The body in this discourse of maternity is effaced. Conceptualised motherhood; motherhood as ideology, as sacrifice . . . is valorised; reproduction—maternity as a physical reality—is disavowed."[16] The rejection of the maternal seems also to take place at the semiotic level, when the girl, after being reproached by the nun for her misplaced curiosity, represses her tears, and, in the immediately following scene, "forgets" to drink her cup of milk. Milk and tears are the most recognizable signs for maternal imagery in general and, in particular, for the representation of the *Mater Dolorosa* since the Middle Ages in the Western world. Milk and tears invest motherhood of an earthly identity. The rejection of these two is a clear rejection of the maternal:

My eyes filled with tears as I wanted her to realise that her recent coolness had wrought havoc with my nerves and my peace of mind.

"What is it?" she said.

I could cry or I could tremble to try and convey the emotion but I could not tell her . . .

I tiptoed back and sat with head down, bursting with fear and shame. Then [the Mother Superior] looked at a tray on which the milk cups were laid and finding one cup of milk untouched she asked which girl had not drunk her milk.

"Me, Sister," I said, and I was called up to drink it and stand under the clock as a punishment. The milk was tepid and dusty and I thought of cows on the fairs days at home and the farmers hitting them as they slid and slithered over the muddy streets. (149)

In the above passage, however, what is rejected is also secretly and unconsciously desired. The emotion that the girl attempts to conceal is, after all, her love for the nun and the kind of security she craves for in that emotion. This predicament somehow represents a replica of the unbound desire of the daughter for the mother. The repression of the maternal, the *heimisch*, the familiar, becomes uncanny because of the effacement of separation and the realization of desire. In O'Brien's echoing of Freud, "there must be, in every man and every woman the desire, the deep primeval desire to go back to the womb. Now physically and technically really, . . . a man partly and symbolically achieves this when he goes into a woman. He goes in and becomes sunken and lost in her. A woman never, ever approaches that kind of security."[17] In the short story's rationale, if Sister Imelda "had a wish it would be to go home for a few hours to see her parents, and her brother"; for her part, the girl "made up [her] mind that [she] would be a nun," "to lead a life unspotted by sin, never to have babies and to wear a ring that singled one out

as the Bride of Christ" (151, 150, 138). Both the nun and the girl seek a
sense of security through alternative expressions of desire: the nun in
the family home; the girl in the walled-in, womblike space of the convent. While her former home provides the nun with a more immediate
arena for the body's expression, to the girl's eyes, the ordered life of the
convent, in which spirituality becomes the paradigm for the regimenta-
tion of desire, also provides a psychodynamic arena for her own self-
fulfillment. Their desire is continuously renewed and, with it, their
sense of loss. Neither one of them, as Edna O'Brien prescribes, will
ever approach that kind of security: the nun will only go home for her
brother's funeral, and the girl, rather than achieving a sense of security,
at the end of the story will feel "a mixture of excitement and dread"
when finally confronted with her broken promise (156). It is precisely
this sense of loss in the expression of love that produces in O'Brien's
work what Freud defined as "the uncanny effect of silence, darkness and
solitude."[18] It is precisely this uncanny sense of loss, or silence, darkness,
solitude, that is central to her work, as she herself states: "my work is
concerned with *loss* as much as with love. Loss is every child's theme,
because by necessity the child loses its mother and its bearings. And
writers, however mature and wise and eminent, are children at heart. So
my central theme is loss—loss of love, loss of self, loss of God."[19]

Love and loss, milk and tears are also relevant personal semiotic
pointers for the author, as she is brought back to her own hegira from
her mother country. While in Ireland, she "had always been a stranger
from what had been [her] life," but in England the perception of Ireland
changed to a certain degree: here the "tepid and dusty milk," the "cows
on the fairs days" and the "farmers hitting them as they slid and slithered over the muddy streets" have for her the unmistakably familiar
flavor of home.[20] On being questioned about her relationship with Ireland, O'Brien admitted to a love-hate connection with her own mother
country. She admitted to feelings that would seem secret and hidden
but have come to light: "As for the country itself, it is no accident that
almost all Irish writers leave the country. You know why? Ireland, as
Joyce said, eats her writers the way a sow eats her farrow. He also called
it a warren of 'prelates and kinechites.' Of course there's the beauty of
the landscape, the poetry, the fairy tales, the vividness. I have shown
my love and my entanglement with the place as much as I have shown
my hatred."[21] As ever, what is repressed returns. Sister Imelda in her
otherness comes into view as mother to the girl. She is the other whom
the girl seeks as shelter and yet, at the same time, she represents the

(m)other the girl wants to escape from. Now, in Freud's view, "we can understand why linguistic usage has extended *das Heimliche* ['homely'] into its opposite, *das Unheimliche;* for this uncanny is in reality nothing new or alien, but something which is familiar and old-established in the mind and which has become alienated from it only through the process of repression."[22] In "The Return of the Repressed" Freud clearly states that in the mother-daughter relationship the daughter grows more and more like her mother, especially when the girl—possibly like the one in the story—will become a wife and a mother:

Take, for instance, the girl who has reached a state of the most decided opposition to her mother. She has cultivated all those characteristics which she has seen that her mother lacked, and has avoided everything that reminded her of her mother. We may supplement this by saying that in her early years, like every female child, she adopted an identification with her mother and that she is now rebelling against this energetically. But when this girl marries and herself becomes a wife and a mother, we need not be surprised to find that she begins to grow more and more like the mother to whom she was so antagonistic, till finally the identification with her which she surmounted is unmistakably re-established.[23]

Gender, the "Double," and Survival

These themes are all concerned with the phenomenon of "the double," which appears in every shape and in every degree of development. Thus we have characters who are to be considered identical because they look alike. This relation is accentuated by mental processes leaping from one of these characters to another—by what we should call telepathy—so that the one possesses knowledge, feelings and experience in common with the other.

     Sigmund Freud, *The "Uncanny"*

What the girl sees and rejects in her mother is the submissive figure of Eve. Yet, she is herself her mother's daughter, she is an Eve figure. What she sees in Sister Imelda, her adoptive spiritual mother, is the antagonistic, energetic form of Lilith, the demon and goddess of Talmudic tradition who, according to legend, was Adam's first wife. Refusing to be considered his inferior, Lilith left him and was consequently expelled from Eden. The root of the name *Lil* in Sumerian means "dust storm" or "dust cloud," and it is a term that designates a ghostly presence whose semblance is, in fact, like a cloud of dust. On one occasion Sister Imelda, with bloodshot eyes, leaves a cloud of dust behind her, running away from the room as if she had wings: "Geometry was my worst subject and indeed a total mystery to me. She had not taken more than four classes when she realised this and threw a duster at me in rage. . . . Her face had reddened and presently she took out her handkerchief and patted the eye which was red and swollen. . . . Suddenly she fled from the room" (140–41). Later on, this aerial image of dust expands into a haunting collective sequence, with all the other nuns in their dark habits flocking down like ravens in the middle of the night, face downward and arms outstretched, in the spectral posture of a deathly but weightless flight reminiscent of Lucifer and the devils in *Paradise Lost* (1:338–55): "At four o'clock in the morning while we slept, each nun got out of bed, in her habit—which was also her death habit—and, chanting, they all flocked down the wooden stairs like ravens, to fling themselves on the tiled floor of the chapel" (144). A mysterious creature of dark appearance, Lilith, referred to as "the screech owl" in the King James Version and as "the night hag" in the Revised Standard Version (Isa. 34:14), is often represented in a birdlike form. The owl is an attribute also associated with the virgin and warrior Athena, whose persona is identified with Sister Imelda during the school's Christmas theatricals: "Then she raised her arm as if depicting the stance of a Greek goddess and walking onto the stage I was fired by her ardour" (146). One more link in the ideology of the selfless, combative Virgin grafted and transposed into a Judaic, Greek, or Germanic setting is provided by the etymology of the name Imelda, coming from a Germanic form meaning "universal battle." The nun is but one link in the authoritative line of Lilith/Athena/Imelda.

In the story the nuns intone a monotonous chant, as owls do, before the morning birds begin their singing, and henceforth are the cause of dismay among the boarders who hear them at night. In the best Gothic tradition, the narrator recalls having suddenly awakened to that lugubrious tune because of a nightmare. As it is possible to deduce from a previous passage, the phantasm that wakens her could in fact be Sister Imelda (or the devouring mother) in the form of an incubus, or succubus, a vampire who creeps inside her, devouring her mind, her passion and heart: "That first morning when she came into our classroom and modestly introduced herself I had no idea how terribly she would infiltrate my life, how in time she would be not just one of those teachers or nuns, but rather a special one almost like a ghost who passed the boundaries of common exchange and who crept inside one, devouring so much of one's thoughts, so much of one's passion, invading the place that was called one's heart" (139).

This secret relation is soon revealed to be a symbiotic one: the girl wonders if Sister Imelda is in the same predicament, lying in bed and dreaming of her. A visible result of such an arcane osmosis is the increasingly emaciated aspect of the nun, as if indeed she were being in her turn vampirized. The nun's marriage ring slipping from her finger therefore indicates that, more than God's spouse, she is "sister" or (m)other to the girl, since they are "in mental and spiritual conjunction all [their] lives":

She looked pale. It may have been the day, which was wretched and grey with sleet or it may have been the white bedspreads but she appeared to be ailing. . . . But I still clung to a belief that a bond existed between us and that her coldness and even some glares which I had received were a charade, a mask. I would wonder how she felt alone in bed and what way she slept and if she thought of me, or refusing to think of me if she dreamt of me as I did of her. She certainly got thinner because her nun's silver ring slipped easily and sometimes unavoidably off her marriage finger. It occurred to me that she was having a nervous breakdown. (148–50)

It gradually becomes obvious, even to the girl, that Sister Imelda is her own double, her shadow or guardian spirit. The name of the girl in Edna O'Brien's story is never revealed in the course of the narration, thus enhancing the sense of doubling (of Sister Imelda and of the author herself) throughout the homonymous story.[24] In Freud's analysis, "the subject identifies himself with someone else, so that he is in doubt as to which his self is, or substitutes the extraneous self for his own. In other words, there is a doubling, dividing and interchanging of the self. And finally there is the constant recurrence of the same thing—the repetition of the same features or character-traits or vicissitudes, of the same crimes, or even the same names through several consecutive generations."[25] At first the nun represents for the girl an antidote against her own sense of loss: as exemplified by Freud, she embodies an insurance against the destruction of her ego, clinging to the girl as soul to body. November, "the month of the Suffering Souls in Purgatory, and . . . their twofold agony, the yearning for Christ and the ferocity of the leaping flames" is a time of "mortification," when the girl in the convent is "in the thick of all these dreads" (140). It seems to be a particularly apt time for fellowship, camaraderie, and intimate familiarity to take place in order to counteract that sense of loss and thus fortify congenial bonds "in that communion of spirit that linked the living with the dead," or, in the best of hypotheses, the people and their guardian angels (140). Sister Imelda radiates this kind of positive energy: "She was radiant as if such austerity was joyful. Maybe she was basking in some secret realisation involving her and me" (146–47). Then, in a similarly ambiv-alent process as that associated with the *heimlich,* the nun "develops in the direction of ambivalence, until [she] finally coincides with [*heim-lich's*] opposite, *unheimlich*."[26] Sister Imelda becomes the uncanny har-binger of the girl's own *unheimlich* fears, destroying her confidence until her love coincides with her fear. In the beginning of the story, having just realized "that there was an attachment between [them]," the girl had found herself "in the thick of all these dreads . . . becoming dread-fully happy" (140). At the end, her love comes together with (and hence is spoilt by) her fear: "My fear of her and my love came back in one fell realisation" (156). A sense of loss, and with it a blurring of boundaries, is consequently established.

The doubling effect also becomes a reflection of the dyad Lilith/Eve that, in Judaic tradition, is one of rebellion versus obedience. Here we are presented with rewritings of myth that break patriarchal conven-tions, and we see for once Lilith and Eve, the antithetical pair of patriar-chal femininity, united in a bond at the heart of which are contemporary women, attracted by the opposite forces of submission and rebellion. If Lilith, although a rebellious and somehow grotesque figure, is power-less being in exile (like Sister Imelda inside the prison-convent), then Eve, traditionally more submissive, is given some possibility of con-frontation and freedom outside the garden, as is the girl outside the con-vent grounds. In O'Brien's rewriting, however, the figure of Eve seems to have lost the courage for confrontation as well as the faith in freedom. Never really challenged by transgression or sin, once she is in the out-side world, away from the convent school and Sister Imelda, she gradu-ally ceases to write to the nun and abandons the project to become like her. She seems instead to have receded to a painfully conscious state of sexual submission. In her words, "Life was geared to work and to meet-ing men and yet one knew that mating could only but lead to one's being a mother and hawking obstreperous children out to the seaside on Sunday" (156).

When some time later she is by chance sitting in the same bus as the nun, she lacks the spirit to confront her. Yet, in that same conclud-ing scene, ambiguity prevails once more. The oxymoronic nature of the Gothic genre promptly returns, as a revitalizing agent, to give gender an-other opportunity for liberation. The fantastic and feminist meet at the crossroads. In the final tableau, populated with symmetrical doubles, Lilith and Eve still travel in tandem, as do the foreign and the familiar, the rebellious and the submissive. Catching a last glimpse of Sister

Imelda leaving the bus with another nun, the girl sees "the back of their two sable, identical figures with their veils being blown wildly about in the wind" (157). In one of the two identical, "wild" figures she probably recognizes the projection of herself, of what she could have become if she had not broken the promise to follow in the nun's steps: the chance she seems to have missed. Had she become a nun, she would have been imprisoned in the convent, and yet free of society's conventional expectations. The Gothic side of Sister Imelda, a veiled subject, stands for the hidden power of femininity. On the other hand, nonetheless, as if reflecting a mirror image, she is accompanied by her inseparable old-time school friend Baba, with whom she attended "the college where [Sister Imelda] had surpassed herself" (155). She still seems to follow in the nun's steps; the opportunity to free herself of society's conventional expectations and therefore to grow into an autonomous, radical, unique being is still in her hands. Baba, whose namesake, St. Bridget, is appropriately associated with thresholds, bridging Pagan divinity and religious sanctity, represents to her another shadow-figure or guardian spirit, another double, another Lilith.[27] Similar to Sister Imelda, her friend is proudly independent: "Baba was the only girl who could stand up to a prefect. When she felt like it she dropped out of a walk, sat on a stone wall and waited until we all came back" (151). Also, Baba shares Sister Imelda's peculiar bittersweet ways of sulfurous bliss, of sweetness and fire, as when in the convent—in an image similar to Sister Imelda's spit sizzling and rising from the hot stove—after eating some sugar, she "threw the remainder into the dying fire so that it flared up for a minute with a yellow spluttering flame" (145). By the end, it becomes consistently clear that the figures of Baba and Sister Imelda converge.

The conclusion of the short story does not unambiguously mark a sense of failure or inadequacy, as various critics or even Edna O'Brien herself seem to imply. Under the surface of Edna O'Brien's text, under its body and hers, under the body of writing and the body of reading, the pair still inseparably survives as if nothing had changed. Embodying and reflecting the archetypes of dyadic femininity for generations (past and still to come)—doubling, dividing, interchanging, redoubling—Sister Imelda/Baba and the girl in their indissoluble filiation represent that bond that the patriarchal order has always attempted to break apart, that subversive and abject disorder that it has always attempted to repress, "like the two forces of an electrical current."

When asked if there was an original for the character of Baba, Edna O'Brien answered, "I think I did have school friends who were the opposite of myself, and they were extrovert and mischievous, more mischievous. I was drawn towards them as I always am towards opposites. But now I think that it was partly my other person, my alter-ego. I had a sort of streak of submersed rebellion in me always, which I never let out, unfortunately; I was really too frightened, too meek. And I don't think that the meek should inherit the earth."[28]

Notes

1. I have here in mind Italo Calvino's *If on a Winter's Night a Traveller* (1979; rpt., London: Martin Secker & Warburg, 1981).

2. All quotations from "Sister Imelda" are from the author's short-story collection *Returning* (London: Weidenfeld & Nicolson, 1982).

3. Edna O'Brien, quoted in Grace Eckley, *Edna O'Brien* (Lewisburg, Pa.: Bucknell University Press, 1974), 26.

4. Maureen L. Grogan, "Using Memory and Adding Emotion: The (Re)Creation of Experience in the Short Fiction of Edna O'Brien," *Canadian Journal of Irish Studies* 22.2 (1996): 10, 13.

5. O'Brien, quoted in Eckley, *Edna O'Brien*, 66–67; Edna O'Brien, *Mother Ireland* (London: Weidenfeld & Nicolson, 1976), 32.

6. Sandra Manoogian Pearce, "An Interview with Edna O'Brien," *Canadian Journal of Irish Studies* 22.2 (1996): 7.

7. Ibid.

8. Hélène Cixous, "La fiction et ses fantômes: Une lecture de l'*Unheimliche* de Freud" [Fiction and Its Ghosts: A Reading of Freud's *Unheimliche*], *Poétique* 3 (1972): 201, 216, 199. All translations from the French are mine.

9. See Tzvetan Todorov, *The Fantastic: A Structural Approach to a Literary Genre* (1970; rpt., Ithaca, N.Y.: Cornell University Press, 1975).

10. Donald E. Morse, introduction to *More Real Than Reality: The Fantastic in Irish Literature and the Arts,* ed. Donald E. Morse and Csilla Bertha (Westport, Conn.: Greenwood Press, 1991), 1.

11. O'Brien, *Mother Ireland,* 36–37.

12. Sigmund Freud, *The "Uncanny,"* ed. James Strachey, in *The Penguin Freud Library,* vol. 14: *Art and Literature* (1919; rpt., London: Penguin, 1990), 345.

13. Gaston Bachelard, *The Psychoanalysis of Fire* (1938; rpt., London: Routledge & Kegan Paul, 1964), 7.

14. See *Oxford English Dictionary,* 2nd ed., under "reverend."

15. Article 41.2 of the Irish Constitution represents a distinct form of sexual stereotyping, as it fails to mention men's duties or to recognize that a woman's place is a woman's choice:

> 1. In particular, the State recognises that by her life within the home, woman gives to the State a support without which the common good cannot be achieved.
> 2. The State shall, therefore, endeavour to ensure that mothers

shall not be obliged by economic necessity to engage in labour to the neglect of their duties in the home.

16. Lorna Rooks-Hughes, "The Family and the Female Body in the Novels of Edna O'Brien and Julia O'Faolain," *Canadian Journal of Irish Studies* 22.2 (1996): 85.

17. O'Brien, quoted in Eckley, *Edna O'Brien,* 30.

18. Freud, *The "Uncanny,"* 369.

19. Edna O'Brien, "The Art of Fiction No. 82: Interviewed by Shusha Guppy," *Paris Review* 92 (1984): 38.

20. O'Brien, quoted in Eckley, *Edna O'Brien,* 26.

21. O'Brien, "The Art of Fiction," 39.

22. Freud, *The "Uncanny,"* 363–64.

23. Sigmund Freud, "The Return of the Repressed," in *Moses and Monotheism,* ed. James Strachey, in *The Penguin Freud Library,* vol. 9: *The Origins of Religion* (1939; rpt., London: Penguin, 1990), 373.

24. To a reader familiar with Edna O'Brien's work, the girl is easily identifiable as Caithleen, Baba's friend in *The Country Girls Trilogy* (*The Country Girls,* 1960; *The Lonely Girl,* 1962 [reprinted as *Girl with Green Eyes,* 1964]; *Girls in Their Married Bliss,* 1964), which was conceived in approximately the same years as "Sister Imelda." The supposed name of Caithleen, associated with the Greek word for "pure," *katharos,* enhances the character's opposition to the nun's uncanny qualities, *heimlich* vs. *unheimlich.*

25. Freud, *The "Uncanny,"* 356.

26. Ibid., 347.

27. In *The Country Girls Trilogy* Baba stands for Bridget. Significantly, though, Baba at a certain point wishes to change her name to "Barbara, pronounced 'Baubra,'" which comes from *barbaros,* the Greek word for "foreign," "strange." The pair Caithleen and Baba (*katharos* and *barbaros*) mirror the girl and Sister Imelda (see note 24).

28. O'Brien, quoted in Eckley, *Edna O'Brien,* 67.

Blurring Boundaries, Intersecting Lives

History, Gender, and Violence in Edna O'Brien's House of Splendid Isolation

DANINE FARQUHARSON and
BERNICE SCHRANK

Interrogating Irish Narratives

By the time *House of Splendid Isolation* was published in 1994, Edna O'Brien had a well-deserved reputation as an author who passionately and eloquently addressed women's needs and desires for liberation and autonomy, particularly in sexual matters. Her short stories and novels are replete with young Irish women coming of age in repressive circumstances, first experiencing the joys of sexual initiation and then enduring the stultification and betrayals of mature domesticized love. Writing in 1974 in the first full-length study of O'Brien, Grace Eckley describes the trajectory of a typical Edna O'Brien novel or short story: "Miss O'Brien's women unhesitantly acknowledge sexual necessity while living independently of public concerns; her feminists rarely recognize that their cause is public. Instead their object is love, and their sorrow is loss."[1] Indeed, the textual worlds O'Brien creates consistently deny women happiness, often leaving them with little more than unfulfilled longing and intermittent regret, the bitter remains of failed relationships.[2]

That O'Brien's characters lack psychosocial grounding and see themselves as floating free of social and historical contexts only exacerbates their feelings of powerlessness and purposelessness. The characters' perceptions of themselves are not, however, synonymous with O'Brien's view of them. In novels such as *The Country Girls, Night,* and *Time and Tide,* and short stories in collections such as *The Love Object* and *Lantern Slides,* it may be inferred that characters' romantic longings and sexual experiments are shaped by the patriarchal world from which they seek to escape. But such a cultural critique is available to the reader (not the characters), and then only between the lines.

Eckley's abbreviated overview of O'Brien's concerns retained its explanatory power until the publication of *House of Splendid Isolation* twenty years later. This novel is unlike any previous O'Brien work. Mahony's observation that *House* is "something of a departure for O'Brien" understates the case.[3] The occasion of the novel is the resurgence of violence in Northern Ireland, with its spillover effects in the Republic. At the center of the novel is the relationship between the octogenarian Josie O'Meara, ill, crotchety, and alone, and an escaped IRA gunman, McGreevy.[4] He is a self-confessed murderer who takes her hostage in her own home, a big, dilapidated house somewhere inside the Republic but also in the imagistic borderland between North and South. Presumably the isolation both of the house and of its lone occupant in part accounts for why McGreevy, on the run, chooses it as his hideout.[5] The key elements here—the old woman, the figure of the gunman, the big house setting—are strong indicators of O'Brien's shifting direction. O'Brien has never focused on a woman as old as Josie; O'Brien has never previously created a central gunman figure; and she has never before used the Big House as artifact or metaphor.

Even more telling in terms of innovation is the novel's direct engagement with (and, as we argue later, deconstruction of) both narrative in general and the narrative of Irish history in particular. The novel relies on and frames its concerns with the metanarrative of Ireland from colonial times through to Independence and into modernity. By projecting the life of the reclusive Josie onto the screen of public events, O'Brien convincingly demonstrates that any conception of a "private" life disconnected from a social and historical matrix is invalid. It is through the character of McGreevy that this background becomes foreground as the constituent elements of Irish history impinge on the present. So, both behind and through Josie, McGreevy and the all-Ireland manhunt for him are conflated with the mythic story of eight hundred years of English occupation and the oppression of an indigenous population whose liberation has been achieved by blood sacrifice (the tradition of insurgency to which McGreevy and his associates belong). Behind as well as through the two protagonists are the consequences of the creation of a new nation in its own way as repressive as what came before (the experience of Josie, whose life exposes the destructive power of the patriarchal arrangements underlying Gaelic and Catholic Ireland and later codified by the post-Independence de Valera government). And, finally, behind and through them is seen the gradual eclipse of nationalism by increasing participation in the global village (the gestalt of the third generation, rebels and police alike).[6] Despite the forceful presence of history in the novel, it is, as we indicate below, contested territory.

The novel's presentation of history is complicated by the persistence of memory, anecdote, diaries (Josie's, McGreevy's, Josie's rebel uncle's), and trace markings, which clarify as well as interrupt, subvert, and threaten to overthrow any anticipated linear sequence of the narrative.[7] Much of the textual density of previous O'Brien novels derives from the richness of her lyrical prose and, in particular, from the exfoliations of her images and metaphors. In *House,* the density and complexity arises in large part from the multiple plotlines, presented as fragmented and seemingly disconnected actions and remembrances, the past spilling into the present, the present repeating the past. The cumulative effect of this shifting, kaleidoscopic style is to deconstruct not only the powerful narrative of Irish history but also to interrogate the existence of truth and the certainty of knowledge. The old Manichaeism at the heart of Irish nationalism, with its orderly categories of English = bad and Irish = good, has broken down, even if characters like McGreevy do not understand the new realities.[8] Indeed, McGreevy is tracked down and eventually caught by Irish police in the Republic. Although the breakdown of the old nationalist mythology does not end the violence, it provides an opportunity for the kinds of transgressions and reconsiderations that allow creative realignments of positions previously deemed static.

Any easy optimism about the future is, however, premature. It is true that O'Brien leaves us without the inevitabilities of the sequential logic of teleology. But, although the components of progressive change may be present in *House of Splendid Isolation,* they have not yet combined so as to enable the emergence of a future significantly different from the past. Indeed, the Big House to which Josie comes as a newly married woman never experiences the presence of children[9] and, in the novel's bookends, the opening and closing sections entitled "The Child," O'Brien suggests that the future (personal as well as national) is already past and dead.[10]

We argue that in *House* there are four narrative lines that disrupt the linear, teleological narrative of Irish history. O'Brien suggests through these lines that an unproblematized faith in linear progress that leads Ireland inexorably from colonialism to nationalism and then to internationalism is misguided. For O'Brien, there are less attractive but equally cogent alternatives to that hopeful metanarrative. These alternatives are linked by violence and conditions of real and metaphoric imprisonment. It is not accidental that the central section of the novel is entitled "Captivity." As an introduction to that section, Josie provides her view of history as a form of entrapment: "dark threads . . . looping back and forth and catching her and people like her in their grip, like snares" (58).[11] The rest of the novel validates Josie's view. So it is that O'Brien's revisions of history are in many ways even less satisfactory than what they challenge inasmuch as the intersection of the different plotlines offers little other than an endless cycle of imprisonment and death.

The four plotlines that underpin the novel are 1) the story of the Big House, a subgenre of the Irish novel, in which the decaying values of an Ascendancy class are exposed; 2) the romance, here rendered as the story of an old woman's unrealized and now unrealizable longings for a full and meaningful heterosexual relationship; 3) the patriotic melodrama of the heroic Irish gunman on the run, prepared to sacrifice his life for the good of the cause, a tale rendered mythic by countless dramatic, novelistic, and cinematic iterations; 4) and, finally, the story about stories in which the multitude of references to misinformation, rumor, folklore, books, notes, and storytelling combine with other plotlines to create a novel that eliminates any possibility of closure or hopeful conclusions. We discuss each of these in the order presented.

Renewing the Patriarchal Order: "What about . . . the big house?"

It has become conventional to identify the Big Houses of Ireland with the genteel drawing-room culture of the Anglo-Irish Ascendancy. According to Jacqueline Genet, these houses "offer an explanation of that class, its style and manners; they set out its relation with its environment and culture, and they plot its eventual disintegration and decomposition."[12]

In recent times, the social meaning of the Big House to which Genet refers has been attenuated by the popular uses to which the image of the Big House has been put. Vera Kreilkamp astutely notes that "the Irish country house has become an iconographic staple of tourist board promotional campaigns rather than an imperial interloper in the countryside."[13]

It is not just that the Big House association with the Protestant Ascendancy is suppressed by such commodification; it is that the unhappy relationship between the Protestant Big House and the majority Catholic population is erased. The playwright Brian Friel insists on their linkage in his play *Aristocrats*: "When we talk about the Big House in this country, we usually mean the Protestant Big House, with its Anglo-Irish tradition and culture; and the distinction is properly made between that tradition and culture and what we might call the native Irish tradition, which is Roman Catholic."[14] Friel's point is surely at odds with the naive pastoralism of "tourist board promotional campaigns." For Friel as for Kreilkamp and Genet, the Big House is deeply implicated in the colonial history of Ireland, an artifact left over from a system in which a minority Anglo-Irish community politically, economically, and culturally dominated the majority Gaelic and Catholic population.

Clearly, then, any discussion of the Anglo-Irish Big House comes with political baggage.[15] According to Otto Rauchbauer, because "the subject has been emotionally charged and still is ideologically controversial in the Irish context," the study of the literature of the Big House has been slow to appear. Nevertheless, Rauchbauer believes (and the collection of essays he edits demonstrates) that the social and economic transformation of Ireland in the last two decades of the twentieth century, that is, its secularization and Europeanization, has moderated those emotions, thereby enabling an examination of the literature of the Big House to proceed.[16] Of course Rauchbauer's gingerly manner signals a certain discomfort with his subject; it is as if he feared being misunderstood as unsympathetic to the oppressed by studying the culture of the oppressor.

Kreilcamp's book-length study of the literature of the Big House, which appeared six years after Rauchbauer's work, is less defensive. Kreilcamp unapologetically summarizes the themes and conventions of the Big House novel and frames that discussion within the broader history of Ireland: "Big House novels represent a major tradition in Irish fiction. Set on isolated country estates, they dramatize the tensions between several social groups: the landed proprietors of a Protestant ascendancy gentry; a growing, usually Catholic, middle class; and the mass of indigenous, rural Catholic tenantry. In the course of two centuries, these novels reveal recurring themes and conventions, most notably the setting of a beleaguered and decaying country house collapsing under the forces of Anglo-Irish improvidence and the rising nationalism of the Irish society outside the walls of the demesne."[17] Kreilcamp's summary indicates that the conventions of Ascendancy Big House fiction rely on an aesthetics of social decline. O'Brien works both within and against these conventions. The house of the novel's title is both the O'Meara family domicile and a metonymic marker for the social and political changes in Ireland in the twentieth century, a means of revealing the weaknesses of the Protestant Ascendancy as well as a way of displaying the limitations of the Catholic succession.

The house is, to begin with, an English Big House. Early on, a farmer in the neighborhood provides Josie with its genealogy: "He traced the various owners for her: the engineer who had built it with workmen in the winter when they weren't farming, built it from a design he saw in a book; a later occupant responsible for the shrubs and flowers, had them sent in a sack from botanical gardens all over the world. . . . English people and half-English people, and one particular Englishman who had brought an Austrian concubine but got sick of her" (41). This same Englishman, having disposed of his Austrian concubine, then took up with an Irishwoman. For a while, according to the loquacious neighbor, the Englishman and his Irish wife had a wonderful time: "bed and hot toddies . . . matinee and evening—and then she got the lonesomes . . . and wanted drives back to the town to her father's pub, and it was all right for a time, and he'd drink and she'd drink with him and they'd be driven home blotto" (41). In this brief sketch, O'Brien evokes the conventions of diminution and decay associated with the Big House in other Ascendancy Big House novels. Compared to the spectacular waste and dissipation depicted in such a prototypical Big House novel as Maria Edgeworth's *Castle Rackrent,* O'Brien's description of the English presence is low-key and their excesses modest. About the worst that can be said of these English landlords is that they were a lackluster bunch. Whatever their faults, they do not destroy the House. The House is still imposing when Josie sees it for the first time: "Any girl," she notes, "would have given her eyeteeth to marry into it" (29).[18]

It is after the House passes into the hands of the O'Mearas, a Catholic family with deep but vague Republican affiliations, that the House falls apart.[19] By the time McGreevy arrives, some sixty years after Josie, the house is no longer the impressive architectural presence that it was when Josie first encountered it. Now, "a warped and pitiless neglect . . . invaded every corner, so that there are flaking walls, missing stair rods, stacks of damp and mildewed newspapers, and over a light switch, like some rustic fetish, a tranche of toadstools ripening in the sun" (76–77). It is, Josie acknowledges, a "decrepit house" (64). The shift in ownership of the House from Protestant to Catholic reflects the larger historical transition of Ireland from colony to independent nation. O'Brien's treatment of that shift in power, based on the decline of the House, is ironic and skeptical.

Inasmuch as the House is a metonymic marker for the history of twentieth-century Ireland, the fact that it decays after independence suggests that independence could not be understood as unmitigated triumph. At the same time that the novel accepts the need to free Ireland from English colonial rule, it also recognizes that the transfer of power did not bring with it full liberation but rather a reconfiguration of oppression. Historically, instead of the old disenfranchisement based on nationality and religion, the Republic, particularly under de Valera (whose successive governments coincide with Josie's marriage), entrenched policies and practices that had as one of their most significant consequences the strengthening of patriarchal arrangements in Ireland.[20] These masculinized policies and practices of the State are enacted in the O'Meara Big House.

O'Brien does more than just ironize the metanarrative of Irish history by emphasizing the new nation's acts of exclusion. She interrogates the very notion of linear historical movement. By focusing on a Catholic landowner with a deeply chauvinist disposition, O'Brien presents "history" as a recycling of the past. We are prodded to remember that not all Big Houses in Ireland were English even during the period of English colonization. As Daniel Corkery points out, "Irish Ireland had become in the eighteenth century a peasant nation, harried and poverty-stricken, with the cottier's smoky cabin for stronghold. But this does not mean that there were no longer any Big Houses, as we may call them, nor well-to-do families in these Gaelic-speaking countrysides." Rather than merely supplanting the English landlord, Jamie O'Meara is renewing the linkage between contemporary Catholic Ireland and its older Gaelic roots, certainly one of the intentions of the nationalist movement. This affiliation rests, as Corkery points out, on a patriarchal view of the world. "These houses," Corkery tells us, "stood for a patriarchal view of life. . . . In the homeliest practices of hall and kitchen it was patriarchal, as well as in the larger aspect of authority and outlook."[21] It is these patriarchal arrangements that imprison Josie.

O'Brien teases out the consequences of male hegemony by scrutinizing the attitudes and behaviors of Jamie O'Meara in his interrelated roles as husband and landowner. At first, he tries to retain the genteel aura of the English colonizers. So he hunts, fishes, and breeds and races horses. He also seeks a wife of some sophistication. Josie has lived abroad (albeit as a servant in Brooklyn), she is a "glamour puss" (33), and she is mistaken for Gloria Swanson (45).[22] He also tries to imitate some of the Ascendancy elegance and ceremony. When he brings Josie home, they arrive in fashionable clothes, she with "a loose fox collar over her velvet outfit," he "jaunty in yellow waistcoat and pigskin gloves" (29). Then Jamie presents Brid, the servant girl, to Josie in a short, formal introduction. Although it is Jamie who puts on airs, Brid directs her irritation at Josie, whose clothes she judges to be inappropriate even though they are not significantly different in style from those worn by Jamie.

This brief scene anticipates the response of the neighbors to Jamie's marriage. Whatever his airs, he is accepted by the local community, a paterfamilias, protected and above criticism. Josie is ostracized. When, for example, she is caught stealing, the delight the shopkeeper feels in humiliating her is typical of the sentiments of the community: "They were pleased to see her so craven, she who had never asked anyone to the big house, who had sat aloof at chapel and called people uncouth, at last brought low" (155). No one in the community is willing to understand that life in the Big House is so nightmarish that it would not be possible, even if Josie had wanted to, to engage in normal social intercourse. So the other farming families fault her for not producing children and for standing apart. The logic of these patriarchal arrangements is that they depend on the complicity of the entire community.

The community is prepared to condone even assault. Jamie's drinking increases. His business dealings become less prudent. Despite the visible evidence of Jamie's physical abuse, the neighborhood turns a blind eye. After one particularly horrible beating, Jamie has a group over for drinks and dinner. When Josie does not appear, he sends one of the hangers-on up to get her:

"Good God . . . you're black and blue." The unctuous voice unable to conceal its pleasure in being lucky enough to be sent up, lucky enough to see the harm for himself and be able to memorise it for his friends in the town. It was the Snooper.

"What time is it?"

"Whatever time it is. . . . The boss says you are to come down and cook a fry. . . . He has company."

"He can fry his own grub."

"He won't, he's bucking.". . .

Down in the front room a fire going and a rough line of jaws, side by side, like men on a chapel bench, except that they are drunk, too drunk and too skittish to even look at her in her bedraggled state, and too settled to go home. She knew them, but never once, not in the pouring of the tea or serving them *as she was obliged,* with fried bread and sausages, did she look in their faces. There was the Snooper, an ex-postman, a knacker called J. J. who dealt in old horseflesh. . . . Egan, the auctioneer, was the only one to give some nod of gratitude when she put the plate before him. . . .

"Feed. Shovel. Ride. Woman and horse," James said, remarking on the likenesses in both but stressing that a horse had more honor.

"Feed. Shovel. Ride," he said, laughing, and *they laughed with him to keep him amused.*

"That's a good mare you have out in the front field," the knacker says.

"I have good mares in all my fields," he says, and seeing her about to depart, he drags her back and says with a galling friendliness, "Not tonight, Josephine . . . Not tonight." (148, our emphasis)

The party continues, the men are lost in "the haze and revelry of the drinking" (150), and Jamie's physical and verbal brutalities, although plainly seen, are ignored. This schmoozy male camaraderie countenances Jamie's transgressions and accelerates his dissipation. These men, after all, are the recipients of his hospitality and his booze. Men dominate the countryside; Jamie dominates the Gaelic Big House. Josie can do no right; Jamie can do no wrong. The Big House is Josie's prison long before McGreevy takes her hostage. Jamie's bankruptcy is more than a commentary on his financial situation. It is a judgment on the quality of the patriarchal arrangements in which he is participant and creator.

O'Brien's use of the Big House setting provides a comprehensive and critical commentary on the history of Ireland from colonial times to post-Independence. Her take on that history is revisionist in that it refuses to endorse the discriminatory practices of the new Republic, especially in relation to women.

The Feminization of the Big House:
"O! Bhean an Tighe" . . ."O! Woman of the house!"

Ruth Frehner argues in *The Colonizers' Daughters* that women exist in an intimate relationship with houses. "Female connotation is . . . apparent in such conjunctions as womb-tomb-home," for example. She goes on to point out Big Houses "have repeatedly and explicitly been compared to women."[23] Although Frehner's work examines women in the Anglo-Irish Ascendancy novels of the Big House, her argument has relevance for *House of Splendid Isolation*. Most obviously, the dilapidated state of the O'Meara Big House is an objective correlative for the deteriorating health of Josie. But more important, Josie is herself an embodiment of Frehner's "womb-tomb-home" configuration, a woman who has been denied sexual satisfaction in marriage, fails to find fulfillment through a passionate affair, and aborts her only child. It is one of the ironies of the novel that Josie finds relief from the isolating and debilitating consequences of these traumatic events in her unfolding relationship with the gunman McGreevy. Through him, she discovers in herself feelings of affection and concern for others as well as a sense of commitment to the world outside her home/body that she has never previously experienced. So McGreevy may be the immediate (if inadvertent) cause of Josie's death, but he also returns her to life. The reserves of feeling that her marriage and her extramarital affair depleted are replenished as she gradually discovers in her relationship with McGreevy the companionship, the caring and the intimacy of a friend, surrogate child, and even lover.[24] McGreevy can, in fact, be understood as the catalyst that transforms Josie's triple captivity—within herself, her house, and Irish history—into a partial and fleeting liberation.

When the novel opens, the age and decrepitude of the O'Meara Big House is a mirror of Josie's own. Like the House, Josie "was wasting" (26). Recovering from pneumonia, Josie has returned to the Big House after a stay in a nursing home. To accommodate Josie's physical needs, Nurse Morissey and Josie domesticate one of the large "gaunt, draughty" rooms, making it into an all-purpose living, sleeping, and eating area with "a makeshift kitchen" (23, 24). From her bed Josie is within easy reach of "cups and saucers, biscuits, a tea caddy, condensed milk, a kettle, and a little stove" (24). These adaptations feminize the setting and lend credibility to Frehner's argument about the feminizing of the Big House, even, in this case, a Gaelic Big House.

But it is not only in its external features that the house is gendered. O'Brien uses the house as a metaphor for Josie's body and spirit. In a very real sense, "the house of splendid isolation" is Josie herself. Imprisoned in a failing body, her husband long dead, her only child aborted, her romantic possibilities frustrated and long behind her, her neighbors indifferent at best, Josie lives alone and measures her days by the brief visits of the nurse. Josie is as emotionally depleted as she is physically sick, afflicted not only with pneumonia but with guilt and loneliness. Without friends or relatives, she turns inward, initiating a process of self-interrogation that appears likely to debilitate her still further: "How would she have lived her life all over again? People often ask themselves that. Would she have married James, or having married him, would she have made the best of it and borne him a child, a daughter who would be calling on her now, fussing, tending, fetching a shawl or a bedjacket, saying, 'Mama . . . Mama?'" (26). Bleakly underlining the absence of any sustaining relationships, this passage demonstrates that Josie's "house" is the kind of womb/tomb to which Frehner refers.[25]

The central failure of Josie's life is her marriage, characterized by its sexual brutality and emotional neglect. Whatever her initial feelings for Jamie, they dissipate as soon as she arrives at the Big House, the romantic allure compromised by her knowledge that the marriage was encouraged by her aunt and uncle as part of a land deal. There is, moreover, a powerful irony in viewing that marriage within the palimpsest of the struggle for Irish independence. Having rejected imperialism in the public domain, Jamie, in many ways a typical Irish man of nationalist sympathies, reenacts the imperial impulse in sexual terms, appropriating for himself the role of colonizer in his bedroom. Sex is for him an exercise of power: "He mounts her without a word because she has got into the goddamn habit of saying no and stop and no. He has taken to holding her lips shut with one hand, clamping the way he might clamp an animal, and he has grown to like it; he likes the power he has over her" (47). In the sexual politics of the O'Meara marriage, Jamie takes possession of Josie's body; as he puts it, he "commandeers her inside and outside" (48).

Just as a colonized people long for freedom, so Josie seeks liberation. Because she lives in a country that did not permit divorce, her long revolt against the confinement of her marriage is complicated, unsuccessful, and ultimately self-defeating. She seeks release through an extramarital affair and an abortion, but these acts of rebellion imprison her in guilt and anger.

In the manner of many other of O'Brien's women who seek sexual gratification and emotional satisfaction outside marriage, Josie's affair is intense and disappointing. One summer, she falls madly in love with the new priest, Father John. Their relationship is passionate but chaste, although Jamie is led by circumstantial evidence to conclude that he has been cuckolded. Furious at Josie's presumed betrayal, he is nevertheless also delighted with the opportunity it provides to pay her back for every real and imagined frustration he has experienced in their marriage. "He beat her for every drink she had ever grudged him; for his poor brother, whom she had dispatched to an exile's death; for the offspring which she had not given him; the mares and fillies she had reviled; but most of all for the dried-up menagerie of her womanhood, the farce that was their bedchamber life" (146). Jamie's beating bruises her body. Father John's subsequent behavior corrodes her spirit. He makes no effort to see her after the beating, although he undoubtedly knows what she has suffered. Months later, Josie catches sight of Father John, but he pointedly snubs her. For Josie, it is a defining moment in which her warmth and yearning give way to a sense of overwhelming deadness: "Just as an instant before all had been soft and moist, there came then the spectre of the charnel house, himself, herself, like lumps of charred dough, but side by side so that she could impart her hatred of him" (159). Although Josie's use of "himself" refers in the first instance to Father John, there is a sense in which the reflexive pronoun refers to all the men in her life, most especially to her husband. Josie's efforts to escape from the lovelessness of her marriage into the excitement and romance of an extramarital attachment leaves her, if anything, more devastated than she was before.

Similarly, Josie's abortion leads not to her longed for liberation but to despair. In a statement Josie has written to be read after her death, she explains the immediate circumstances surrounding her decision to have the abortion (illegal then as now in the Republic) as well as the terror and pain that accompanied it. She states, first, that "she was not ready for a child." Then she notes that the crib her husband provides belonged "to his people. It felt alien" (211). She displaces onto the crib what she feels about the child. Given the nature of her marriage, she regards a child not as a source of joy and love but as tangible evidence of Jamie's conquest and humiliation of her. From Josie's point of view, the imperial logic of her marriage makes the duties of motherhood unbearable. Josie understands the abortion as a means of achieving autonomy and control of her own body. It is also her revenge for Jamie's mistreatment of her, her means of denying him the proof of his virility and the heir to his estate. But, as she soon appreciates, although undertaken to liberate her from her husband, the abortion enslaves her to guilt. Perhaps even more distressing than the guilt, the abortion cuts her off from the future, from the comforts of family and from the companionship of children in her old age.

Whatever the guilt, O'Brien insists that there be some acknowledgment that the abortion takes place within a historical context in which blood sacrifice is often the fate of the young, and, in such a context, abortion is not a uniquely criminal event. In the opening and concluding sections of two pages each, O'Brien gives voice not only to Josie's aborted child but to all the other dead Irishmen and -women, victims of the unceasing hostilities of the past eight hundred years. Every one of the dead in Ireland's long struggle for independence, O'Brien points out, was someone's child. In these two framing sections, O'Brien explicitly conflates the political and the personal, so that Josie's abortion may be understood as enacting on her body the political violence of the nation.

The voice of the Child in these two sections is disembodied and elegiac, invoking the broad panorama of Irish history, with its common theme of violence. History is inescapable, we are told and "everywhere. It seeps into the soil, the subsoil. Like rain, or hail, or snow, or blood" (3). That the Child, who should embody the future, is the spokesperson for the past carries its own terrible irony and provides a telling corrective to a too-easy belief in any narrative that sees Ireland inevitably progressing from the problems of the past into the promise of the future.

Despite the emphasis on the past, the Child also addresses the future, speaking generally of "things past and things yet to be" (3), but it is unclear from what is said whether history will serve as a cautionary lesson or a goad to further violence. The Child expresses the desire "for all the battles to have been fought and done with" (3). As the novel is brought to a close with Josie's death and McGreevy's capture, it is more than possible that the doomed dynamic of Irish history will loop back on itself, as the novel does by returning in the final section to the dead Child.

Indeed, the last words of the novel, cryptic and dense, belong to the Child, and these words suggest, however contradictorily, that hope may be found even in such despair. There comes a time when the killing is so close, so intimate (as in abortion) that it provokes an urgent desire for peace: "Everything is riddled. The doer and the done-to. 'As the killer is close to him whom he kills.' From the near and the far past a wailing and a gnashing. Graves and mounds and more graves and a statue and a dyed carnation to mark where the sudden carnage has been. It seeps, the land does, and small wonder. But the land cannot be taken. History has proved that. The land will never be taken. It is there" (232). To this point, the passage encapsulates the long torment of Irish history, indicating the degree to which the oppressor and the oppressed are bound together in exhausting and destructive conflict. Lest this observation be taken as heaping blame equally on both parties to the conflict, the Child insists that all efforts at conquest and colonization are inherently futile, that the centuries of blood sacrifice demonstrate that Ireland will never be "possessed." The Child then comments about killing in a manner that breaks down the distinction between the political and the personal: "'As the killer is close to him whom he kills.' That's in a book. But to be close in body or bayonet is not enough. To go in, within, is the bloodiest journey of all. Inside, you get to know—that the same blood and the same tears drop from the enemy as from the self, though not always in the same proportion. To go right into the heart of the hate and the wrong and to sup from it and be supped. It does not say that in the books. That is the future knowledge. That knowledge that is to be" (232). From the Child's perspective as well as from the novel's, when the womb has literally become a tomb, progressive exfoliations of history are impossible. Yet, at the same time, the Child suggests that the intimacy and force of Josie's pain, the pain of any mother who experiences the death of a child, brings with it the possibility of understanding and release some time in the future. Nevertheless, the Child's prophecy contains the implication that, at least in the short term, the circle of violence will continue, that history will go on repeating itself.

Josie's encounter with McGreevy is in some ways a testing of the Child's prophecy. The insertion of the gunman figure into Josie's House is disruptive, dissolving into the public and political her perception that she leads an exclusively private life, haunted by loneliness and regret, cut off from the larger social world. The developing relationship with McGreevy forces Josie to recognize that she must connect to the larger world and redefine her life in terms of its needs as well as her own. Her decision to "give the house over to young people, a youth hostel for those who travel, a place to be lived in" (194) is a measure of her new openness. She wishes to offer to the young people from all over the world the hospitality of her Big House. At the metaphoric level, Josie's plan for the Big House, if realized, would ally her to a future in which national boundaries and gender distinctions have lost their force.

Having achieved this level of awareness, Josie feels obliged to take some action to prevent McGreevy from carrying out his attack. In trying to disrupt McGreevy's plans, Josie seeks to make amends for the death of her child and the death of her husband as well as to forestall the deaths planned by McGreevy. Josie's determination energizes her, pushes her out of the House and establishes new human connections, but her actions also alert authorities and lead to her own demise as well as McGreevy's apprehension. Her accidental death demonstrates the insufficiency of goodwill to overcome the cycle of violence and undermines any easy faith in progressive change.

Confronting Irish Nationalism: "I'm trying to save my fucking country"

McGreevy brings violence back into Josie's space. He is a gunman on the run and that violent character type has a long narrative history. O'Brien is in no small way responding to and revising that character lineage. Primarily escaping or hiding from the forces of law and order, the gunman on the run is most often a figure of romance; he is sheltered by people (invariably women) who believe in his cause and who fall for his Byronic allure. Having said that, the gunman on the run in fiction and film is also overwhelmingly described using the language and imagery of confinement or entrapment. Two examples of the narrative enclosure of the gunman on the run, which have narrative echoes in O'Brien's *House of Splendid Isolation,* are Johnny in Carol Reed's 1947 *Odd Man Out* and Fergus in Neil Jordan's 1992 *The Crying Game.*[26] These two films will be discussed briefly by way of engaging O'Brien's characterization of McGreevy.

A man who has spent little of his adult life outside of a jail cell, Johnny in *Odd Man Out* is wounded in an IRA robbery attempt, abandoned in his comrades' escape, and made to make his way to safety in Belfast during a surreal, hallucinatory nighttime. He is pursued by the police, the IRA, and the woman who adores him (she has a devotion to him similar to Creena's admiration of/love for McGreevy). Although he may be out of prison, Johnny is now outside the protective circle of the IRA and an outlaw from law and order. His travels during the Belfast night are shot in black and white with film noir flair, and *Odd Man Out*'s plot is delineated by the many encounters between Johnny and the people of the city.[27]

In the dark and confining spaces of Belfast, Johnny has a particularly telling encounter with an artist who learns that Johnny is hiding in an enclosed booth in a pub. Lukey, a painter, sees Johnny as an object worthy of aesthetic consideration and artistic rendering. He is attracted to the violent beauty of the man as well as the danger of hiding him from the authorities (the attraction of Creena to McGreevy can be described in similar terms, although she is not an artist per se). Lukey is drawn to Johnny not only because of the danger and violence Johnny represents but also because he is running, trying to escape capture. Johnny is struggling not to be caught, and the artist is trying to "catch" him and to capture his essence on the canvas. That Lukey has a sidekick who walks around with a bird in a cage is the more obvious visual image of Johnny's physical and metaphoric confinement. The film ends with Johnny being taken away by the bird-man to Kitty, the love interest, and the caging continues. Kitty and Johnny are ambushed by the police and both are killed in the film's shoot-out finale.

Johnny is little but an object of other people's perceptions of him, and his character is really a cipher with which director Reed is able to profile a city in the midst of violent upheaval. The city is more the subject of the film than Johnny. In contrast, Fergus in *The Crying Game* is a character in search of subjectivity. His escape from Ireland after the botched IRA hostage-taking scheme, and his hiding out in London, facilitates a profound and violent personal metamorphosis for Fergus.

When Fergus leaves Ireland and goes to England because he "needs to lose [himself] for a while," he changes his name, gets a haircut, and seeks out the now-dead hostage's girlfriend in order to honor the dying man's last request.[28] While Fergus may be on the run in England, he finds and retains love despite the prison walls that will separate him and his lover at the end of the film. Unlike many other gunmen on the run, Fergus does not end up dead or alone. He falls in love with Dil, and their relationship, as complicated as it becomes, is the primary locus of Fergus's humanization process.

Fergus is being hunted by the IRA, in particular the cold-hearted, maniacal femme fatale, Jude. When she discovers Fergus in London, he refuses to help her (and the IRA), telling her he's "out" for good. Jude replies that "you're never out," warns him to "stay in one place" and to "keep the faith." Fergus resists all such limitations. He has already left Ireland, he loses his faith in the cause, he renounces his former identity, and he kills no one. When Fergus protests Jude's threat on Dil's life, Jude replies: "Jesus, you're a walking cliché." The irony of this statement is that Jude is the cliché, not Fergus. Jude is allowed little room to maneuver past stereotypes of the killer bitch or the vicious terrorist. She is what Fergus might have become had he not broken away from the rigidity the film portrays as indicative of the IRA and, by extension, any and all polarized positions.

Even though Jude (as threat, menace, evil) is killed in the film's penultimate scene, it is far too easy to conclude that the film's message is that if you love, then you live, and if you hate, then you die.[29] Jody is a loving character, and he is killed by his own British forces. The film also insists that the viewer acknowledge the presence and power of social and political barriers to love. While Fergus rejects many of the rigid boundaries that restrict his identity and he and his lover survive, their bond of love and understanding (and their willingness to negotiate and accept each other's difference) is still blocked and prohibited by external forces. Dil may have shot Jude, but Fergus takes the blame in an ironic moment that mocks both the mythic Irish rebel-tradition of self-sacrifice and the musical cliché of "Stand by Your Man." Because of his sacrifice, Fergus ends up in prison behind the glass barrier reserved for "dangerous criminals." Ironies are further layered in the final shot of the film as Fergus is imprisoned for being exactly that which he tried to escape: an IRA gunman.

The glass wall separating Fergus and Dil at the end is a visual echo of the opening sequence (Jordan's film is framed with a similar narrative technique as O'Brien's Child chapters). The film begins with a long, wide-angle pan of a fairground by the water. Cutting across the screen, however, is an iron bridge. A bridge certainly connotes crossing over or passage, but in this opening sequence it functions so as to block our sight; it prevents us from seeing the full picture (just as O'Brien's fragmented narrative style prevents any complete history from being told). The iron bridge establishes an extended visual metaphor of confinement and obstructed vision. The camera looks through windows and doorways; shots are framed and obscured by furniture, scaffolding, and bars. Dil's apartment is a maze of diaphanous curtains and mirrors. Jordan's consistent use of mirrors emphasizes the importance of appearance, but the mirrors also create a sense of the constantly receding self—there are so many different images of the characters that their unique, individual identities become confused, doubled, multiplied. If you get the chance to see around or beyond the structural barriers, you can never be sure of what, or who, it is you are looking at. Even though the barriers in the visual text become increasingly transparent—to the point where the walls are glass at the end—they remain barriers.

Spatially, the two lovers are separated, despite whatever emotional and psychological union has occurred. In this way, the film may detest rigid definitions of identity, but it also mocks individual agency.

Separated from the organization they joined or that gave their lives purpose and meaning, the gunmen on the run wander or run for their lives. McGreevy's character can be read as a hybridization of the objectified Johnny and the subject-coming-into-being of Fergus. Like Johnny, McGreevy operates in the early part of the novel as an ever-changing text or object that is read differently depending on the reader. In his encounters with Josie, McGreevy finds companionship and a kind of love similar to what Fergus finds with Dil. But McGreevy is as doomed as Johnny and Fergus to the fate that joining the IRA seems to dictate.

There is an interesting irony in O'Brien's representation of the gunman on the run. In both *Odd Man Out* and *House of Splendid Isolation,* the gunmen are primarily hiding from the forces of law and order (whereas Fergus is running from the IRA).[30] The narratives in which they exist, however, are overwhelmingly concerned with encounters the gunman has with people; the connections, both failed and successful, he makes with those he meets along the way. *House* presents a series of seeming opposites thrown into conflict in the novel: an old woman and a young man, truths and fictions, memory and history. Josie and McGreevey may be in conflict, but they also find in each other something of their own lives and their own pasts. Narratives about gunmen on the run are about being found.

There are other narrative echoes from *Odd Man Out* in the opening pages of *House of Splendid Isolation* beyond the images of marginalization that both titles conjure. O'Brien introduces her IRA man, and the various people he encounters on his journey from the North to the South of Ireland in his escape from the authorities, just as Reed's film depicts different community reactions to the wounded Johnny. McGreevy is aided by a farmer, despite his wife's pitiless anger at the fugitive's invasion of her home. The story of his escape is watched on the television by a guard and his family: the young son, Caimin, "remembering a hero from his schoolbook," compares the gunman to Cúchulainn (12–13). The guard, who will hunt the gunman through the novel, offers McGreevy credit for eluding the law and refers to him as a "pimpernel." McGreevy meets an IRA contact who responds to McGreevy's claim that "I'm going to fuck away off someday and chuck this" with the threat — so often articulated — that "we'd find you" (20). And a young girl takes the gunman toward Limerick in her van out of fear and intimidation.

Like Reed's film, O'Brien offers a number of different perspectives of McGreevy; but unlike *Odd Man Out,* which never allows the character of Johnny any depth, O'Brien quickly focuses her novel on the developing relationship between Josie, the isolated, lonely, neurotic, and near-suicidal woman, and McGreevy, a gunman on the run.

All of the encounters in the first part of the novel are integrated into the personal stories of Josie and McGreevy in what has become a signature style of O'Brien's. From collections of short stories to her novels, Edna O'Brien frequently offers narratives that reveal unexpected connections between people's lives and the past and the present. The argument between the farmer and his wife, for example, is echoed in a memory Josie has of her husband demanding they assist one of their farmhands in hiding guns for the IRA. The wives are defensive and do not want trouble; the husbands are determined to offer assistance. Josie's husband's determination, and his "resurrecting every bit of Fenian feeling he ever had" results in his being shot (57). Once again in the present, Josie is in a situation in which she has choice but to tolerate a fugitive. Whereas in *Odd Man Out* Johnny is the one trapped, in *House* it is the people inevitably implicated in McGreevy's activities who are imprisoned and helpless.

McGreevy's decision to hide out in Josie's deteriorating house changes both of their lives. Josie, previously so lonely that she has contemplated suicide, finds herself developing strategies for dealing with her invader and tapping into energy reserves she thought long gone: "She who had been too weak to hobble down the stairs a few days before was now dragging the brown chest of drawers across the floor . . . she believed she had at least shown some spunk" (71). It is not only energy and spunkiness that Josie feels in herself with the arrival of McGreevy but also "swarms of memory." The memories of her troubled past are "back now with a vengeance, the chains of history, the restless dead and the restless living, with scores to settle" (78). McGreevy, one of the restless living who reminds Josie of the restless dead, is a catalyst for change and awareness. His presence, almost predictable in this narrative defined by inevitable returns, is the embodiment of memory, of Josie's past as well as the incarnation of the living with "scores to settle." Such are the chains of history that dictate all the lives in the novel; the repetition of patterns with no escape is one of *House of Splendid Isolation*'s primary concerns.

McGreevy, who is described and defined in a vast array of metaphors (Josie thinks of him as an impudent pup; the guards describe his as brutal, savage, and psychotic; Creena and her mother think of him as a romantic patriot), is humanized, like Fergus, through the interactions with another human being.[31] Josie offers McGreevy various gifts (her uncle's letter from 1921, when he too was a gunman on the run, and her husband's collection of fishing tackle) and these gifts open up their conversations: "everything happens then" (99). They often speak of ghosts, the ones supposedly haunting the house and the ones haunting their lives, and the sharing of their grief and their guilt creates a bond between them.

This is not to suggest that their relationship is a kind of sweet, melancholic meeting. Josie taunts McGreevy constantly in an attempt to gain control over him. She calls him the "brave soldier" with sarcasm and refers to his guns as "your babies," while challenging his courage to kill her (87, 120). The "splendidness" of isolation is the narrative space and the fleeting narrative moments in which these two people, so different and opposed in age, class, and gender, can talk. At first hesitatingly, Josie and McGreevy share thoughts about death, politics, life, mistakes, regrets, and they connect with each other. The cruel irony is, of course, that these moments and their splendid space are doomed to be invaded again, this time by the forces of law and order in pursuit of McGreevy. Even more cruel is that Josie dies in the chaotic shooting of the attempted capture just as her husband died years ago trying to protect Paud, his brother. Josie wants to save McGreevy because she has come to know the complexity of his life. He is no legend, stereotype, or construction of propaganda: "his life has many chapters to it and many evolutions" and because of this complexity he "must be taken alive" (221). The violence of his life destroys the protective "isolation" that Josie built around her, but McGreevy's invasion allows her to remember the wonder of life's changes. Unfortunately, her awareness of the complexities of life leads to her own death. It seems a bittersweet commentary on the nature of human connections and relationships, but the novel is also a brutal exposition of those characters who never attempt to read beyond the stereotypes, who are never granted the splendid space and time to discover the complexities of others or themselves.

No Endings, No Closure, No Future: "Talk of the word"

House of Splendid Isolation is a novel about incomplete stories, fleeting moments of connection, and the often violent consequences of misreadings. O'Brien fills her pages with references to unfinished letters, such as the ones Josie attempts to write to her unrequited lover, the priest; with fragmented stories, such as the incomplete fairy tale Rory tells his daughter or the partial story about St. Caimin that Josie reads; and with notes that directly result in violence, such as Josie's note to the police about Paud's involvement in the IRA and the note in her corset that leads to the brutal beating by her husband. The unfinished tales, combined with O'Brien's own style of fragmented subchapters, suggest that part of the impulse behind *House* is to challenge narrative omniscience, to dispute all claims to know everything: no story is complete and most especially not the story of Ireland. By looking at examples of O'Brien's fragmented narrative we argue that the metanarrative of *House* is one in which all texts are shown to be inadequate and that the possibility of a better future (for Ireland, for storytelling) requires a radical change in the way we read.

There are two epigraphs to the novel, and both make declarations about the inevitable end to violence in Ireland and the vanquishing of the Irish enemy. Both are wrong. The first is a quotation from a letter sent by Sir John Davies to the Earl of Salisbury in 1606 claiming that the "genius" of the British crown would see to it that "all those generations of vipers [Irish rebels]" will be expelled from Ireland. The second epigraph is the famous quotation from Lloyd George in dispatching the Black and Tans to Ireland in 1920, stating optimistically, "we have murder by the throat." In the first pages of the novel, in the Child section, to which we have already referred, there is the italicized quotation from *The Valley of the Pigs* about the "last battle" and how a "woman with a shawl" will be able to knock down the men in battle. The quotation ends thus: "It says that in the books." This heavy handed reliance on quotation early in the novel invites the questions: are the books and the sources in the epigraph to be trusted? Are these prophesies to be fulfilled or are they naive and wrongheaded assertions about an end to conflict and violence in Ireland? Given that the end of O'Brien's incomplete and fragmented stories is the violent death of Josie and the capture of McGreevy, it is the second option that seems most credible.

Perhaps the most powerful indictment of the impotence of texts and storytelling is the inability of language to adequately describe violence. In the chapter called "The Present," the domestic world of Rory, the guard who will hunt McGreevy, is depicted in terms of its reactions to news stories of IRA/Gardaí violence. What is most disturbing to the family is the possibility of the violence invading their home, but O'Brien's treatment of this scene presents the ultimate ambiguity in any

telling of violent events. This brutality has no name and no face. Its effects are tangible, yet its fighters are elusive and ethereal, floating in
and out of skirmishes. The indefiniteness of the war Rory fights against
the IRA is clear in the media description of recent violence: "these faceless men with their guns and their hoods. One had been shot dead on a
road not far away. It was in the papers, a photograph of the very spot,
details of the rounds of ammunition, the nickname of the victim, his
comrade who got away. . . . It was well known, well reported, discussed
again and again: the number of rounds fired, the angle at which the
Guard shot, the type of wound, the length of time it took your man to
die" (9). This description of a shooting is telling in a number of ways.
First, Rory's wife, Sheila, is by no means comforted by the details of the
story in the papers or the accompanying photos. The violence remains
haunting and terrifying in its essential unknowability. Reading about
the number of rounds of ammunition used does nothing to allay her
fears for herself and her family. Second, the event was "well reported,
discussed again and again," and encourages the transformation of re-
portage into tall tale replete with distortions, enlargements, and embel-
lishments. Third, the absence of an identity for the felled gunman (he
has a nickname but remains faceless) allows the gunman to retain his
shadowy and menacing "otherness" as well as his separation from normal social intercourse. The news report (and what happens to "news"
as it enters the consciousness of the community) creates a deeply threat-
ening atmosphere of anticipated violence, and it also encourages the
sense of the inevitability of violence.

The inability of language to deal adequately with the threat of violence is elaborated just a few pages later. A story about a "terrorist"
who has escaped (McGreevy) comes on the news. Rory responds in
anger ("Jay-sus . . . Christ Almighty!") to the announcer who is telling
in a "dry and polished voice" how the gunman had jumped from a
moving vehicle and disappeared (11–12). Rory's response to the story is
complex (and at odds with the announcer's detachment); his reaction is
indicative of media power and the complexity of Rory's relationship to
the men he hunts:[32]

Kneeling now, close to the set, he asked the lady announcer who was reporting
war in another part of the world to tell him how the British Army, the Royal Ulster Constabulary, the Garda, and an entire operation could let a guy who had
got away before, who was known to be a pimpernel, go into a field and vanish.
How, unless he was a fucking buccaneer. Even in his outrage he gave the fella
credit and said, "That's my boy McGreevy, that's my baby."

"Maybe he's a spaceman," his little daughter Aoife piped up.
"I hope he comes this-a-way," he said, waving his fist at the television.
"I hope he doesn't," Sheila said. (12)

Rory directs his words to the inanimate TV set, the screen on which the violence is played out for the vast number of people in the community. His daughter speculates on the otherworldly nature of the escapee as if he were a character on the Space Channel. His wife articulates fear. Neither the family nor the news report, however, is able to speak the violence into comprehensibility. The violence and the men involved remain mysterious and unknowable. Without such knowledge, the community is unlikely to be able to deal effectively with that violence.

Despite McGreevy's violence and disruptiveness, there are intratextual moments of connection in the novel that imply, albeit ironically, that some understanding is possible. But with the exception of the shared intimacies between Josie and McGreevy, these moments are tenuous connections at best and do not lead to changes in perception or action: they are textual correlations. Rory's son, for example, is named Caimin. Josie reads a story about St. Caimin later in the novel.[33] But there is no sense that this metaphysical association influences either narrative progression or character. In another similar example, the boy Caimin says to his father that McGreevy may be Cúchulainn. Pages later McGreevy says to a fellow IRA comrade, "I'm not fucking Cúchulainn" (19). The analogy is a link, but, of course, McGreevy's denial immediately disrupts the linkage. While there may be a metanarrative dialogue going on in the novel, the characters whose comments appear as though echoes or responses to each other never meet eye to eye. Gaps of time and space and culture continue to divide the characters, except for the brief moments of communion between Josie and McGreevy.

O'Brien associates connection between people, failed or otherwise, with writings and texts. Josie uses a fragment of her uncle's journal about the War of Independence and his flight from British authority as a way of reaching out to McGreevy. While initially impressed by the man's courage and devotion to the Republican cause, McGreevy rejects Josie's gesture of friendship. We as readers, however, see the connection between the two men all too readily. The death of the uncle in the 1920s seems to foreshadow the narrative end of McGreevy, but even this apparent certainty does not pan out as anticipated. McGreevy is captured, but it is Josie who is shot dead. There is an implied lesson for readers here about making facile assumptions and jumping to conclusions in their reading process.

The lesson about the dangers of misreading and of making assumptions is reiterated in the legend that grows up around McGreevy. Stories and rumors about him abound in the early pages of the novel. He is called many things, among them beast, pimpernel, buccaneer, savage, and desperado. The hype that surrounds McGreevy magnifies his stature; yet, to the surprise of readers and the police, McGreevy turns out to be a small man in physical size. His legendary status is what enhances his personal stature, and such legends are also augmented by the charged atmosphere that surrounds him and encounters with him.

Take the case of Teresa, the young woman whose life is altered to her detriment when McGreevy hijacks her lunch van and she ends up telling her story to the police. She is as terrified of the guard as she is of McGreevy or the IRA. Giving information is not straightforward. The police suspect Teresa of being a willing accomplice to McGreevy's escape; she is terrified to provide information to the authorities because the police do not appear to believe her and because word might get back to the IRA that she has informed. Teresa begins to cry under interrogation: "big cumbersome tears dropping onto everything, onto the miserable notes he has made, and he thinks, Torched. . . . She hasn't a clue what the word is, but she knows what the fear is and she re-encounters it every time she steps out of her house" (23). Teresa is intimidated by her fear both of the IRA and of the police; she is doubly terrorized. It is clear from this early incident that McGreevy's stature is a function not of his physical size but of his fearlessness and his fierce commitment to armed struggle.

Just as the possession of information is dangerous to Teresa, so Martin's possession of knowledge becomes a threat to Josie and McGreevy's relationship, their splendid isolation. Martin, who enacts another kind of invasion of Josie's home, is an informant and he is destructive. In a moment of rage when Josie figures their game is up, she lashes out at McGreevy: "I have been telling myself that you are a nice young man . . . and that you wouldn't kill and that you haven't killed. I've been telling myself this fairy tale." McGreevy points out the cold truth behind her delusion: "I told you I've killed" (119). McGreevy, for all his political intransigence and cold ideological commitment, knows the distance between what people want to believe and other versions of the truth. In his letter to Josie he writes, "they think we're cowboys or animals or worse" (121). He refutes such ideas based on his experience of camaraderie among his fellow hunger-strikers and prisoners in Northern Ireland: their bravery, their laughter. From such encounters, McGreevy claims to derive an unswerving devotion to the cause. It "only takes

being with people like that and one's faith is invincible" (122). Despite
such assertions, McGreevy's beliefs are shaken more than once in his
life and in the novel. But even in the face of his own occasional doubts
and hesitations, McGreevy is determined to persevere with the armed
struggle.

Whether the televised news briefs or the testimony of individuals,
verbal language and images are inadequate to express the fear people
feel about violence. In a moment of parallel narration like the news
bulletin and Teresa's testimony, the story of Paud and the guns is told
in fragments: "a cache of arms, a simpleton, Guards, darkness, bungle,
and no one knowing exactly what happened, opinions varying at the
inquest" (57). Similar to the earlier details of a another shooting, this is
a list of great specificity with no indication as to how such information
is to be comprehended. No one knows anything exactly, and opinions
vary. This type of incomplete story not only is repeated in the novel but
is the form of *House of Splendid Isolation* itself.

Incomplete stories are then directly connected with the historical
narrative of Ireland and any historical narrative: "the dark threads of
history looping back and forth and catching her and people like her in
their grip, like snares" (58). The story that Paud tells McGreevy years
later about the "Queen of the Munster Fairies" is made ridiculous when
McGreevy encounters Josie in her home, which he has invaded. The romantic longings and imaginings of Paud (and by extension characters
such as Creena) are made foolish by two factors: reality and the lapse of
time. The house of the title hangs in a temporal suspension wherein
past and present can merge if even for a moment, but McGreevy's invasion eliminates the possibility of any continued suspension or isolation.
McGreevy comments on Paud's lack of knowledge: "How little he
knew. How little anyone knew when they joined up. How little that
woman up in the bed knew" (68).[34] This same sentiment is repeated by
Josie in reference to McGreevy. Josie writes in her diary, "The saddest
bit is that we're the same stock, the same faith, we speak the same
tongue and *cannot know*. Language to each of us is a Braille that the
other *cannot know*. Words like justice or love or bread turned inside out
or outside in" (93, emphasis ours). Later she writes, "I thought I knew
this part of the country. I thought I knew the people up in the village
and every house around, but I don't. All is confusion" (105).

Josie's confusion and the community's fear and speculation lead to
the question of control. Who are the authorities? During the first few
days of Josie and McGreevy's forced cohabitation, she thinks that he

has "chilling authority" (80). Both his coldness and his authority fall away as they get to know one another. He shows kindness by asking after her health and taking her to safety after she loses her way in the fog. She undermines his commitment and his assurance about his role in the IRA and the missions he undertakes. There are, in actuality, no authorities in the novel. The police are at most times ridiculous. When all the guards are collecting for the big manhunt, there are numerous references to the Wild West and Hollywood icons: "Bandit country" is used more than once and one officer is referred to as "the Quiet Man" (182–83).[35] To call one of the protectors of civil order "the Quiet Man" is to cut him down to size. Such references undermine the seriousness of the guards' mission to capture McGreevy; or, perhaps more accurately, they undermine some of the figures of authority engaged in the manhunt.

In the logic of the novel, wherein there is no clear authority and no discernable control, it is not surprising that Josie would consult an alternative text for meaning. In the section "A Love Affair," when Josie is fatefully pursuing the priest, she picks up "the yellowed book" and "his hands went up in defense to signify no" (140). The book is a fortune-telling guide using Celtic runes: "It was a very old book which she had found in a trunk and which she often consulted. Different symbols, painted in black, signified a different set of destinies. By asking a certain question and then, blindfolded, putting one's finger on one of the symbols, one knew which answer to consult. He did not want to know his future, he was quite happy with the present" (140). Runes are a mysterious language within which fragments, such as the different symbols, combine with readerly intent to create meaning. In the case of Josie's book, the meaning is the future or one's destiny. This scene is a delicate moment between the two possible lovers in which they can, if they choose, create a private yet shared language of love. In refusing to participate, Father John gives warning of their ultimate failure to sustain communication.

Notes, like letters and books, point to the difficulties and imperfections of communication. Josie slips a note to the police informing on Paud's activities, and the violence she hoped to prevent ensues. Josie keeps a note in her corset that is a "love-like-hate-adore-marry game" not unlike the runes book (146). The accidental recovery of that one results in violence. Notes are dangerous; information leads to violence. The abuse Josie endures from James and the humiliation in the eyes of the community ends with her beginning "letters that were left unfinished" (153). The unwritten note, the unresolved conflict, is reflected in absent texts. The ultimate condemnation of texts and readings is misreading. The grossest violation of truth occurs when the guards who watch Josie's house believe they are seeing her and McGreevy having a "bit of last-minute fun" (206). McGreevy is now a perverse "Valentino" (207). The guards are very wrong, dangerously wrong. Their eyes betray them as they read the images incorrectly.

This is not to say that *House of Splendid Isolation* presents texts and language as signifying nothing; rather, it is a novel that takes up the modernist belief that texts and language are insufficient to depict the complexity of the human condition. *House* is also postmodern in its textual self-annihilation: it is a story about the incapability of stories to communicate full and unambiguous meaning. Thus the four plotlines discussed in this paper all portray the tenuousness and fragility of communication. The decrepit Big House, the unrealized romance, the shallow nationalist myths, and the absence of an ending that is not a repetition—all these elements articulate the problem but do not resolve it. As the voice at the end of the novel states, the problem is in part that no one goes deep enough. No one asks for or thinks about context. Communication is all surface: TV screens and movie theaters. The only suggestion as to how to alter the cycles of violence and the chains of history is "to go right into the heart of the hate and the wrong and to sup from it and to be supped. It does not say that in the books. That is the future knowledge. The knowledge that is to be" (232). Josie and McGreevy do go to the heart of the hate and the wrong, but only momentarily. Their moments of splendid isolation do still end in violence, death, misunderstanding, and imprisonment. But the moment was worthy of narration—the moment is a key to some "future knowledge" that is not in the books.

Edna O'Brien's *House of Splendid Isolation* is arguably her most politicized novel. Tackling issues such as abortion, domestic abuse, tourism, the violence in Northern Ireland, and the history of the Irish novel, *House* ruptures any notion of linear progress or any hope for immediate reconciliation. And while the novel depicts the looping strands of history catching its characters in a snare, the voice of the Child (albeit an aborted child) does offer something. Taking up the Joycean image of Ireland as a sow who eats her young, O'Brien's narrative voice tells its readers to sup from the hate and the wrong, to know it well, to consume it and so perhaps by exposure and immersion, to transform it. But, coming from such a fragmentary text as this one, this advice and knowledge will not be easily learned.

Notes

1. Grace Eckley, *Edna O'Brien* (Lewisburg, Pa.: Bucknell University Press, 1974), 10.

2. For an examination of O'Brien's variations on the theme of unfulfilled longing, see Bernice Schrank and Danine Farquharson, "Object of Love, Subject to Despair: Edna O'Brien's *The Love Object* and the Emotional Logic of Late Romanticism," *Canadian Journal of Irish Studies* 22.2 (December 1996): 21–36. For another perspective, see also Sandra Manoogian Pearce, "Redemption through Reconciliation," *Canadian Journal of Irish Studies* 22.2 (December 1996): 63–72.

3. Christina Hunt Mahony, *Contemporary Irish Literature Transforming Tradition* (New York: St. Martin's Press, 1998), 214.

4. Edna O'Brien, *House of Splendid Isolation* (New York: Plume, 1995). All references to the novel are taken from this edition.

5. He is also drawn to the house by the story he has heard from Paud, who, as a young man many years before, had fallen in love with Josie and been involved in an IRA action that involved burying guns on the O'Meara property. Unbeknownst to Paud, it was Josie who reported the activity to the local police, thus precipitating a raid in which her husband was fatally wounded. Paud fled to the North and later encountered McGreevy, to whom he raves about Josie as the "Queen of the Munster Fairies . . . her husband and herself martyrs for Ireland" (67). Paud has gotten it all wrong, as McGreevy realizes the moment he sees the ancient Josie so very different from the idealized woman of Paud's memory. Memory (what O'Brien characterizes as "the yeast of memory" [129]) is the springboard of the action, but it is a flawed memory of an event only partially understood by one of its participants. O'Brien's point here (and elsewhere in the novel) is surely the durability of memory in all its contexts—personal, political, and historical—coupled with its unreliability.

6. The whole machinery of the manhunt with its stakeouts, telephone taps, and night surveillance speaks to a Hollywood and television culture, which is given expression in casual remarks. Take, for example, the Disneyesque American colloquial form Detective Horan gives to his irritation and nervousness because the reports about McGreevy are so vague: "'Last seen . . . last seen . . . Mickey Mouse stuff'" he complains (100). What is true for the police is true also for the secret army. Dyed-in-the-wool Republican Creena (who has Gaelicized her name, which was originally Margaret), who would "do anything for McGreevy" (127), has a picture on her wall of James Dean, on whom she has a crush. To her he is not just James Dean, but the more familiar "Jimmy Dean" (126). In Creena's mind there is an emotional equation between McGreevy and Dean. Another of these throwaway lines reinforcing the sense that Irish culture is being shaped by international influences occurs in the early stages of the manhunt when a wig, which McGreevy has used as part of his repertoire of disguises, is found in a yard. The none-too-bright Guard Flynn tries to discover how the wig came to be there and suggests that perhaps it was "theatre folk" who lost it. This is the response Guard Flynn receives to his suggestion: "'Unfortunately, we have no theatre folk; the television has destroyed our culture,'

Miss Cusack says peevishly" (73). Miss Cusack's peevishness nevertheless points to the power and pervasiveness of their postnational world.

7. A good example of the way O'Brien uses such traces is in the attention she gives to initials carved into a tree. Walking through her fields, Josie "remembered how on her wedding day he [her husband] had marched her out there and showed her the two names, his being the first and most decisive, the J O M carved into the pinkish trunk" (86). The names are of her husband and Mick. As Josie remembers the event, she believes her husband's demonstration is intended to show that he and his brother possess the land, and the force of the demonstration (she remembers being brought to the tree as a march, with its military connotations) indicates to her that he meant to possess her too. Later, when Martin the Snoop brings Josie the news that one of the trees on her land is rotten, we are told that "the M the J, and the O'M [are] as clear as if they were carved today" (114). Despite the unhappiness of Josie's marriage and her many efforts to break free of it, Martin's report that the tree may fall over pains her, reminding her of the ephemeral and bittersweet qualities of all life and of the markers of life. Such traces of the past, although threatened by erasure, persist in the present with considerable (and, as this instance indicates, unexpected) force. But these traces are inseparable from the unreliable and unstable memories they evoke. Josie's two responses to the initials carved into the tree show just such variation and change.

8. As Josie points out to McGreevy, "'The Ireland you're chasing is a dream . . . doesn't exist anymore. . . . It's gone. *It's with O'Leary in the grave*'" (208).

9. One of the O'Mearas' neighbors explains about the house to Josie soon after she arrives: "'Never any children, though,' he said, sorrowfully, adding that though her husband's parents had two sons, they died leaving these infant children to be fostered out to cousins, so that the house had not known the cheerfulness of children. . . . 'A couple of children, that'll lift the curse,' he said" (43). But Josie and James have no children. The child that Josie conceives is aborted. Obviously, the discussion of children, as well as the use of the image of the child, carry with them the temporal concern about the future.

10. This framing device will be discussed in greater detail below. It is worth noting here, however, that O'Brien has always acknowledged her debt to James Joyce. In this novel, particularly in the opening and closing sections, she relies, however inadvertently, on Stephen Dedalus's image of Ireland as an old sow who eats her young. O'Brien's indebtedness to Yeats has not yet been given much attention; Yeats's play about the Big House, *Purgatory*, represents Irish history as an endlessly repeating tragic cycle, a view with which O'Brien, at least in part, concurs.

11. The image of the snare is particularly potent because it links Josie to her doppelganger, McGreevy. Both are hunted and trapped. It also ties Josie to the male-dominated life of rural Ireland, in which hunting, fishing, racing, drinking, and carousing with "the boys" take precedence over other activities (domestic, cerebral, emotional), which might provide her with some scope and fulfillment. In particular James O'Meara enjoys snaring rabbits. Indeed, Josie identifies with those ensnared rabbits, an identification anticipated when, early

in the marriage, her husband and brother-in-law take her with them to empty the traps. As the men empty the snares, each dead rabbit is carried back to Josie and laid at her feet. Although, after nine kills, Josie wants to leave, her husband insists that she stay, and he drapes her shoulders with two dead ones, "the fresh blood warm and simmery" (45). Symbolically, to Jamie, Josie is a rabbit he has caught, and their marriage, a deadly snare.

12. Jacqueline Genet, *The Big House in Literature* (New York: Barnes and Noble, 1991), ix.

13. Vera Kreilkamp, *The Anglo-Irish Novel and the Big House* (Syracuse, N.Y.: Syracuse University Press, 1998), 261.

14. Qtd. in Genet, *Big House in Literature*, ix.

15. The influential Irish critic Seamus Deane, for example, pooh-poohed the reemergence of the Big House novel as a sign of cultural exhaustion. It is hard not to read into Deane's assessment a distaste for the subject (*Celtic Revivals* [Boston: Faber and Faber, 1985], 32).

16. Otto Rauchbauer, ed., *Ancestral Voices: The Big House in Anglo-Irish Literature* (New York: Georg Olms Verlag, 1992), vii, 11–12.

17. Krielkamp, *Anglo-Irish Novel*, 6–7.

18. Counter to McGreevy's nationalism, the novel, through the House, suggests not only that the English are gone but that the English colonial presence was not totally destructive.

19. O'Brien does not provide dates. It is not clear exactly when the O'Mearas take title of the property. What is clear is that by the time of Jamie's marriage the Troubles have passed and the guns buried on the property are part of a post-Independence IRA action. O'Brien allows inferences about time to be drawn from allusion, slang, clothing. Josie would seem to be in her early twenties at the time of her marriage, and, given the style of her clothes, it suggests that the time is perhaps the mid- to late 1920s.

20. From 1923 to the late 1950s, postcolonial Ireland fashioned repressive domestic policies in support of rural life, patriarchal domestic arrangements (no divorce, no contraception, no abortion), small shopkeepers and farmers, artistic censorship, and the Catholic religion. See: Terence Brown, *Ireland: A Social and Cultural History, 1922 to the Present* (Ithaca, N.Y.: Cornell University Press, 1985); David Cairns and Shaun Richards, *Writing Ireland: Colonialism, Nationalism, and Culture* (Manchester: Lanchester University Press, 1988); and Roy F. Foster, *Modern Ireland: 1600–1972* (Harmondsworth, Middlesex: Penguin, 1988).

21. Daniel Corkery, *The Hidden Ireland* (Dublin: M. H. Gill and Son, Ltd., 1956), 30, 37.

22. This identification is made by a passenger on the boat from America. Jamie is proud of her looks and encourages her to tell his brother about the mistaken identity. It is a measure of Irish insulation from Hollywood at this time that Jamie's brother "had not a clue who Gloria Swanson was" (45). In the novel's present, Gloria Swanson might have been forgotten, but other Hollywood icons are familiar (see note 3, above). One of the ways O'Brien records the change from Irish isolation to internationalization is through the increasing familiarity with American culture. Her use of Gloria Swanson in particular may

also be an intertextual reference to one of Swanson's most famous films, *Sunset Boulevard,* in which an aging and reclusive actress uses a young man (played by William Holden) to choreograph a screen comeback.

23. Ruth Frehner, *The Colonizers' Daughters: Gender in the Anglo-Irish Big House Novel* (Tubingen: A Franke Verlag, 1999), 10–11.

24. The sexual undercurrent of the Josie/McGreevy relationship is given substance, albeit parodic and humorous, as the police, who have surrounded the Big House, watch the activities of Josie and McGreevy through the window. They conclude, erroneously, that what they see is McGreevy and Josie engaged in some indecent sex play. Cormac, one of the policemen, says to Matt, another:

> "He's touching her."
> "What? Where?"
> Together now they jockey for it, each pushing the other aside to get a glimpse, each able to reassure the other that yes, they're on the ground, the woman and the boyo. A man about to do a grim and grisly deed having a bit of last-minute fun with the woman.
> "Oh, the Biddy . . . Oh, the Biddy," Matt says as he sees them fall to the floor and the man's arms come around her. (207)

What has actually happened is that Josie and McGreevy hear a sound and think they are being attacked. To protect Josie in a gesture of self-sacrifice and love, McGreevy pushes her to the floor and covers her with his body. It transpires that what they have actually heard is the buzzing of two wasps. That the police surveillance transforms this scene of profound affection into an illicit dalliance and that they treat it as if they were watching a forbidden pornographic movie ("each pushing the other aside to get a glimpse") undermines their claims to moral superiority over McGreevy and denies them any credibility as upholders of law and order.

25. The nurse is Josie's only visitor, and, despite Josie's entreaty that she stay longer ("'Don't go yet,' Josie says [24]), she declines to linger. But even her companionship is compromised by a mean-spirited satisfaction that Josie, who she regards as socially privileged, has been brought down a notch or two: "To think that once this woman wouldn't wipe the floor with her or her kind, this woman with her style and her finery, flashing eyes that matched the deep blue glass of her rosary beads which she dangled in chapel" (24–25). When Josie dies, we are told in the voice of her aborted child that the "nurse took my mother's belongings in a suitcase but wore the coatee with the velvet collar, *sported it*" (our emphasis, 232). The nurse, whose ostensible duty it is to care for Josie, sees the advantage to herself of Josie's death.

26. We mention cinematic examples of the gunman on the run because of O'Brien's use of Hollywood, television, and American popular culture as part of her system of allusions. In describing the situation of his men surrounding the house, Rory (the guard leading the assault on Josie's house) says: "This is cowboy country and we're cowboys here" (184). In the mind of one of the most important police officers involved in the search and apprehension of McGreevy, the peculiarly Irish context has dissolved into a Western action movie. Further, there is the film-star poster on Creena's wall. But Dean is the quintessential

"rebel without a cause"; McGreevy is the quintessential rebel with a cause. On the one hand, Creena's linkage of McGreevy with a Hollywood heartthrob glamorizes the gunman; on the other, it undercuts his commitment. There are, of course, other textual examples of gunmen on the run: Johnny in O'Casey's *Juno and the Paycock* or the shadowy revolutionary in *Shadow of a Gunman* and Frankie McPhillip in Liam O'Flaherty's *The Informer* are all objects of a manhunt. Characters such as Cal in Bernard McLaverty's novel of the same name and Tod in Danny Morrison's *The Wrong Man* are both running away from their involvement in the IRA.

27. Reed's most famous film, *The Third Man* (1949), was made two years after *Odd Man Out.* Film critics such as Laurence Miller consider both films to be pivotal moments in the cinematic history of film noir, with their emphases on a deterministic universe and the lack of human agency in a malevolent world. Laurence Miller, "Evidence for a British Film Noir Cycle," in *Re-Viewing British Cinema, 1900–1992: Essays and Interviews,* ed. Wheeler Winston Dixon (Albany, N.Y.: SUNY Press, 1994), 155–64.

28. All references to *The Crying Game* are from Jordan's published screenplay in *A Neil Jordan Reader* (New York: Vintage, 1993).

29. The logic of loving = living and hating = dying is refuted in *House* as well. At the moment when Josie learns to communicate with another person and begins to love, she is killed. Both *The Crying Game* and *House* present the insufficiency of love as a cure-all to the world's problems. Both texts also question the validity of individual agency.

30. The gunman on the run also has a narrative relationship to outlaws, Wild West gunslingers, and bandit heroes such as Butch Cassidy and the Sundance Kid. A recent article in the *New Yorker* looks at the varied histories of Billy the Kid and proposes that the legendary Western outlaw was actually a transplanted Irish terrorist. Fintan O'Toole, "The Many Stories of Billy the Kid," *New Yorker,* 28 December–4 January 1998–1999, 86–94.

31. Fergus's transformation in *The Crying Game* begins with his connection to an IRA hostage.

32. O'Brien makes a connection between Rory and Josie's husband through their mutual love of hunting: "Rory loved to get up early on a Sunday morning and go into the woods with his rifle, to track and shoot deer" (9). Rory also hunts McGreevy, and thus McGreevy is linked by a complex pattern of association to the felled deer and the bloody rabbits James and his brother drape on Josie's shoulders.

33. Josie's reading of St. Caimin is the third reference to a hermit or recluse in the novel. Josie is, of course, the main isolated figure. Then there is the allusion to Gloria Swanson and by extension the reclusive character she played in *Sunset Boulevard,* and finally St. Caimin—an Irish saint known for being a hermit. That the young son of Rory is named for that saint possibly implies that O'Brien sees little in the next generation to suggest a moving away from isolationism and an opening up of boundaries.

34. The lack of full knowledge is extended to a critique of the tourism industry as well. Ma Hinchy, who is involved in the conversation about the wig and its possibly scandalous origins, calls out to her husband to help her remember

the name of a film star. The husband is too busy to answer: "He's off to the bog to collect turf, because the tourists go mad for turf fire and the smell it gives out, have themselves photographed in front of it" (72). The implication is obvious: Mr. Hinchy is only cutting turf for a tourist's idea of what Irish country living is, or should be, not what it is. That wig becomes the subject of another conversation about incomplete knowledge. The guard takes the wig to the police station and after a rather comic discussion of what it is, the police sergeant reprimands the young officer for tampering with evidence. A later phone call to Dublin Castle is all about the procedural difficulties with incomplete evidence: "A fact," says the Dublin detective, "in the lines of inquiry, would be where is the bag" (101). Of course, the police have no idea where the bag is.

35. *The Quiet Man* is a famous film starring John Wayne and Maureen O'Hara that details Wayne's venture into the Irish landscape. It is also considered a gross stereotype of the pastoral beauty of Ireland's rural communities and its feisty, red-haired inhabitants.

On the Side of Life

Edna O'Brien's Trilogy of Contemporary Ireland

SOPHIA HILLAN

The plot of *Wild Decembers*, Edna O'Brien's third and final novel in her recent trilogy of life in modern Ireland, might seem far-fetched, if the very horror she describes had not occurred and, with almost eerie synchronicity, been reported in the press within weeks of the book's publication in 1999. The central event of the novel is the crazed killing by a farmer of his neighbor and former friend. It caused one Irish reviewer to write that "O'Brien often seems out of touch with the locality about which she writes."[1] Yet, barely one month later, a newspaper account reported the horrific murder by a man of his neighbor and his neighbor's wife, because the man felt "under siege" from his neighbor. The writer of the account reports that "over five years he made four or five complaints to local gardaí over what most people would consider minor problems. Differences of opinion over trees and bushes and a leaky septic tank . . . were typical examples. But in [his] mind the small things formed a pattern that added up to what he described as 'abuse.'"[2] Chillingly, the report tells us that the killer "was 'very forthcoming when arrested' and expressed 'great sorrow and regret' at what had happened, according to the gardaí. He told them, however, he 'couldn't allow the abuse to continue.'"

The scene could have come straight out of *Wild Decembers*. There, having killed his neighbor and sometime friend and having risked killing his own sister, the crazed brother confesses in terror and remorse to the gardaí that he has "shot your man up in the yard." When, disbelieving the normally mild man, the police probe further, he replies, "Twas him or me," saying, "from the day his tractor pulled into our yard everything went bust. . . . He broke us" (228).[3] This being so, it is hard to agree with Hayden's view that O'Brien's "vision of Ireland is still rooted in the fifties and sixties." In a recent profile of the author, Nicholas Wroe confirms that O'Brien's trilogy dealing with three key issues in modern Irish life, "the IRA, abortion and land . . . [has] . . . seen her castigated as out of touch with modern Ireland and her heightened prose style as out of touch with modern readers."[4] Perhaps the opposite is true: it may prove to be the case that Edna O'Brien is utterly in touch, under the guise of near-magical realism, with the very issues that still lie at the heart of Irish life. Two hundred years after Carleton's "Wild-goose Lodge" and "Denis O'Shaughnessy Going to Maynooth," it seems that the sectarian violence, sexual repression, and what used to be called "the land question" are still central to Irish life.

There is irony in the recollection that, thirty years ago, O'Brien was in equal trouble for being too far in advance of the ordinary reader. Of her eighteen published novels, the first six were banned in the Republic of Ireland. Undeterred, O'Brien has continued to write. Before *Wild Decembers*, she published the first two novels of a trilogy of contemporary Ireland: *House of Splendid Isolation* (1994), in which she addresses the difficult subject of the rationale behind political extremism and its effect on those compelled to live with it; and *Down by the River* (1996), where the abortion debate and the shadow of the Kerry Babies provide the basis for a candid, compassionate, and poetic examination of some of the darkest places of Irish life.[5] Before the publication of *Wild Decembers* in October 1999, her most recent work, published in June 1999, was a study of James Joyce, whom O'Brien acknowledges as a most profound influence on her work

Like her mentor Joyce, she journeys in her novels—as she has in her life—in and out of Ireland. Her first and most endearing heroines, green-eyed Kate and her sparring partner, the brazen, irrepressible Baba, move throughout the *Country Girls* trilogy from Clare, to Galway, to Dublin, and then on to London, from innocence and exuberant mischief to saddened gravitas and a resilient worldly wisdom. *August Is a Wicked Month* (1966) moves its heroine to the Continent, and *Casualties of Peace* (1966) returns to London. The setting in *A Pagan Place* (1970) is again Irish, recalling the tone and style of a text often echoed and alluded to in O'Brien's work, Joyce's *A Portrait of the Artist as a Young Man*. She continues her Joycean journey in *Zee and Co.* (1971) and *Night* (1972), where her central characters essentially continue and develop the soliloquy begun by Molly Bloom at the end of *Ulysses*. With *Johnny I Hardly Knew You* (1977), she brings us to London, Scotland, and Italy, exploring the relationship between an older woman and a man young enough to be her son, a theme to which she returns in great depth in *House of Splendid Isolation.*

After the publication of *The Country Girls* (1960)—which "wrote itself" in her first weeks in London when, as she recalls, "I was crying a lot because I had left Ireland, although I was not driven out"—O'Brien found herself hurled into a bewildering round of parties. She was besieged by fame verging on notoriety and recalls that, hearing Elizabeth Bowen's description of her as "talented but completely mad," her reaction was to think "even then that madness is no drawback to a writer." O'Brien added a caveat: "Obviously, if, like Virginia Woolf or Gogol, you cross the frontier then that is fatal. The hope is to 'come back from the Azores' as Joyce said of himself."[6]

It is in this journeying to and from the Azores that the key to Edna O'Brien's writing lies. In her first trilogy she carried out the novelistic equivalent of Seamus Heaney's digging down and back into her own past and that of the island of Ireland. As with Heaney's early work, this digging took the writer beyond itself to the wider world, and then back to Ireland, described by O'Brien as "a state of mind as well as an actual country" (144).[7] She is in no doubt that the country of origin is a starting as well as an ending place, ultimately a resting place, and that to be Irish conveys membership in the European world, with all of its history and its myth. She reminds us in *Mother Ireland* (1976) that Ireland was "originally a land of woods and thickets, such as Orpheus had seen when describing the voyage of Jason, through a misted atmosphere . . . thought to have known invasion from the time when the ice age ended and the improving climate allowed deer to throng her dense forest" (12).

Mother Ireland is an impressionistic, subjective study of the mercurial nature of the Irish temperament and of the country that nurtures that temperament while making it impossible for its natives to live there. "There must be something secretly catastrophic about a country from which so many people go, escape," she says, and goes on to speculate on the nature of the contradiction: "Loneliness, the longing for adventure, the Roman Catholic Church, or the family tie that is more umbilical than among any other race in earth? The martyred Irish mother and the rollicking Irish father is not peculiar to the works of exorcised writers but common to families throughout the land. The children inherit a trinity of guilts (a shamrock): the guilt for Christ's Passion and Crucifixion, the guilt for the plundered land, and the furtive guilt for the mother frequently defiled by the insatiable father" (32). In the first trilogy, O'Brien makes her first cuts, digs her first layer. Thereafter, the characters from *August Is a Wicked Month* onward are—if Irish—Irish in a wider context: living in England, married to citizens of other countries in Europe, or sojourning on the Continent. With her latest trilogy, she has brought them home.

A long gestation period led up to this. O'Brien's last novel before the trilogy was *Time and Tide* (1992), a moving evocation of the love and grief of a woman on the death of one son and the loss through natural growing away of the other. O'Brien had explored the theme of the mother and son relationship to powerful effect in *Johnny I Hardly Knew You*, and in *House of Splendid Isolation* it is even more carefully examined. There, the pivotal relationship is between an older woman, a widow of the Big House, and a young, ruthless, betrayed IRA fugitive with whom, as his hostage, she is forced to live and for whom she comes to have a deep love that ultimately costs her her life. The plot is loosely based upon the case of Dominic "Mad Dog" McGlinchey, one of a number of IRA prisoners whom O'Brien visited in prison while researching this novel. Her impression of him and his story provide the stimulation for an investigation of the "trinity of guilts." *House of Splendid Isolation* opens with the words, "History is everywhere. It seeps into the soil, the sub-soil. Like rain, or hail, or snow, or blood. A house remembers. An outhouse remembers. A people ruminate. The tale differs with the teller" (3).[8]

History, in this novel, operates at several different levels. There are first the land, the house, and all that they remember. Then there is the woman, Josie, brought young to the house, and her recorded memories of the kind of Irish marriage that lies at the heart of Edna O'Brien's novels—where the woman is object of both desire and repulsion, at once trophy and slave. These form the background to the unfolding drama of Josie's brief but profoundly affecting time with McGreevy, the McGlinchey character. Having married to escape a life of domestic servitude in Manhattan, Josie finds she has entered another kind of imprisonment in rural Ireland, under the rule of her husband and her husband's brother. The land is all of life to them, and for that reason, there must be children. Indeed, the desire for children, expressed through the man, his brother, and their friends who come to play cards, recalls the obsessive, atavistic desire to produce an heir for the land that permeates Marcel Pagnol's novels and films *Jean de Florette* and *Manon des Sources.* Josie has "married into the best family in the county," as her husband's unnervingly familiar friend Jacko, a former boat-maker, informs her. While telling her this, he makes frightening and unwelcome advances, saying, "not everyone could control her, only three people, her husband, her brother-in-law, and yours truly" (37). O'Brien sums up, in Josie's thoughts on her husband and the bargain in general, the dilemma of the woman who has thought to escape drudgery and servitude in America, only to find it in her longed-for haven: "He was not a cross man, not a vexed man, but a ravenous man. She thought of Brooklyn and thought, what a mistake she had made to come home. The card parties, the card games, the winks from her husband were gall now. Her uncle and aunt, who were promised free grazing, would not find it very satisfying to learn that she was dumped in a day" (38).

Jacko goes on to tell the history of the house, in which no child has ever been raised. It was constructed by an engineer "who had built it with workmen in the winter when they weren't farming, built it from a design he saw in a book . . . with rooms where others had slept, husbands and wives, English people and half-English people, and one particular Englishman who had brought an Austrian concubine but got sick of her" (38). It is a Castle Rackrent-like house, full of anger and violence, including one suicide. Her husband, rather like the couple in Frost's "Witch of Coös," hears "chains on the stairs at night" (95). All but deserted on the first day of her marriage when her husband resumes his routine pursuits, Josie regards her new home as a house with a curse. Marriage brings not the love for which she had hoped, but joyless and often violent sexual congress. Yet, her husband is not an entirely unsympathetic character. Like many of O'Brien's unhappy and abusive men, his own loveless past means that he can express himself no other way: "Up in the village he is a gentleman, talks to people, buys buns for girls and sings a song if asked. When he isn't buying buns or cracking jokes, there is in his eyes, in all of him, a vacancy, like a lost stunned animal, far from home. He either buys all the commodities and repents or buys them and flings them down and that night or the next he is gone and days later he is carried back and in bed he groans and in the morning he mounts her with a lingual gusto, commandeers her inside and outside and still and feck it, she does not get with child" (44–45).

That is her marriage. Josie learns to accommodate herself to it and to see with a kind of despairing compassion that she has been maimed by life like "one of his ailing horses in whom spirit has been quenched" (59). Following this, and despite her own largely imaginary and ultimately unconsummated affair with the local priest—for which her husband punishes her brutally—she contrives to live fairly peacefully with him until his death. Then, old and odd, finding herself held hostage by McGreevy, a dangerous terrorist, she discovers at last the redemptive power of love and giving, at first tentatively and then without stint, because she finds the criminal is a gentle man, a gentleman. From *The Country Girls* onward, O'Brien's heroines look for and often find, however briefly, "Mr. Gentleman." It is a leitmotif in Edna O'Brien's work that when Mr. Gentleman is found, in whatever unlikely guise, he can have everything the heroine has to give, even if he is, almost inevitably, on his way somewhere or to someone else.

O'Brien sets out to penetrate McGreevy's consciousness and through this to seek an understanding of the deeper conflict taking place in the country of her birth. When asked in an interview whether she thought the Irish were "prone" to "war in the house, war in the land, war in the heart," she replied:

> I certainly think they're more turbulent. They're more turbulent by disposition and by language. And their history has made them suffer a hell of a lot. I have written about strife between mother and child, between husband and wife and in *House of Splendid Isolation,* between two parts of a country. An IRA man [*sic*] told me once, "When you're shooting, you don't feel. But when you've shot him, you do feel, because half of you hopes you got him, and the other half hopes you didn't. Because we're all Irish under the skin." That to me was a story about war. War, whether it's between a man and a woman, or different parts of a country, or different nations, is always, always more complicated than just the two sides. It is *that* I want to write about. It's the dilemma and the conflict within the obvious dilemma that matters.[9]

Therefore, when Josie finally settles down to talk to her captor, she does not ask him how he can do what he does and still say he loves his mother and would hate to upset her. She thinks those things, but her question is different. She asks instead what part he aims for when he shoots. His reply, "The biggest part," shocks her deeply because she hears in his voice, "no tremor . . . no inconclusiveness, simply the reply, the biggest part, like shooting a wall" (96). Yet, to her, he is gentleness it-self, and she, who has known so little in her life of tenderness, responds to that. She sees in him the child he tells her he once was, someone ex-cited at coming across the border for holidays, who thought "every-thing was better—the lemonade, the holly berries." She asks, "And now?" to which he replies, "The South forgot us" (99–100). O'Brien touches here upon a sore place in the Irish psyche, voicing the generally unspoken view that little was done in 1969 by the Dublin government to help the beleaguered and bewildered people of the North. Moreover, she deliberately takes the reader into the mind and heart of a man who has killed. This is part of her stated intention: "In the case of *House of Splendid Isolation,* I wanted to write about an IRA soldier, not from per-ceived opinion of him, but to explore his thinking, rationale, conflict, ruthlessness vs. idealism, etc. and for this I saw many prisoners who talked to me openly. The character of McGreevy is more rounded, com-plex, and probably truthful than any of my former male characters."[10] Her IRA man's wish for himself is "not to have grown up in hate, not to have been Papist leper scum, not to have been interned at fourteen and fifteen and sixteen, not to have been in the Crum and Long Kesh and waiting to go on the blocks." That, to him, "would have been out of this world" (113).

A delicate and improbable love story unfolds between Josie and McGreevy, intercut with snatches of fairy tale and magic, various inter-weaving subplots providing counterpoint. We see curious neighbors calling, not out of kindness, but to see what is going on; we meet a young girl, Creena, who loves McGreevy, knowing that he is mourning his murdered wife, and who nurses Josie for McGreevy's sake.

Most tellingly, O'Brien shows us how this situation affects the gardaí, normally occupied with agrarian and domestic crime. It falls them to track down McGreevy and his accomplices. One of them, echo-ing the words of the garda who talked to O'Brien, finds out what it really means to shoot a man:

The guy is shouting. He does not know whether he is asking to give up or whether it is a trick.

"Drop your gun," he shouts back, his voice lost in the oncoming hammering and hoping and praying now that his chamber will not give out, he rises, rushes it and sprays the bonnet of the car as if someone, someone is impelling him to do it. He sees an arm go down, and something float like a big bird and he thinks that's his hood and realises that the man is down. That's all he knows, that the man is down. The sudden silence is appalling. . . . Moving across he sees the body slumped over the car but twitching, twitching and he thinks, "If I have to shoot point blank, then I'll have to shoot point blank." The ebbing of the life, even in that darkness, was like seeing an electric current fizzling out, the jigging getting less and less, then nothing, only a heap. A still heap and looking in over him he hears nothing. Least of all a breath. (166–67)

A little later, still in shock, he says the words the real-life garda said to O'Brien: "Half of you hopes you got him, and the other half hopes you didn't." And his colleague also speaks the original words: "I know. . . . I'd be the same. . . . We're all Irish under the skin" (177).

On the wild night on which it all ends, Josie is alone in the house after McGreevy has disappeared. She is grieving for him, like a mother for an errant but much-loved child, wishing he can neither be harmed nor cause harm. Then he comes back, unexpectedly, and the action moves to its climax. McGreevy tells her how his wife was shot as he lay in prison, how his baby died without his being permitted to see her. She wonders "what want in him" has caused him to return (182). Later, as the police stake out the grounds, McGreevy dreams of his dead wife. When they come to take him, Josie puts on an old raincoat and goes barefoot to intercede with them, to explain to them, because she understands him, that they must not kill him, that "his life has many chapters to it and many evolutions" (205). The guard, seeing an asexual figure in a raincoat, shoots her. The violence of her death recalls the horror of Carleton's "Wildgoose Lodge," where the woman pleading for her baby's life is stopped midsentence by a bayonet through the mouth.[11]

McGreevy, wounded, is taken; Josie lies dead. The guards, heart-sickened and scarred by what has happened, pick up the pieces. The novel's last words, presented in the voice of a seer, muse on questions neither McGreevy, Josie, nor the guards can understand: "To go in, within, is the bloodiest journey of all. Inside you get to know. That the same blood and the same tears drop from the enemy as from the self, though not always in the same proportion. To go right into the heart of the hate and the wrong and to sup from it and be supped. It does not say that in the books. That is the future knowledge. The knowledge that is to be" (216).

It is this inexplicable and perhaps unteachable "knowledge that is to be" that informs the second book, perhaps the heart of the trilogy, *Down by the River.* Its two epigraphs reflect the thought of the epilogue to *House of Splendid Isolation.* The first, deliberately heavy with inherited Irish guilt, is from Joyce's *Ulysses:* "Darkness is our souls do you not think? Flutier. Our souls, shame-wounded by our sins." The second, by ironic contrast, joyously celebratory, is from the Song of Solomon: "And thy belly be like a heap of wheat set about with lilies." At the novel's heart is what was known as "the X case" of the young girl who, having fled Ireland in 1992 to England for an abortion after being raped by a family friend, was brought back amid a tumult of outraged Irish morality. The child in *Down by the River,* Mary MacNamara, is a girl not quite fourteen years of age who knows and yet does not know what is happening to her the first time her father rapes her: "his essence, hers, their different essences one. O quenched and empty world. An eternity of time, then a shout, a chink of light, the ground easing back up, gorse prickles on her scalp and nothing ever the same again and a feeling as of having half-died" (4).[12] Shocked and bewildered, Mary tries to live her life outside an incomprehensible horror. "To go in, within, is the bloodiest journey of all": this is the journey undertaken in saddest innocence by the young heroine of *Down by the River.* She goes "right into the heart of the hate and the wrong" and lives "the future knowledge." In a disillusioned way, she is Kate again, and she has her Baba in Tara, touchingly innocent in her assumed sophistication about sex and men, all learned from forbidden magazines.

Many of the themes of the earlier novels surface in *Down by the River.* It is as though O'Brien is revisiting the territory of her own earlier writing and looking at it, like Lear's Cordelia, "with washed eyes." As in the early novels, we find the Joycean mother, terrifying in death; the doctor who carries on despairing affairs with his patients, including the heroine's mother; and the convent that seems at first a haven but holds its own traps and snares. To these themes are added new ones: the police who, like their counterparts in *House of Splendid Isolation,* are shocked and permanently marked by what they are called on to do in the name of the law; the members of the legal profession and the politicians whose double standards cause them few scruples; and, worst of all, the "right-thinking" women who, in a parody of nurturing Mary and her unborn child, damage both far more than the abuse of her father could. He, at least, bent and broken and tortured like the husband in *House of Splendid Isolation*—indeed like so many fathers in earlier O'Brien novels—loves his daughter somewhere in his self-hatred and despair. The women, with few exceptions, lack compassion.

The leader among them, Roisin, is at first sight a candidate for the "Rose of Tralee" beauty competition or its cynical counterpart, the "Lovely Girls" competition of the acclaimed Irish television series *Father Ted,* the bitter satire of which moves, in a direct line from Flann

O'Brien, through the fanatical devotion to the church and motherland so clearly delineated in this novel.[13] Roisin comes to a meeting held in one of the women's homes to give a talk on the horror of abortion. She arrives by the back door, "her tread so light that everyone jumped and most were startled to see such a beautiful girl with such lovely hair and very special eyes, grey eyes that shone, as if silver polish had been poured into them" (22). The women, although they are fascinated by Roisin, fear her, yet still follow her as their leader.

As *Down by the River* gathers momentum, circumstances force the helpless Mary into contact with her father until the inevitable happens. The women form a kind of chorus, and the action upon which they comment is as terrifying as in any Greek tragedy. From the outset the child has little hope of rescue. Her father's need and dependence, especially after her mother's death; the unwitting conspiracy of all around to keep her at home with him; and Mary's own impulse of friendship, which sends her home to another rape, resulting in her pregnancy—all conspire to maintain the status quo. Even Betty, the well-intentioned widow of the Big House, who tries her best to help Mary, even bringing her to England in the hope of securing an abortion, admits in the end: "We all knew, all along. . . . But we were dumbfounded" (222).

Part of the reason for everyone's reluctance to believe in the horror before their eyes is that they feel compassion for Mary's father, James MacNamara, and cannot think beyond his obvious loneliness, which so clearly needs his daughter's presence. He is their neighbor; they believe they know him. They cannot bear to believe that he is carrying on an incestuous relationship with his young daughter. O'Brien treats this with great delicacy. James is not portrayed as a monster. She is deeply compassionate toward him, while sparing us none of the horror of his actions. We know he rapes his daughter brutally, time and again; we know he terrifies her and almost destroys her emotionally and mentally; we know he has been equally cruel toward his wife.

Yet, we also see his moments of kindness, his near-tenderness, and his profound despair, most obvious in his post-coital "outcast's forlornness," which Mary witnesses and which causes her to feel "a shame lurching into sorrow" (85). He is a grief-stricken widower, a daughterless father. It does not matter that he has brought these griefs upon himself. He has to see his only child outside his window, realizing that she will not come in to see him, will never come to see him again, and know that "of all the wrenchings of his life it was the worst" (219). He feels the final emptiness of his house, "all his ruinous life coming to a head in him as he looks about a room that bore all the trademarks of a once breathless bride" (223). When finally cornered and driven to confess what he has done, he reveals that at the time of his wife's death, dimly knowing that somewhere in him all this darkness lay, he "asked them to send me somewhere. . . . An infirmary . . . anywhere . . . but they wouldn't" (219).

Most poignant of all, as in *House of Splendid Isolation*, is to see the side of MacNamara that is strong and tender. Just as McGreevy on the run takes time to deliver, expertly and with great care, a laboring cow of its calf, so does James save a horse and her foal with "taut and terrible delicacy" (*House of Splendid Isolation*, 62). His care and attention to detail are again highlighted in the account of his suicide, as he reflects that his nylon rope will not make his neck itch, that the stones on the top of the wall on which he will stand are sufficiently loose not to hold him, "telling them that when he kicked they were to go, saying that he mustn't botch it. He must not be heard roaring like a ginnet to the surrounding countryside" (249). Little could prepare the reader for the terror and horror of his realization that he is to die:

It was when the ground went that he began to holler. Ground gone, stones gone and he up there in a worse nowhere, crater and cradle, beginning and end; out, back and around, crazed bumps-a-daisies. It was then he shouted, it was then he knew it, it was then the words came, a great welter of words from the entrails, the help word, the hate word, the blast word and the love word, known to all men, compressed into the one word because it was only minutes, less; his breathing going and him still sashaying backwards and forwards, the blood leaving his face in waves, the expression furious and piteous; lips lifted over the teeth to say the first and last thing which man craves to say and ending in a terrifying hosanna that was in the old tongue. He sought then to undo it and with a tugging that exceeded human might he pulled and pulled but the rope had already commenced the steady, mathematical snapping of bone and the neck piping to be free was soon a crust of raw stigmata. (249)

James MacNamara is a tragic figure here; Sophocles would have recognized him. Yet, he is not so notably of the classic Greek tradition as is the novel's Medean chorus of women who, under the guise of piety, bring about, ironically, a spontaneous abortion, a miscarriage. "We all love you to death," they tell Mary, with deadly accuracy (152). Seeing her bleeding almost to death, beautiful Roisin spits, "May you rot in hell" (259). When Mary is brought, bewildered, home from England, they say, "We're glad to have got you home. . . . Your father is glad and every right-minded person in the country is glad" (151). Those who are "glad" form a panoply of satirically well-drawn characters: a politician with a mistress of long-standing who asks him, "Why one law for us and one for some poor girl?" (159); the complacent members of the legal profession "men of honour, men of *gravitas*" who regard it as a case of "some little slut about to pour piss on the nation's breast," who "want this under wraps," knowing "that it is in everyone's interests including the girl's that nothing gets out" (167–68); the police who are, just as in *House of Splendid Isolation,* appalled and sickened by the case (229–30).

In the midst of it all is the little girl named by the media "the Magdalene." O'Brien deliberately uses the New Testament names adopted with fervor by Catholic Ireland. Mary the Virgin; Mary Magdalene, a woman taken in adultery; and Veronica, who wiped the face of Christ on his way to Calvary, now become the relentless torturers of the innocent. This motherless girl is trying to grow up, trying to find an adult to help her among the nuns, the neighbors, and among the "right-thinking" women who have ultimate care of her. A lifeline is extended to her by Mrs. B, "the only friend among them" (250). Despite Mrs. B's slight assistance, the Magdalene's journey continues on its ordained path. On her way she finds other waifs and strays, and they, too—the young girl who goes through with her abortion, the gentle hippy boy who shelters Mary and is punished for it—suffer through association. Bewildered, driven to attempt suicide, and brought back again by the interference of the relentlessly good, Mary survives and ends the novel on a night of snow like that which covers Ireland at the end of Joyce's "The Dead"; singing into the emptiness in a night club, "a paean of expectancy into the gaudy void"; breaking the hearts of those who hear her as she speaks to the unutterable in them. In spite of all the brutality she has endured, she touches their deepest hearts because she knows the unknowable: "Her voice was low and tremulous at first, then it rose and caught, it soared and dipped and soared, a great crimson quiver of sound going up, up to the skies and they were silent then, plunged into a sudden and melting silence because what they were hearing was in answer to their own souls' innermost cries" (265).

In *Wild Decembers,* the souls' innermost cries are, yet again, almost drowned. In *Down by the River,* the crushingly virtuous Veronica exhorts Mary to remember "we must not forget our roots, our woods and our rivers and our history above all" (178). Breege, the heroine of *Wild Decembers,* learns in her depths of silence the truth of words of the preface to *House of Splendid Isolation*—"A girl loves a sweetheart and a sweetheart loves her back, but he loves the land more, he is hostage to it" (*Wild Decembers, 3*). Her love for her brother's friend, their neighbor Michael Bugler, is great. So, too, is Bugler's almost unacknowledged but deep and growing love for her. Yet, the land hunger that devours both her brother and her lover seems to be more powerful, and it all but destroys love. Fear of famine, the atavistic tendency to that which will keep want at bay and ensure the survival of the genes, drives these men to a terrible battle over "fields that mean more than fields; fields that translate into nuptials of blood; fields lost, regained and lost again in that fickle and fractured sequence of things . . . the warring sons of warring sons cursed with that same irresistible thrall of madness which is the designate of living man as though he had to walk back through time and place, back to the voiding emptiness to repossess ground gone for ever" (1). Mary MacNamara in *Down by the River* faces "the gaudy void" of a future first sullied then almost emptied for her by interference. Here, Breege Brennan is left as the faithful "spirit that remembers" almost, though not quite, devoid of a future. Yet, like Mary and Josie, she is, as O'Brien tells us at the end of this final novel of the trilogy, "shaped by that place and by that loneliness" (242). Unlike Mary, who loses her child, and, for a long time, her hopes for the future, and unlike Josie, who has no child but the late-found gunman whom she loves like a son, Breege loses her lover and her brother. She keeps, however, the child growing within her and faces the future with calm, gentling the past and nurturing hope for the future. The trilogy culminates in this study of "stranded selves," and the burden of its message is that all can be, however unlikely it may seem, "harbingers of love" (242).

All these unhappy families of dedicated farmers and their women hark back to the ancestors who had to settle on the mountain to survive and then let themselves be slaves to "the sacred fetters of land and blood" (7). At the heart of the tale is a woman—like Josie and Mary, solitary of spirit—who lives on an inhospitable side of a mountain with her kind, erudite, reclusive brother Joseph. Referred to as "Ivory Mary" by the Crock, their crippled, equally well-read but bitterly malevolent neighbor, Breege keeps house for her brother, who is in a sense like his namesake Joseph, her "most chaste spouse." Until Bugler comes, Joseph lives in a world peopled by ancient myths. The old tales of the Red Branch Knights and *Idylls of the Kings* are more real and precious to him than anything but his land. He is hurt and surprised to find that his neighbor, Bugler, first friend then bitter enemy, is also beloved of his sister. This intruder, this knight on a tractor, is at first a fascination to him, a model, almost a hero; but when all he holds dear—his land and, to a lesser extent, his sister—stands to be lost to him, he comes first to hate Bugler and then to kill him.

Breege—whose name recalls Saint Brigid, Ireland's own Mary—is a trembling bird among hunters, and her frailty, masking a steadfast spirit, is sketched throughout the novel in delicate and swift strokes. While still friends the men watch in the woods "the dusk through which the small and secretive bird will fly for its evening food" (17). Once they have shot the bird—as they will combine to injure Breege— once "the little parcel of invisibility comes teetering down," they look on it with compassion, and Joseph explains with a kind of tenderness: "'They are a solitary bird. . . . They fly alone, they eat alone, the only time you see a pair is when the mother has a chick under her breast.' 'Under her breast!' Bugler said, touched" (18–19). Joseph displays a similar double-edged tenderness toward his delicate, fawnlike grey-hound, Violet Hill, "more like a changeling than a dog" (110). He loves her as he might a baby, but teaches her to desire and chase the scent of blood. When the greyhound, on one of her mad dashes, is run over in the road, she dies like a child in Joseph's arms. Bugler finds her and brings her home, where he stands with Breege, both silent in forebod-ing, and they hold the dog between them "as if somehow holding her they would keep her alive but letting her go would bode the end of everything" (125). Joseph, inevitably, blames Bugler and, in one of the most moving scenes in the novel, gives Violet Hill her last rites: "He did not roar, he did not speak, he closed his eyes for several seconds, then came down the stairs, took Violet Hill in his arms and with his hands he gripped the stiffening face and held it and saw. He began then to help her die, to allow her to die, telling her it was not dying at all, it was run-ning faster and faster into the free and untrammelled emptiness, under the dew and the rain and the stars where none could wound or kill her because she had gone from flesh to spirit" (125).

Throughout this novel, as in *Down by the River,* a strong element of magical realism pervades the narrative, as if this were a story by the Brothers Grimm being played out in everyday life. There are such evil characters as the Crock, at once pathetic and menacing in his Caliban-like revenge upon the beautiful girl he covets for himself. There are the siren sisters, Reena and Rita, who lure and seduce men, including Bugler, and then blackmail them into parting with their property or goods. There is also the thread of poignantly joyful magic in the relation between Bugler and Breege, from the time of their first meeting, when

Bugler shows Joseph and his sister the wondrous tractor. Breege climbs up on it and feels a sensation "like being up on a throne with the fields and the low walls very insignificant" (5). Bugler, mistaking her embarrassment for fear, reassures her: "'You're OK. . . . You're OK. . . . It won't run away with you,' Bugler said softly and leaned in over her. Their breaths almost merged. She thought how different he seemed now, how conciliatory, how much less abrupt and commanding" (6). The magical connection thus begun continues, and the tractor is transformed into a chariot as Bugler literally carries Breege away from her brother. This innocent journey becomes, through the alembic of Crock's malice, her having "gone up the mountain" with Bugler. Joseph confronts her like a jealous lover, describing her as he has seen her in his mind's eye "like Cleopatra on her barge" (63). He is frustrated, because she did not, while on the mountain with Bugler, point out to him "the boundaries between his land and ours." Moreover, he fears for her honor and, by association, his own. Angry and afraid, Breege rightly foresees that "they would hunt her down and with a bloodthirst they would take away from her that lit taper of hope" (64). Yet, somehow, the lit taper continues to burn, and when Bugler and Breege embrace, hiding in the hay from the wicked sisters, there is a stolen kiss as magical and mystical as in any fairy tale or romance: "With his hat Bugler brushed her down and with his hand he removed wisps of hay from her hair, fingering each strand as if he were unbraiding it. Then he moved very close to her, the shape of his mouth searching out the shape of hers. The kiss withheld for so long, given, taken and retaken. Their ripe lips. Unfolding once more. Once more. Silently wooing. Silently clasped. He held her then and the constraint that was between them was gone" (142). Although he is known to be engaged to an Australian girl, standing "in that radius of astonishment," they know they belong together, that "a promise was struck although no words were said" (143).

Inevitably, with all the forces of interference activated, their path becomes difficult. The Australian fiancée, Rosemary, instinctively uneasy, seeks reassurance over the telephone, and Bugler thinks of these two women who make him tremble: "Rosemary, who always referred to herself as a witch, and Breege, light as a leaf yet full of passion, passionate" (144). He fears "the unthinkable, two women, having to fail one or the other, or both" (145). Yet the love of Breege and Bugler continues, and they find themselves one night in the eerie light of a ruined island church. She feels at home among the graves, sure that it is the only place she will ever have lasting peace. When she disappears for a moment,

and he, suddenly fearful, finds her, they finally make love: "in that nas-
cent nearness in which self is lost, self and other becoming one against
cold desperate death and cold ravenous life, in that nimbus of heat and
light that ravish of courtship, that covenant that would be theirs for
ever and yet never theirs like flowers that are hatched in the snows"
(161). Their happiness is brief. Rosemary announces her imminent arrival, and, shortly thereafter, Breege is rebuffed by Bugler but, paradox-
ically, is certain in the moment of rejection that he loves her. Then, meeting Rosemary and seeing the proof of her gaudy engagement ring,
Breege is obliged to stand "feeling the cold truth of things run up and
down her body," and thereafter is struck dumb (188).

What saves her is what saves Mary in *Down by the River,* a song. For
Breege, it is "The Castle of Dromore," the haunting melody sung by
Mary MacNamara's mother as she lies dying. It has been sung, too, to
Breege and Joseph by their mother now long dead. Bugler sends Breege
the verses after their first glorious tractor journey. After Breege's col-
lapse and discovery, like the Christ child, in the church crib and her
nightmare incarceration in a mental asylum where no one, including
Bugler, can reach her, her silence breaks only though her song: "her
voice . . . clear and pure and trilling down the length of the ward" (204):

> Bring no ill wind to hinder us, my helpless babe and me—
> Dread spirit of Blackwater banks, Clan Eoin's wild banshee,
> And Holy Mary pitying me, in Heaven for grace doth sue
> Sing hush-a-bye, lul, lul, lo, lo, lau,
> Sing hush-a-bye, lul, lul, loo.

With echoes of "The Lass of Aughrim" in Joyce's "The Dead," the song
of the girl abandoned with her baby outside the great house in the cold
forcefully reminds us of Mary's courageous effort at survival in her
song at the end of *Down by the River.* For both Breege and Mary, the
music takes them to the point where they can endure.

In her will to survive, Breege is stronger and more fortunate than
either her brother or Rosemary, the apparently hard Australian fiancée
who has traveled the world to claim her man, only to lose him by her incessant neediness and fear-driven tantrums. Rosemary's case is as sad
in many ways as that of Breege. She never discovers the deep reaches of
love, preferring to wage a traditional battle for her lover on the familiar
and well-trodden stones of custom and cliché. She never loses herself in
love, keeping herself with a grim determination in the center of a story
of her own making and, as a consequence, never sees things as they are.

Most tragic of all, she never truly realizes that Bugler loves her, in a different, more urgent, less mystical way than he loves Breege. She never sees that she has no need to test him, that Bugler would have kept his agreement to marry her. Like the foolish and greedy sisters in the classic fairy tales, she gives nothing and loses all.

Joseph, described by Breege as "my brother, my highly-strung brother. Always on about the sacred fetters of land and blood," his mind full of nervous protection of all he loves, deranged by the thought that his land and the sister will be taken from him by a friend turned enemy, finally loses his reason and freedom (7). His pursuit of the deeds on which his claim to the land rests brings about his descent into madness. His final act of despair is the killing of Bugler. So, Joseph, in Mountjoy Gaol, pines for "the fields and the fresh air" and dreams of Yeats's "To a Child Dancing in the Wind" (243). Breege is left to hold the land he loved in trust, like Josie in *House of Splendid Isolation,* and, unlike Mary in *Down by the River,* is allowed to carry within her the child who may so dance, who may inherit the land. Of all these "stranded selves" found throughout O'Brien's novels, and in particular in this last trilogy, Breege is the character who most clearly knows what must be done. Like the characters in Yeats's Noh plays, she is dreaming back, gathering within her the wisdom of the generations and trying to ensure that her child will be as she is, as Josie and Mary are, a warrior of the spirit. At the end of *Wild Decembers,* questions are left unanswered. We do not know if the child, like those who came before, will love the land more than people or whether love may yet prevail. O'Brien presents us at the end, not with an answer but with a passionate expression of hope that Breege and her child and all who have gone before them may transcend all that would snare them and, like Joyce, "fly by those nets": "Shaped by that place and that loneliness she thinks that the longing which ran in her listening and ran in her veins was answered so and holding her belly she reaches back, back to those nameless and spectral forces of which she is made and reaches to him too in the hope that there is communion between living and dead, between those, who even in their most stranded selves are on the side of life and harbingers of love" (244).

Like the three heroines of her trilogy, Edna O'Brien recognizes the necessity of facing the "gaudy void." She is not afraid of it; rather, she welcomes it. Proud to be Irish, she has taken her own voyage, like Ulysses, out to the beyond and back. She is not fooled by what she has described as Ireland's "misted atmosphere," seeing it instead as a land "ancient, turbulent, and beyond pity."[14] She echoes the verbal dexterity and deadly wit of Joyce, and, indeed, what she writes of him in her recent study may be said of herself: "A writer . . . both feels more and less about human grief, being at once celebrant, witness and victim, if the writing ceases, or seems to cease, the mind so occupied with the stringing of words together is fallow."[15] This trilogy, written after a long period of silence, confirms that the mind of Edna O'Brien is not lying fallow. She is an admirer of Joyce's "total honesty and perseverance," and, in her own writing perseverance and honesty are channeled through elegant and enduring prose into a body of work that has, in the words of Nuala O'Faolain, "changed the reality of women's lives in Ireland."[16] In her latest novels, she demonstrates not only an unerring sense of the fundamental issues that have rocked the safe certainties and demolished the old myths but also a mature compassion for all men, women, and children whose lives are marked or marred by this disintegration. In the end, however, it is O'Brien's country girls—not their fathers, their husbands, or their brothers—who inherit the land. Neither Joyce's old sow nor Mother Ireland herself can stand in their way, for, like the fragile and courageous daughter of an Irish clergyman whose poetry provides the epigraph to *Wild Decembers,* and, indeed, like that of Edna O'Brien herself, theirs is "the spirit that remembers."

Notes

1. Joanne Hayden, "Unveiling Naked Truth of Rural Life," *Sunday Business Post,* 26 September 1999.

2. "The Simmering Rage that Led to Row over Pebbledash and Ended in Double Murder," *Irish Times,* 23 October 1999.

3. Edna O'Brien, *Wild Decembers* (London: Weidenfeld & Nicholson, 1999).

4. Nicholas Wroe, "Saturday Review," *Guardian,* 2 October 1999.

5. Toward the end of 1984, following the abortion amendment to the constitution, the "Kerry babies" case brought infanticide to the attention of the Irish public. A baby with multiple stab wounds was found washed up on a beach in County Kerry. An investigation into the identity of the mother led to a confession by Joanne Hayes, a single mother, but the discovery of the body of a second baby on the farm where she lived raised questions about this confession. The gardaí claimed that Joanne Hayes was the mother of both babies, but scientific tests showed that she was not the mother of first baby. The mother of that baby has never been identified. A subsequent investigation revealed perjury and gardaí intimidation and exposed Hayes's relationship with a married man from another town. Wrongly accused, Joanne Hayes attracted considerable public sympathy, and the attendant news coverage made her a symbolic victim of patriarchal control over female sexuality, which forced her to conceal the

birth of her child. See *The Encyclopedia of Ireland*, ed. Brian Lalor (Dublin: Gill and Macmillan, 2003), 585.

6. O'Brien, quoted in Wroe, "Saturday Review."

7. Edna O'Brien, *Mother Ireland* (London: Weidenfeld & Nicholson, 1976).

8. Edna O'Brien, *House of Splendid Isolation* (London: Weidenfeld & Nicholson, 1994).

9. Interview with Edna O'Brien, *Salon Magazine*, www.salonmagazine.com, 2 December 1995 (accessed April 2000). O'Brien has recently corrected a detail in this interview as quoted: "*Salon* actually got it wrong many years ago. The remark about all being Irish under the skin was *not* made by the IRA man but by the guard who shot him," e-mail, Edna O'Brien to Sophia Hillan, 21 May 2000.

10. "On Tour: Edna O'Brien," *Hungry Mind Review*, www.bookwire.com/HMR/Review/tobrien.html (accessed April 2000).

11. William Carleton, *Traits and Stories of the Irish Peasantry*, vol. 2 (Dublin: William Curry & Co., 1844; facs. ed., Gerrards Cross: Clin Smythe, 1990), 360–61. See also, Raymond Murray, *The Burning of Wildgoose Lodge: Ribbonism in Louth, Murder and the Gallows* (Armagh: Cumann Seanchais Ard Mhacha, 2005).

12. Edna O'Brien, *Down by the River* (London: Weidenfeld & Nicholson, 1996).

13. Graham Linehan and Arthur Mathews are the writers of *Father Ted*. This bitingly witty Irish series, mocking every tradition in Irish clerical life, appeared first on British television's Channel 4 and only afterward on RTÉ.

14. Edna O'Brien, *Time and Tide* (London: Weidenfeld & Nicholson, 1992), 123.

15. Edna O'Brien, *James Joyce* (London: Weidenfeld & Nicholson, 1999), 176.

16. "A Schooling for Scandal," *Independent* (London), 12 June 1999. Nuala O'Faolain's comment was mentioned in correspondence with Sophia Hillan.

Contributors

Index

Contributors

WANDA BALZANO graduated in English from the University of Naples (Italy) and received her master of arts and doctorate from University College Dublin, where she researched and lectured on Irish studies and feminism. She was then awarded a postdoctoral fellowship from the Irish government. She came to Wake Forest University as a visiting professor in 2004 before taking up the directorship of the Women's and Gender Studies Program there. Her publications range from Samuel Beckett and James Joyce to Irish women's writing, art, and film. With Moynagh Sullivan she is presently editing a special issue of *The Irish Review* on Irish feminism

KRISTINE BYRON has a Ph.D. in comparative literary and cultural studies from the University of Connecticut and is assistant professor of Hispanic cultural studies at Michigan State University. She has published articles on Latin American literature, Cuban history, and Irish literature and has recently completed a comparative study of women, revolution, and life writing.

LISA COLLETTA is the author of *Dark Humor and Social Satire in the Modern British Novel* (2003) and the editor of *Kathleen and Christopher: Christopher Isherwood's Letters to His Mother* (2005). Her work on humor, modernism, gender, and the twentieth-century novel has been published in various collections, journals, and newspapers, and she is currently finishing a book on British novelists in Hollywood. She is assistant professor of English at Babson College.

DANINE FARQUHARSON is assistant professor of Irish literature at Memorial University in St. John's, Newfoundland, Canada. She has published and presented papers on artists such as Neil Jordan, Seamus Deane, and Liam O'Flaherty. She is particularly interested in issues of masculinity and violence (men with guns).

MICHAEL PATRICK GILLESPIE is the Louise Edna Goeden Professor of English at Marquette University. He has published books on the works of James Joyce, Oscar Wilde, and William Kennedy. His latest book is *The Aesthetics of Chaos.* He is currently working on a study of Irish film.

SOPHIA HILLAN lives in Belfast, Northern Ireland, where from 1993 until 2003 she was associate director of the Institute of Irish Studies at Queen's University. Her research interests include the literary and cultural history of Ireland in the nineteenth and twentieth centuries, and her work covers aspects of the writings of Michael McLaverty, Seamus Heaney, William Carleton, and Sam Hanna Bell as well as Edna O'Brien. She has won several prizes for short fiction, was short-listed for a Hennessy Award in 1981, and was runner-up to John Arden in the Royal Society of Literature's V. S. Pritchett Memorial Prize of 1999. Her work is included in the 2005 *Faber Book of Best New Irish Short Stories,* edited by David Marcus. She is author (as Sophia Hillan King) of *The Edge of Dark: A Sense of Place in the Writings of Michael McLaverty and Sam Hanna Bell* (2000) and *The Silken Twine: A Study of the Works of Michael McLaverty* (1992), editor of *In Quiet Places: The Uncollected Stories, Letters and Prose of Michael McLaverty* (1989), and coeditor, with Sean McMahon, of *Hope and History: Eyewitness Accounts of Life in Twentieth-Century Ulster* (1996).

MAUREEN O'CONNOR lectures in the department of English in the National University of Galway, Ireland. She has published widely on Irish writing, including the work of Oscar Wilde, Sydney Owenson (Lady Morgan), "Speranza" (Lady Wilde), Edna O'Brien, Frances Power Cobbbe, and Maria Edgeworth. She has recently completed a study of Oscar Wilde's literary matrilineage and is currently an IRCHSS Government of Ireland Post-Doctoral Fellow at the Centre for the Study of Human Settlement and Historical Change, NUI Galway. She is the coeditor, with Tadhg Foley, of *India and Ireland: Colonies, Culture, and Empire,* forthcoming from Irish Academic Press, and, with Kathryn Laing and Sinéad Mooney, of *Edna O'Brien: New Critical Perspectives,* forthcoming from Carysfort.

REBECCA PELAN is senior lecturer and director of the Women's Studies Centre, National University of Ireland, Galway. She was born and raised in Belfast but moved to Australia with her family in 1969. Rebecca lectured for eleven years at the University of Queensland, principally in literature, drama, women's studies, and communication and cultural studies before returning to Ireland in 2001. She has published extensively on the subject of Irish women's writing, Edna O'Brien's fiction, feminist/literary theory, and women and "the Troubles."

BERNICE SCHRANK is professor of English language and literature at Memorial University of Newfoundland, where she has taught since 1969 in the areas of Irish and American literature. She has written many articles on Irish drama, fiction, and autobiography. Her most recent full-length study, *Sean O'Casey: A Research and Production Sourcebook,* was published by Greenwood Press in 1996. Her recent work in American studies includes articles on the role of the Rosenbergs in American political culture, the life and writings of William Z. Foster, labor organizer and one of the founders of the American Communist Party, and the construction and treatment of the "Jewish nose" stereotype in contemporary American literature, television, and cinema.

HELEN THOMPSON, a native of Darlaston, England, is assistant professor of English at the University of Louisiana at Lafayette. She is coeditor, with Caitriona Moloney, of *Irish Women Writers Speak Out: Voices from the Field* (2003) and has completed a book-length manuscript on Edna O'Brien, *Territories of Desire: Reconstituting Irish Womanhood in the Works of Edna O'Brien. Having Our Own Field Day: Essays on the Irish Canon* will be published in 2006 by Edwin Mellen Press.

Index

Irish Studies in Literature and Culture